MODERNIZE
YOUR CAREER
SERIES

3RD EDITION

T0051620

MODERNIZE
Your Resume
Get Noticed ... Get Hired

MASTER RESUME WRITERS

Wendy Enelow &
Louise Kursmark

Modernize Your Resume
Get Noticed ... Get Hired

Copyright © 2023 by Wendy Enelow and Louise Kursmark

ISBN 978-0-9966803-7-0

 EMERALD CAREER PUBLISHING

Publisher: Emerald Career Publishing
               590 Valverda Street SW
               Supply, NC 28462
               www.emeraldcareerpublishing.com
               434-444-4714

Cover & Interior Design: Deb Tremper, Six Penny Graphics
http://sixpennygraphics.com

Distributor: Cardinal Publishers Group
www.cardinalpub.com

Printed in the United States of America

CONTENTS

INTRODUCTION

If you're like most job seekers, writing your resume can be daunting. It is your challenge to create a resume that communicates *who* you are, *what* you can do, and *how well* you do it.

Everywhere you turn, you read different advice about how to write, format, and design your resume. How do you know what to believe—how to handle specific circumstances and challenges of your career, best showcase your qualifications, and highlight what is most relevant to your current objective?

What's more, you must understand the current technology and hiring trends that will affect your job search:

- **Today's readers demand quick rewards.** If your resume does not deliver critical information quickly and clearly, it is unlikely to be selected for deeper reading.

- **Electronic scanning dominates the job application process.** Your resume is likely to be read first by a computer, so it must be written and designed to pass an Applicant Tracking System (ATS).

- **Job search channels have multiplied.** You can post your resume online, reply to posted openings, upload to databases, email to prospective employers, and apply from your phone or tablet.

- **Companies screen candidates more thoroughly.** Just about everyone can be found online, giving hiring authorities the chance to learn more about you before you ever get a call for an interview.

If it sounds overwhelming—relax! We've been writing resumes for decades and keep current with all that has changed and continues to evolve.

One thing that has not changed: The starting point for any successful job search is a resume. In this 3rd edition of *Modernize Your Resume*, we eliminate the confusion and show you exactly what you need to know and do to create a modern resume that meets the 3 critical standards of today's job search market:

- **Content** that is tight, lean, and clean.

- **Format** that showcases your career and accomplishments.

- **Design** that distinguishes your resume in a crowded field of candidates.

In addition, you'll find 4 chapters for people facing unique job search challenges and opportunities: **Career Change; Consulting, Freelance & Gig Work; Military-to-Civilian Transition;** and **Return-to-Work.**

Finally, a **comprehensive chapter on strategies and techniques for writing LinkedIn profiles** truly enhances the value of this book. It includes sample profiles that demonstrate those tools in action.

Resume writing is not a formulaic process. That's why this book is so valuable, helping you navigate the complexities of all that is involved in creating a powerful and on-brand resume.

PART I:
The Modern Resume

We get it … you want a fast, easy process to create a great resume and land a new job.

With this book, we give you everything you need—and more. Looking for inspiring resume samples? Check. Fresh design ideas? Check. Great resume and LinkedIn (LI) profile content? Of course. The latest advice on keyword-scanning Applicant Tracking Systems (ATS)? That too. It's all included and presented in an easy-to-understand and easy-to-manage process.

How to Use This Book

Divided into 9 distinct parts, this book provides both quick answers and deep, more thoughtful explanations for everything you need to know to create your own modern resume and LI profile.

- **Part I—The Modern Resume.** We tell you and show you what's different about resumes today, explain the various sections in a modern resume, and give you guidelines for your specific circumstances—from graduating student to senior executive to career changers and everyone in between.

- **Part II—Modernize Your Resume Content.** The 4 chapters in Part II discuss, in depth, our 4 Core Principles for writing modern resume content while providing best-in-class samples of those concepts in action. You'll learn to:
    - Start with the Wow!
    - Put Your Objective in the Driver's Seat
    - Write with Meaning and Power
    - Write Tight, Lean, and Clean

- **Part III—Modernize Your Resume Format.** The 4 Core Principles in Part III, along with the accompanying resume samples, guide you through the many decisions you'll need to make as you organize, structure, and format your content so that you can:
    - Showcase Your Career with the Right Resume Structure
    - Follow the Rules of Good Formatting
    - Improve Readability and Skimmability
    - Format for Human Readers and Applicant Tracking Systems (ATS)

- **Part IV—Modernize Your Resume Design.** Never to be overlooked—or its value underestimated—is the visual presentation of your resume. You'll see unique, eye-catching, and remarkably distinctive resume samples that follow our 4 Core Principles to help you:

- Capture Attention in a Flash
- Follow the Practices of Good Page Design
- Match Design Elements to Your Industry, Profession, and Career Story
- Be Distinctive

- **Part V—Resumes for Challenging Situations.** Many job seekers face unique challenges that can make resume writing more complicated or require a different approach. In the 4 chapters in this section, you'll find detailed instructions for how to write and format resumes if you are:
  - Changing Careers
  - Pursuing Consulting, Freelance, and Gig Economy Opportunities
  - Transitioning from a Military to a Civilian Career
  - Returning to Work after an Extended Absence

- **Part VI—LinkedIn Profiles for Everyone.** LI has become the #1 site for companies and recruiters to source candidates for hire. It's also the #1 site for candidates to network and uncover opportunities. In fact, companies and recruiters will review your LI profile to learn more about you … even before they reach out to connect. We share strategies and samples to help you create a profile that will attract opportunities and convey your unique value.

- **Part VII—Resume Portfolio.** These 40+ modern resumes, written for job seekers of all levels in a wide array of industries and professions, illustrate the core principles discussed in Parts II, III, IV, and V. Review the portfolio for new and fresh ideas to write, format, and design your own resume.

  Heartfelt thanks to our professional colleagues who shared their very best resumes with us and with you! Each resume shows the contributor's name and contact information, and we encourage you to reach out to these talented writers if you're in need of professional resume assistance.

- **Part VIII—Resources.** As you put theory into action and begin to write your resume, you'll find these tools and resources extremely valuable:
  - **Goal-Setting Worksheet,** a tool that will help you define your career objective(s).
  - **Career Vault,** a structured guideline for gathering your resume information.
  - **Dig-Deep Questions** to uncover, quantify, and write about your accomplishments.
  - **Verbs with Verve,** a list of **440 action words for your resume.**

- **Part IX—Resume and LinkedIn Profile Index.** Use this easy tool to find resumes and profiles that match your profession, industry, or circumstance.

Our Commitment to You

Follow our guiding principles, study the samples, and move step-by-step through the process, and we promise that resume writing, formatting, and design will be easier, faster, and better.

With a modern resume in hand, you'll be a more empowered job seeker, confident in your qualifications, able to articulate your value, and prepared to outperform your competition and win the job!

CHAPTER 1:
Welcome to the World of Modern Resume Writing

6 Hallmarks of a Modern Resume

- Clear and concise, written and designed to appeal to today's readers
- Laser focused to each individual's job targets
- Rich with keywords that resonate with employers and ATS
- Specific in describing achievements rather than general capabilities
- Contemporary in appearance and visually distinctive
- Linked to email, online profiles, websites, and social media

Are you ready to take your first step toward your next great career opportunity? It begins with a shift in mindset—how you think about the process of crafting your resume and LI profile.

To begin, you must understand the significant changes that resumes have gone through over the past decade. Rapidly, they have evolved to meet our modern world of job search—characterized by unprecedented competition; a massive shift to virtual work; a global workforce; and technologies that have forever changed how we communicate, find new job opportunities, and select candidates to interview and hire.

Follow our *Modernize Your Resume* guidelines, and we're certain you'll be one of those candidates.

Modern Resume Content, Format & Design

In a tough job market, you must do everything you can to shine brighter than your competition. To help you do that, we've devoted the 3 major sections of this book to the 3 core elements of the modern resume—**Content, Format,** and **Design**—all of which are essential to help you *get noticed* and *get hired*.

PRO TIP: First, you need to hook your readers with the design and appearance of your resume; then you can reel them in with content that is powerful, interesting, engaging, and relevant.

Before we dive in, let's review some essential guidelines to help you develop a solid infrastructure—a foundation—for your resume. In fact, we've included 3 different infrastructures for 3 different categories of job seekers: Graduating Students and Young Professionals; Mid-Career Professionals; and Senior Managers and Executives.

After you've reviewed your relevant guidelines, be sure to read the discussion on page 9 of all the other categories—or sections—you might include on your resume. Those will round out the primary sections to paint a complete picture of all that is unique and valuable about you.

> **PRO TIP: Does your career reflect unique circumstances—Career Change, Consulting or Freelancing, Returning to Work, Military-to-Civilian Transition?** If so, in addition to the guidelines in this chapter you'll want to devote close attention to Part V (pages 117–143), which includes recommendations and samples tailored to you.

Guidelines for Graduating Students & Young Professionals

- **Professional Skills Profile** (Summary). Start your resume with valuable information that positions you as a strong candidate—a short paragraph, a few bullet points, or a brief listing of your most notable skills, education, and experience as they relate to your target opportunities.

- **Education:** List your degree, college/university, location, academic honors, leadership activities, sports, and other distinguishing information. This will likely be the meatiest section of your resume because your education is your primary qualification, and employers will want to know what you did both in and outside the classroom.

  Does high school matter? Possibly. It matters if you were valedictorian or at the top of your class, had a unique and important internship or related experience, or attended a private high school whose alumni often look to recruit talent from their alma mater.

- **Internships:** Create a separate section if you've had one or more internships that relate to and support your professional objectives. Be sure to mention if you've interned with impressive companies, had notable responsibilities or achievements, or had multiple internships.

- **Project Highlights:** If you have important information that you think will attract prospective employers to you, be sure to include a separate section to showcase notable projects, courses, and assignments that support your current career goals.

- **Employment Experience.** Your work experience may not tie directly to your professional job objectives, but it communicates that you have a strong work ethic and possess other valuable workplace skills. You can also include internships here, rather than in a separate section.

John Newsmith Resume—page 5

John's resume incorporates many of our modern resume guidelines. Following a Summary that clearly identifies his qualifications, the most significant part of his resume is Project Highlights. This strategy elevates his class projects into truly meaningful experience that gives him valuable professional skills and relevant achievements even though they were acquired in school and not on the job. Two faculty testimonials are powerful additions.

Guidelines for Mid-Career Professionals

- **Professional Qualifications or Career Profile** (Summary). Begin your resume with a strong overview of your qualifications, achievements, and other notable information that is on-brand, distinctive, and memorable in positioning you for your current job targets.

JOHN NEWSMITH

Orlando, FL 32300 • 803-888-1234
j.newsmith@gmail.com • LinkedIn.com/in/JohnNewsmith

ACCOUNTING GRADUATE • CPA CANDIDATE

High-performing accounting graduate, prepared to assume role as Associate or Staff Accountant. Energetic professional with a tireless work ethic and determination to excel. Quick to step up and take on leadership roles. Mesh easily with diversified teams to support and emphasize problem solving and project excellence.

- Advanced Analytic Capabilities
- Commitment to Continuous Learning
- Intensive Attention to Detail
- Expert Computer Skills

 Mr. Newsmith has consistently produced outstanding work. He presents excellent communication and interpersonal skills, and he always exhibits a sense of responsibility and integrity." — Anthony A. Jones, CPA, Faculty Instructor in Accounting, Florida State University

EDUCATION

Bachelor of Arts in Accounting, Florida State University, Tallahassee, FL   December 2022

Honors & Awards
- 3.85 GPA • magna cum laude • President's List
- Academic Achievement Award in Business Administration

PROJECT HIGHLIGHTS

Strategic Management 2, Florida State University, Tallahassee, FL   Fall 2022

Led team in capstone consultancy project for a local tech startup. Delivered positive and lasting impact for real-world client.
- Produced 120-page business plan, including new mission statement, short- and long-term goals, and marketing and human resources plans.
- Analyzed revenues and expenses, reviewed financial breakdowns, and proposed new financial processes and procedures.

 John took the lead and acted as the group liaison, facilitator, and main presenter. The group's plan gave the business owner sound strategic concepts that, when implemented, helped the business establish a strong competitive advantage." — Dr. Rick Smith

Strategic Management 1, Florida State University, Tallahassee, FL   Spring 2022

Member of a stellar academic team that produced and presented innovative corporate strategy for ABX Corporation in Orlando, FL. Gained competencies in data analysis, teamwork, audits, and risk detection.

ASSOCIATION MEMBERSHIPS

Students for the Advancement of Management (SAM)
Florida Institute of CPAs (FICPA)

Linda Gibson, M.A., CPRW • Career Helm, LLC • careerhelm.com

- **Professional Experience or Employment Experience.** Detail your work experience—job titles, employers, locations (maybe), and dates (*almost* all of the time). Briefly summarize your areas of responsibility but, most importantly, highlight successes and achievements of each position. Clearly and concisely communicate the value you bring to an organization.

- **Education.** List your degree(s), colleges/universities, and distinguishing academic honors, along with relevant training, certifications, licenses, and other professional credentials. Don't waste space with details that don't matter (e.g., played lacrosse), but do include any truly distinguishing information from your academic career if you believe it will work to your advantage.

- High school no longer matters, unless fellow alumni can open doors for you in your job search.

Jason Stewart Resume—pages 7–8

The top half of Jason's resume is rich with relevant detail, beginning with a short Summary after a powerful Headline that clearly communicates *who* Jason is and the value he delivers. The Notable Skills & Achievements section puts his key accomplishments front and center, and the right column (Expertise) is rich with keywords that provide a quick overview of his strongest qualifications.

Jason's Professional Experience includes more details of the "Notables" mentioned in the Summary and is the largest portion of the resume—as it generally is for mid-career professionals. Notice the Education—a great example of showcasing important credentials in a very concise presentation.

Guidelines for Senior Managers & Executives

- **Career Profile** (Summary). Use this section of the resume to position yourself, communicate who you are (the "brand" that is you), and briefly share your most distinctive, memorable, and relevant career achievements.

- **Professional Experience.** For senior managers and executives, this section is the most extensive. Detail your experience—job titles, employers, locations (maybe), dates (*almost* all of the time), and overall scope of responsibility. Most critically, showcase your achievements, focusing on the big-picture items … the things you've done to improve operational and financial performance and other key impacts. Your achievements are what will set you apart from other talented senior managers and executives vying for the same positions.

- **Education.** List your degree(s), colleges/universities, and distinguishing academic honors, along with relevant training, certifications, licenses, and other credentials. If you do not have a degree, consider omitting this section entirely.

  High school no longer matters. You may want to reach out to individual classmates if there is still a strong alumni network, but you don't need to include on your resume.

- **Board Appointments, Consulting Engagements & Professional Affiliations.** These categories can be strong additions in branding yourself, building your visibility, and increasing your reach. Include the organization and your role, activities, and achievements most relevant to your current search. Whether you combine all of this information in a single section or create individual sections, and where you position them on your resume, should be dictated by your current career goals.

Jason Stewart

Start-Ups. Large Enterprises. Open Source. Digital Creative.

206-522-3999 ▪ jasonstewart@gmail.com ▪ linkedin.com/in/jasonstewart

PRODUCT DESIGN LEADER | USER EXPERIENCE CHAMPION

INSTITUTE DESIGN PHILOSOPHY AND BUILD CREATIVE TEAMS WITHIN GLOBAL COMPANIES

Influence integration of design-first strategies for product and solution development in both start-up and established organizations, boosting business value and enhancing customer experience through a passion and belief that
"technology is nothing without experience."

NOTABLE SKILLS & ACHIEVEMENTS

☑ **15+ years of progressive product and design expertise** in both small and large enterprises across different industries. Involved in digital from its initial start.

☑ **Built multiple product design and creative teams of 80+** from the ground up, including the world's largest open-source design team.

☑ **Introduced and fostered "balanced design" approaches** and end-to-end user experiences that reduced customer support calls 45% and improved user-facing processes and experiences.

☑ **Generated product solutions by leaning on design** to streamline processes, eliminate challenges, and smooth out experiences.

☑ **Created 60-person, new $65M digital business line.**

EXPERTISE

User Experience Design (UXD)
Customer-Focused Solutions
Empathy-Driven Design
Product Design
Team Leadership
Strategic Planning & Execution
User Experience (UX) Practices
Client Contracts
Product Release Strategy
Sales & Marketing
Stakeholder Communications

PROFESSIONAL EXPERIENCE

RED TOP COMMUNICATIONS - SEATTLE, WA | 2010–Present

SENIOR MANAGER, GLOBAL USER EXPERIENCE | Principal Interaction Designer/Manager
Operating Budget: $10M | Supervise: 75+ | Products: 20+

Called upon to champion the creation and expansion of a centralized global user experience design (UXD) function and team within the organization. Continue to drive adoption of design-first approach into all product design processes. Advocate for UXD at various global events. Foster team growth and advancement, managing budget and operations. Collaborate closely with senior executives, marketing, and sales during ongoing company growth.

Started and Grew
Centralized User
Experience Team

4150% in 7 Years

- **Built largest open-source design team in the world, creating a 3-, 6-, and 12-month plan to drive initiative forward:**
  - → Collaborated with executives and staff to educate on UXD value and advantages.
  - → Grew the team from the ground up, expanding from 2 to 85 people in 7 years.
  - → Awarded 50% more requisitions than all other groups, valued up to $2.4M annually.

- **Strategically influenced engineering-heavy product development process to embed design balanced approach,** achieving buy-in from 100% of the group to establish UX as a core philosophy within the company.

- **Lowered UXD-related customer support calls 45%,** creating an end-to-end team to manage customer user experience from purchase to support. Expanded breadth of user experience beyond product use.

Jason Stewart

CONNEXION INC. – SEATTLE, WA | 2004–2009

DIRECTOR, DIGITAL PRODUCT SOLUTIONS
Operating Budget: $10M | Supervised: 60

Specially requested to drive integration of digital and interactive technologies into the events of this 150-person brand experience agency to enhance event offerings and generate new revenue stream. Together with a partner, created successful new digital business line, supporting all aspects of product design through to sales.

- **Built a 60-person, $65M digital business for the company in just 3 years:**
  - → Evangelized digital into a non-technical organization by initiating internal sales training program.
  - → Improved staff comfort with the value and capabilities of digital within the event production space.

> Launched Digital Business from
>
> **$500K to $65M**
>
> in just 3 years

- **Increased sales call closures 85%,** personally supporting calls to introduce digital abilities and promote return on investment to new and existing customers.

- **Boosted product appeal and sales with a profit margin of 45%,** reusing base code to create an event application that could be easily customized for client requirements.

MISSION INTERACTIVE – SEATTLE, WA | 1998–2003

VICE PRESIDENT, CREATIVE TEAM LEAD
Budget: $1.5M | Supervised: 25

Recruited to build out a creative team from scratch for this new digital creative agency, supporting organizational growth to a 50-person company, with global clients, over 5 years. Managed hiring, training, company promotion, sales, profitability, and budgeting for all agency projects during times of market transition and challenges.

- **Built out successful and robust creative team, expanding from 0 to 50 people in 5 years:**
  - → Promoted organization at industry events to attract top talent.
  - → Maintained nearly zero staff attrition in 5 years by fostering a work environment that empowered staff to push creativity with long-term concepts and commitment.

Grew Sales from

$0 to $7M

In 4 years

- **Generated $7M in peak sales, implementing a strategic plan to differentiate company from competitors:**
  - → Instituted design philosophy and product offering centered around "Influencing User Experiences," pioneering digital campaign offerings that attracted clients.

EDUCATION, PROFESSIONAL DEVELOPMENT & INVOLVEMENTS

Bachelor of Science, Management & Marketing – University of Washington

Member, User Experience Professionals Association
Board Advisor, Digital Information Society

Matthew Marsh Resume—pages 10–11

For this senior executive, the Summary accurately identifies his executive level and areas of expertise. It's followed by Professional Experience, which is appropriately the longest, richest, and most detailed. Many of the achievements are quantified, and the chart on page 1 is powerful and eye-catching. The resume is formatted to include a lot of text in an easily readable presentation. Notice that his earliest positions are just briefly listed, without details, to show his full career history.

Additional Sections—For Your Consideration

Many people have bits and pieces of information that don't quite fit into any of the major resume sections. Depending on your past experience and current objectives, you might find it beneficial to add categories that allow you to more clearly and fully present your distinguishing and relevant details.

- **Technology Qualifications or Technology Profile.** If you're a hands-on tech professional, demonstrate your technical proficiency by listing your technical qualifications in detail.

- **Board Appointments.** If you're an executive who has served on Boards of Directors, be certain to include that information. It instantly communicates a strong message of talent and achievement.

- **Honors & Awards—Publications—Public Speaking.** All 3 of these categories represent third-party endorsements of your expertise and are valuable additions. Create a separate section for each, integrate into your Summary, or add to the appropriate work or school listing.

- **Project Profile.** If you work in a profession where projects are the mainstay, or if you're a consultant or freelancer, detail your most notable projects—name of project, scope of work, project partners, budgets, and results. You can do this in a separate section or integrate with your jobs.

- **Professional Affiliations.** Your involvement with professional associations relevant to your industry can be extremely valuable. Mention any leadership roles, committees, or notable contributions.

- **Community Leadership & Memberships.** These items can be a nice addition to your resume, particularly if you're looking to remain in the same geographic region. Include any leadership roles, committees, achievements, or other contributions.

- **Languages.** If you speak, read, or write multiple languages, prominently showcase them—particularly if you're looking for a job where they will be important. Present your language skills in the Summary for instant recognition or create a separate Languages section.

- **Personal Profile.** US residents, do not include personal information such as marital status or number of children on your resume, and don't list interests if they are not distinguishing. Outside the US, follow the customary rules for the country in which you live or work.

The Great Date Debate

Should you include dates on your resume? In most cases, yes. Dates help tell your story and show the progression of your career.

But sometimes, depending on your age, your experience history, your college graduation year, and your current career objective, the question is not so straightforward. Here are a few scenarios to consider:

MATTHEW MARSH

Englewood, NJ 07631 | 201.555.4444 | MMarsh@gmail.com | www.linkedin.com/in/MattMarsh

EXECUTIVE MANAGEMENT

HEALTHCARE | SENIOR SERVICES | NON-PROFIT

KEY AREAS OF EXPERTISE

Restructuring & Revitalization

Joint Ventures & Alliances

Business Development

Negotiations

Startups & Turnarounds

Strategic Planning & Branding

Employee & Labor Relations

Financial Analysis & P&L

Hands-on Director with an empathetic approach to the population served and advocate for the employees needed to deliver high-quality care.

Change Agent with proven history of increasing profitability, rescuing faltering organizations, and finding innovative solutions to complex issues.

Business Partner who excels at building collaborative, cross-functional relationships that improve healthcare outcomes, enhance customer experience, and drive up annual profit margins.

Innovative and Compassionate Leader with 20+ years of experience in highly competitive and diligently regulated industries.

CAREER HISTORY

Patterson Healthcare System, Patterson, NJ   2019 to Present
Community-based healthcare provider and continuing care retirement community.
***Total Beds/Units:** 650 | **Combined Budget:** $28M | **Employees:** 600*

EXECUTIVE VICE PRESIDENT, SENIOR SERVICES

Oversee total operations for Patterson Healthcare. Recruited during leadership transition as organization sought a change agent with strong, strategic, and visionary thinking. Pioneered initiatives to break down silos between senior communities and medical center.

- Propelled Patterson's revenue by $700K in 2022 by conceiving and executing Senior Services post-acute strategic plan that included recognizing need for additional sub-acute beds, a more defined referral process, and better integration of support and clinical services.

- Created system strategy for affiliation with VNA Health Group. Affiliation resulted in the following:

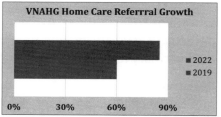

  ⇨ Secured $80K grant from Centers for Medicare & Medicaid for nurse coaches to assist patients through continuum of care transition.

  ⇨ Ensured all acute care discharges were seen at home within 24 hours.

  ⇨ Increased Visiting Nurses Association Health Group (VNAHG) home care referrals from 60% to 85% in first 3 years of affiliation.

- Led task force in forming Geriatric Fellowship Program in concert with Princeton Medical School. To date, program has graduated 14 fellowship doctors.

Kaiser Foundation Hospital of New Jersey, Cherry Hill, NJ　　　　　　2008 to 2019
NJ-based hospital and part of multiple non-profit health systems providing a continuum of care.
***Total employees:** 400 | **Overall Budget:** $30M*

PRESIDENT / CHIEF EXECUTIVE OFFICER

Hired to turn around underperforming institution. Immediately launched initiatives to address major deficit spending, improve quality of care, revitalize fundraising, and determine long- term strategy and direction.

- Developed strategic plan and gained consensus from Board of Trustees to downsize from 290 to 220 beds.

- Hired new nursing management team and implemented new quality assurance program. Combined efforts slashed annual NJ Department of Health and Senior Services survey from 15 deficiencies to zero.

- Reduced annual deficit $850K in fiscal year 2013 and $1M in 2016 by reengineering staffing patterns in all departments and reducing overall supply expenses by 5%.

- Increased inpatient sub-acute days 12% by strengthening admissions and marketing departments and streamlining referral process.

- Directed launch of $12M capital campaign in collaboration with Board of Trustees and fundraising consultant. Generated $1.5M in donations through active solicitation of key donor and board contacts.

South Jersey Health System, Ocean, NJ　　　　　　2003 to 2008
Integrated delivery system comprising 3 acute care hospitals.
***Total beds:** 180 | **Overall Budget:** $15M*

SENIOR VICE PRESIDENT, SENIOR SERVICES

Recruited to lead newly formed Senior Service division, a joint effort with 2 hospital systems, and to develop 3 skilled nursing facilities. Merged 2 divergent cultures.

- Oversaw design, construction, policies, budgeting, hiring, regulatory process, and approval to ensure timely implementation of 14-bed, hospital-based, sub-acute unit.

- Consolidated 2 health care systems' senior programs into a single 8000-member organization.

- Integrated acute care rehabilitation department into both outpatient and post-acute services. Process resulted in expense reduction by eliminating use of outside rehab agencies in post-acute setting.

VICE PRESIDENT, SENIOR SERVICES, Northern Jersey Health System, Bergen, NJ
VICE PRESIDENT, OPERATIONS, Little Silver Community Health Services, Little Silver, NJ
ADMINISTRATOR, Southern State Community Health Services, Atlantic City, NJ

PROFESSIONAL ASSOCIATIONS

Board Member, New Jersey Association of Non-Profit Homes (5 years)
American Hospital Association – Long-Term Care & Rehabilitation Governance Council (3 years)
Joint Commission on Accreditation of Healthcare Organizations – Advisory Council (4 years)
New Jersey Hospital Association – Long-Term Care Advisory Committee (9 years)

EDUCATION AND LICENSES

Master of Public Administration, Hofstra University, Hempstead, NY
Bachelor of Arts, Health Education—Minor: Public Administration, Rutgers University, New Brunswick, NJ
Licensed Nursing Home Administrator – New Jersey and New York

- **You don't want to appear old.** For job seekers 50+, age discrimination is a concern. To show all of your experience but *not* your precise age, briefly summarize your earliest career experiences *without* dates. If you choose this approach, be certain to also omit your date of college graduation.

- **You don't want to highlight lengthy unemployment.** Instead of using dates, use number of years—for example, "5 years" instead of 2012–2017. Employers will probably assume that you're currently not working, but you've still communicated an impressive number of years of employment.

- **You want to bring prior experience to the forefront.** Let's say you're making a career switch back to something you did years ago, and your more recent jobs are unrelated. Position that great prior experience prominently—in a Related Experience section that comes before Additional Professional Experience. If you do that, consider omitting dates entirely or using the years-only technique.

- **You've heard it's best to delete graduation date.** Sometimes that's true, but be careful that you are not inadvertently aging yourself. Let's say you graduated in 2005 and deleted that year from your Education. Yet you began working that same year—2005—and included that date. Readers will assume there *is* a gap and that you are older than you are.

- **You want to fit in with an older or younger crowd.** Are you targeting startup high-tech companies? Youth is an asset! In other jobs and industries, you don't want to appear young and immature. Understand the culture of the companies and industries you're interested in, and use the date strategy that positions you appropriately for that specific audience.

There are no definitive rules about when to use dates and when not. As with most of resume writing, the answer to everything is "it depends"—on you, your career, your objectives, and more.

Of course, you should never lie or misrepresent. But neither do you have to bare all. Create the right perception by choosing the right information and best way to present that information to support your current objective.

PRO TIP: As a rule, include years of employment and education—not months and years. Readers want to see the progression of your career, from one position to another, and the dates make that clean and simple. But don't waste space with months—they're not essential at this point.

In some cases, though, short-term jobs are the norm. For example:

> You're a graduating student with several part-time jobs and internships.

> You're a young professional and are showing a combination of part-time jobs during college and permanent employment since graduation.

> You're an independent contractor with a variety of projects and assignments that overlap and/or take only a few months.

If you find that including the months tells a more cohesive story, by all means do so. Make the decision that presents your information in the clearest and most beneficial way for you.

The Modern Resume: Principles in Action

In the chapters that follow we will introduce you to 12 core concepts and share more than 100 samples to help you create your own modern resume. As an introduction to everything you'll learn, let's begin with an illustration of how a traditional resume was rewritten, reformatted, and redesigned to align with today's principles that guide modern resume writing.

Andrew Lawson Resumes—pages 14–15

Look at Andrew's "before" resume on page 14. By today's standards, it is outdated in both content and appearance:

- He's used a small size in a font (Times New Roman) that is old-school and has been widely overused.

- The resume starts with a Career Objective rather than a Summary. An Objective tells an employer *what you want* from them. When you start with a Summary, you're telling the employer *what value and expertise* you bring to their organization—a much more powerful introduction.

- Andrew worked at the same school system for 8 years, yet his first position (year 1) is listed as a separate job. That makes the content repetitive because the jobs entailed the same responsibilities. Merging them into a single listing (as in the "after" resume) is a much more effective presentation.

- Andrew's email address link is not live, making it impossible for employers to click and connect.

- The LinkedIn profile link is not live—contrary to what we recommend for today's resumes.

- There are quite a number of grammatical, spacing, and punctuation errors throughout Andrew's resume. Sloppy resumes communicate sloppy work performance, and that is certainly not the message you want to communicate. Be sure to proofread carefully—several times.

Look at page 15 and you'll see Andrew's new, modern resume. You'll notice:

- It includes live links (email and LinkedIn) but does not include a home address—an increasing trend. Many job seekers want to be open to opportunities in numerous geographic locations, so there is no need to include a location that could potentially keep you out of the running.

- It starts with a powerful Headline and Summary that is loaded with keywords that are directly relevant to corporate training and development (his target). By taking those skills out of the classroom environment, strengthening the language, and positioning them at the top of the resume, Andrew instantly positions himself as a qualified corporate trainer.

- His important technology qualifications are listed at the end of the summary, bringing them from the very bottom of the resume on his original to the top, to demonstrate his tech knowledge and capabilities.

- Making a career change means including all information on your resume that could be relevant. For Andrew, it's very important to include 2 prior jobs listed under Early Career Positions. This section showcases Andrew's corporate experience in addition to skills that are attractive to corporations as he transitions from public school teaching to corporate training and development.

- The visual presentation—format, font, and design—is much more distinctive and modern.

Before

Andrew Lawson

999-382-8383 / andrewlawson8282@gmail.com

CAREER OBJECTIVE

Passionate, dynamic, organized and highly knowledgeable educator with excellent management and communication skills seeking position in corporate training and development. My commitment is to inspire a continuous love of learning through a wide variety of engaging activities that meet each individual where they are in the learning process. I want to inspire others to believe in their capabilities and strive for greater success in all they set out to accomplish.

PROFESSIONAL EXPERIENCE

Darwin County Public Schools, Chicago, IL

Educator   July 2015 – Present

Management of classroom operations and all aspects of learning, including planning, communication, evaluation, monitoring and adapting educational strategies to maximize effectiveness while meeting curriculum requirements; these efforts have impacted over 600 students.

- Develop and adjust curriculum and learning opportunities to accommodate the individual needs of students
- Utilize and integrate technology and multi-media applications into daily instruction and assessments
- Foster a caring, collaborative learning environment that is conducive to achieving success
- Collaborate alongside both Intervention and Special Education teams in order to facilitate appropriate learning for at risk students
- Analyze individual and school wide data to determine student, classroom, grade level and school wide goals for both academics and behavior
- Serve as grade chair and collaborate with team to create and implement learning strategies that work toward continued growth and development
- Sit on the scheduling and field trip committees to assist in planning and creating the yearly schoolwide schedule for on campus and off campus instructional learning
- Selected as staff liaison in order to effectively communicate events, staff requests, as well as school needs aligned to the parent teacher association

Educator   January 2014 – June 2015

- Implemented district wide curriculum standards in Language Arts, Mathematics, Science and Social Studies to students in a Title 1 school environment
- Utilized assessment data to create small, highly individualized literacy and math groups
- Collaborated with grade level team to create student learning cohorts which were based on need for daily mathematics instruction, intervention, enrichment
- Attended professional learning development meetings with both grade level co-workers as well as co-workers in grades above and below to meet student academic needs.

EDUCATION

Master of Arts in Teaching, University of Chicago, Chicago, IL
Bachelor of Arts in Psychology and Child Development, Colorado State University, Boulder, CO

ADDITIONAL SKILLS

Microsoft Office Suite – Word, Publisher, Excel, Power Point
Google Drive – Docs, Forms, Sheets, Slides, Meets, Classroom

After

ANDREW LAWSON

999-382-8383 | andrewlawson8282@gmail.com | LinkedIn Profile

TRAINING, DEVELOPMENT & LEARNING PROFESSIONAL

Curriculum Design & Development	Educational & Teaching Strategies
Classroom & Virtual Teaching Methodologies	Instructional Tools & Technologies
Performance Measurement & Reporting	Learner Needs Assessment & Evaluation
Special Events Planning & Coordination	Educator Training & Development
Classroom & Student Management	Program Planning, Scheduling & Logistics

Outstanding presentation, communication, and interpersonal relationship skills. Collaborative training and leadership style with ability to inspire others to achieve. Dedicated to advancing educational innovations to drive learner success.

Technology: MS Office—Word, Excel, Publisher, PowerPoint | Google Drive—Docs, Forms, Sheets, Meets, Classroom

PROFESSIONAL EXPERIENCE

Educator, Chairperson & Staff Liaison | Darwin County Public Schools, Chicago, IL   2014 to Present

Classroom Teacher responsible for design, customization, and delivery of group and individualized learning programs. Staff Liaison to educational teams, administrative personnel, learners, association members, and others.

Recently appointed Learning Chairperson, guiding other educators in defining educational strategies and integrating technology tools to drive continuous growth and development. Taught 650+ students during tenure.

- **Increased student learning performance year-over-year, averaging 80%+ for 5 consecutive years.**
- Produced Master Schedule for entire school and all personnel, facilities, instructional materials, activities, and more, impacting 600+ learners and 100+ faculty and staff annually.
- Successfully managed immediate transition from in-person to virtual learning during pandemic. Minimized learner disruption, created digital teaching and multimedia tools, and fostered student engagement.
- Partnered with other educators, administrators, and management teams to drive forward learning innovations.
- Led ongoing data collection, analysis, and reporting functions to assess learner behavior and performance, training program effectiveness, and quality of both on-campus and off-campus instruction.

EARLY CAREER POSITIONS

Sales Associate, Recruiter & Trainer | Modern Design, Inc., Chicago, IL

Built 18-person field sales organization into one of the top-performing networks in nationwide company.
Managed recruitment, training, and management functions for new hires and seasoned sales professionals. Led sales presentations, developed customer outreach communications, and grew sales by average of 18% annually.

Assistant Director | Gifford & Miller Academy, Inc., Rainier, IL

Dual responsibility for training and managing 30 employees and for developing curricula and teaching classes.
Coordinated recruitment, training, and development for professional and paraprofessional staff, directed administrative affairs, and managed purchasing, inventory control, facilities, recordkeeping, and reporting.

EDUCATION

MA – Teaching | University of Chicago, Chicago, IL

BA – Psychology & Child Development | Colorado State University, Boulder, CO

Resume Mindset

Maintaining a positive and confident attitude when writing your resume, LinkedIn profile, and other career communications is essential but can sometimes be difficult. Use these tips to keep yourself motivated and moving forward.

- **Think about what you *do* have, not what you don't.** Make your resume all about your assets—your value, distinguishing credentials, relevant experience, and unique achievements. Prepare and practice your success stories for use in your resume and during interviews. (Refer to Career Vault, page 244, for more on success stories.)

- **Match your value to employers' needs.** How will you benefit your next employer? Approach resume writing and interviewing from the viewpoint of "I'm here to help." Being helpful makes us feel valuable and in control, and that translates to confidence in your job search and the workplace.

- **Know why you're a great fit for a specific role.** Learn as much as you can about the job, the company, and the industry, and be able to clearly express how your specific skills and experiences fit the need. It's easier to focus on the positives when you really know—and can address—what's involved.

- **Recognize that all candidates have drawbacks.** There's no such thing as a perfect candidate! It's easy to fall into the trap of thinking that "everyone else" is more qualified. Companies weigh the pluses and minuses of each candidate and then hire the one who can help them *now*.

- **Understand "fit factor."** A lot of hiring decisions are based on fit, which is hard to define but easy to feel. Even when you're an ideal candidate, you might not get the job because someone else just fit better into that company's culture. It's outside your control, so accept it and move on.

- **Deal with your demons.** Much of what you might worry about ends up being a minor point in your job search. Nonetheless, you must be prepared to address all questions and issues that might arise. Create a plan for how to respond—you'll worry less and be much more confident and relaxed during your interviews.

PRO TIP: In our experience, all too many job seekers focus on the negatives. They worry about current unemployment, or past job gaps, or lack of the right education and credentials. Certainly, some situations present challenges, but they are almost never insurmountable!

Personal Branding & Resume Writing

A current, high-profile trend in resume writing is personal branding. Simply stated, a branded resume tells an interview-attracting story of qualification and success while demonstrating passion, personality, work style, leadership style, and other unique characteristics. It's a bold way of stating definitively—*THIS IS WHO I AM—THE BRAND THAT IS ME.*

A branded resume generally starts with a strong branding statement at the very beginning. This statement, in conjunction with the headline, communicates your unique value proposition in such a way that it's clear, concise, and recognizable to every recruiter, hiring manager, and decision maker.

Here are 3 examples of resume headlines with their accompanying branding statements:

ENTRY-LEVEL SALES & MARKETING ASSOCIATE
Self-starter with strong competitive drive

QUALITY TEST ENGINEER
Committed to innovating safer, cost-effective solutions that leave smaller carbon footprints.

RETAIL EXECUTIVE

Building Multi-State Retail Enterprises that Blow Away the Competition

> **PRO TIP: Even if you don't start with a specific branding statement, you can create a branded resume.** Every modern resume is branded because it powerfully communicates who you are, how you're unique and distinguishable from other candidates, and why a company should hire you. Your brand will shine through.

For examples of well-branded resumes, you can look at every single resume sample in this book.

In general, the personal brand of each individual that is showcased at the top of the page is reinforced and supported in every other section of the resume. The theme is consistent: *This is who I am, what I'm good at, and why you can believe me. This is how I do things and what makes me different from—and better than—other candidates.*

Next Steps

Now that you've dipped a toe into the world of modern resume writing, it's time to plunge in wholeheartedly so you can move forward with your job search.

As you work through the guidance in the following chapters, the lessons we share about the core resume-development principles, combined with expert resume samples, will inspire you to create your own powerful resume so that you will *get noticed* and *get hired!*

PART II:
Modernize Your Resume Content

The 4 Key Principles of Modern Resume Content
- Start with the Wow!
- Put Your Objective in the Driver's Seat
- Write with Meaning & Power
- Write Tight, Lean & Clean

A great resume starts with great content. No matter how visually dazzling or neatly organized, no resume will help you achieve your goals unless it instantly communicates your value in the workplace to recruiters, employers, and other decision makers.

One reason that resume writing is so challenging is that most people don't do it very often! You might put together a new resume when you enter the workforce and then every 2 to 5 years when you are looking for a new job. Like anything else, practice improves skill, and the reality is that most people don't get that much practice.

In the following chapters you'll learn how to write strong resume content that showcases you—your skills, qualifications, achievements, work experiences, educational credentials, and all of the other tangible and intangible assets you bring to the employment market.

We'll teach you what professional resume writers do and we'll show you how we do it so you can apply the Principles of Modern Resume Content to write your own great resume.

> **PRO TIP: All of our content principles and guidelines are valuable for everyone**—from the senior executive to the graduating student, from the career changer to the return-to-work mom or dad, from the classroom teacher to the global sales associate, and virtually every other profession, industry, and job search challenge or situation.

CHAPTER 2:

Start with the Wow!

What is the wow? It's what's most impressive, important, and valuable about you as a candidate— the top few things that you want readers to instantly know about you, so they'll be impressed, interested, and eager to learn more.

Your unique "wow factor" information distinguishes you from others with similar skills and qualifications. Be sure to prominently position it on your resume so readers can't possibly miss it and you create an instantly positive first impression.

To clearly demonstrate the difference between the wow and the not-so-wow, here are 2 examples:

> **Not-So-Wow:**
> *Responsible for turning around stagnant sales region and returning it to profitability.*
> **Wow:**
> *Grew sales by $34M in first year, a 220% increase over prior year.*
>
> **Not-So-Wow:**
> *Wrote software programs and applications for new technology releases.*
> **Wow:**
> *Pioneered next-generation technology architecture for Microsoft's newest suite of laptops.*

As you can see, wow statements are specific—they tell what *you* did, not what someone with a similar job might have done. They make your resume (and you) memorable, and that's step #1 to getting interviewed and hired.

Wow content can go virtually anywhere in your resume, including the following sections:

Summary. When you add wow statements to your Summary, you're starting with your best foot forward. In just a glance, readers will quickly learn what you have accomplished.

Tips for including wow statements in your Summary:

- Limit your items to 3–4. If you have too many, you diminish the impact that you are trying to create.

- Or use just 1 "big wow" and position it right at the top of your resume, either above or below the headline that boldly states *who* you are.

- Keep each wow statement to 1 line if possible. Fewer words draw more attention.

- Save details for later. Your wow statement is a quick hit of impressive information. You can expand on the achievement in the appropriate section of your resume.

Experience. In all too many resumes, position descriptions begin with an overview of job functions to define overall scope of responsibility. That's important information, of course—but it's not the most interesting.

Instead, consider starting each job description with the #1 achievement of that job—the big, overarching success story. When you do that, you communicate an instant message of success. You can then follow the wow with a brief description of your job responsibilities and other notable achievements of that position.

Education. If you're a recent college graduate with limited work experience, Education becomes the showpiece of your resume. Make sure that you wow your readers by highlighting what it is that makes you a uniquely qualified young professional—perhaps your notable academic performance, leadership activities, special projects, internships, or volunteer work.

Honors & Awards. Distinguishing honors and awards are a great enhancement to your wow factor. They can be listed in a separate category—either near the beginning of your resume or at the end; they can be added to the Summary with an honors and awards subheading; they can be integrated into the jobs where you won them; or they can be highlighted in Education.

Other wow information that may be relevant to some job seekers includes publications, board-of-director affiliations, media mentions, public-speaking engagements, patents … anything that tells readers you are an expert in your field, recognized by your peers, and valued for your contributions and accomplishments. As with honors and awards, this information can be included in separate sections or integrated into your Summary, Experience, or Education.

> **PRO TIP: Ask yourself these questions to help uncover your wow achievements:**
>
> When have I been first or best?
>
> What is the #1 thing I achieved in each position?
>
> When did I help turn a failure into a success?
>
> Which of my achievements have the most impressive numbers?
>
> What have I been publicly recognized for?
>
> What major business successes have I contributed to?

Following are 2 resumes that clearly exemplify how to start with the wow. The moment you begin reading, you're instantly drawn in and impressed with the success of both job seekers.

Sally Clairborne Resume—pages 24–25

Sally's resume includes a number of wow factors that create an immediately positive first impression that is reinforced by the strong content throughout her resume:

- A bold graphic at the top immediately signals that Sally is in the healthcare field.

- The branding statement underneath her headline highlights her success in "practice transformation."
- Shaded boxes set off the Summary and concise job descriptions, creating immediate visual distinction between sections.
- Attention-getting headings are set in reverse (white) type in a bold black box.
- Bullet points in the Summary and Experience are introduced with bold type that draws attention to her expertise and achievements.
- The strong visual impression from page 1 carries over to page 2, where a graphic illustrates her related technical achievements.

Tricia Maxwell Resume—page 26

Tricia's resume (also shown in color on the back cover of this book) uses several "wow" techniques to capture and maintain each reader's interest:

- A headline instantly describes her as an "Award-Winning Sales Executive."
- An endorsement from her prior manager provides a third-party testimonial to her success.
- A dedicated Career Highlights and Awards section draws maximum attention to the many times she stood out from her peers.
- A powerful Revenue Growth graphic captures the eye and reinforces achievements (numbers) that are highlighted in bold in the bullet points.
- The 1-page presentation is an added bonus for Tricia, giving readers a wealth of information in a single glance.

Sally Clairborne

Evanston, IL 60201 | 847-522-4810 | sclairborne@gmail.com | LinkedIn

HEALTH CARE INDUSTRY CHIEF OPERATING OFFICER
Practice transformation for multi-site health/ambulatory care networks

Senior executive with track record of success developing and implementing health management programs and operational strategies in the changing healthcare landscape.

→ **Change driver** in pivoting organizations from single to multi-service and expanding brand footprint through innovation and strategic partnerships.

→ **Champion** of technology that promotes efficiency and cost savings and improves the patient experience.

→ **Fiscal watchdog** who unearthed millions of dollars in operational savings and created/extended revenue streams adding millions of dollars to optimize patient services and programs.

Expertise: Service/Program Development | Revenue Cycle Management/Enhancement | HIT/EHR Implementation

Quality Improvement & Compliance Coalition Building | Meaningful Use Compliance

340B Drug Discount Start-up & Compliance | Patient-Centered Medical Home Building

Accountable Care Organization Readiness/Optimization | Population Health/Care Coordination & Management

Grant Writing/Management | Budget & Staff Management

PROFESSIONAL EXPERIENCE

MERCY HOSPITAL & MEDICAL CENTER | Chicago, IL | 2012 to Present
Multi-site community health/ambulatory care network with 5 primary care programs serving 60,000 patients annually.

Chief Operating Officer
Lead daily operations and promote practice transformation through integration of health information technology, medical home model, and affiliations with other community-based organizations. Budget $10M; Staff/Providers: 100+

➕ **Rescued organization from bankruptcy and added close to $500K in revenues in 12 months.** Uncovered $250K in unprocessed claims and recovered another $250K in past-due claims.

➕ **Drove strategy to secure $440M in funding to reinstitute dental services following a 5-year lapse.** Created business rationale, wrote grant proposal, and oversaw entire infrastructure build and recruitment process. Service manages 5,000+ visits per year and is one of the only services of its kind in the area.

➕ **Captured $300K in incentives and garnered close to $200K in funding by digitizing all patient records.** Ensured seamless transition and realized dramatic improvements in objective measurements of patient care.

➕ **Secured $150K to launch a chronic disease management program** and developed strategic partnership with Methodist Hospital's *Health Works* program to deliver services and reduce costs.

➕ **Created first-of-its-kind initiative to encourage primary care appointments and reduce ER visits.** Program provided counselors to educate patients using ER for reactive low-level visits to transition to proactive visits with primary care doctors. Program is currently under consideration at other area health networks.

➕ **Sourced and implemented technology that significantly improved healthcare screening process.** Software is projected to expedite process for health screenings and trigger faster reimbursement for services.

Barbara Safani, NCRW, CPRW, CERW, CCM • Career Solvers • careersolvers.com

METHODIST HOSPITAL OF CHICAGO | Chicago, IL | 2009 to 2012
$110M, 24-site ambulatory care network managing 500,000 patient encounters annually.

Assistant Vice President, Ambulatory Care Division
Planned, developed, and delivered enterprise-wide strategic initiatives. Designed, organized, and implemented new programs and services to increase access to care and achieve organizational growth objectives. Key advisor to senior administration on operational initiatives and regulatory compliance. Budget: $110M

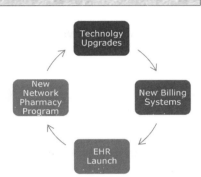

- **In just 6 months, added $700K in Medicaid revenue** related to inpatient services provided by outpatient MDs by implementing new billing processes and procedures.

- **Increased pharmaceutical program revenues by $150K annually** by working with vendors to restructure network's discount pharmaceutical program and pricing model.

- **Identified a $250M annual revenue opportunity** by co-creating a workers' compensation injury care program.

- **Secured funding for launch of a $5M Electronic Health Record system,** later implemented network-wide.

- **Proposed/opened an innovative on-site health clinic** for low-income employees at Hawthorne Race Course.

ADVOCATE TRINITY HOSPITAL | Chicago, IL | 2008 to 2009
Multi-site community health/ambulatory network managing 77,000 patient encounters annually.

Administrative Director
Oversaw specific grant and operational programs. Staff: 3

- **Built infrastructure to support creation of a 340B Pharmacy/Discount Drug Pricing Program** budgeted to increase revenues by $100K annually.

- **Managed state and federal grants totaling ~$17M.** Orchestrated 3 new grants during tenure.

- **Coordinated relocation of 6 outpatient departments to new facility,** improving continuity of care and increasing accessibility to clinical and counseling services.

- **Developed profitable state-sponsored Comprehensive Health Evaluation for Children (CHEC) Program** to coordinate the medical, developmental, and mental health care services for children in out-of-home placement in Illinois. Managed service development across multiple departments from RFP to start-up.

- **Coordinated Congress-mandated tabletop and live emergency preparedness exercises** for Department of Homeland Security's Top Officials Three Exercise (TOPOFF 3).

Earlier roles include **Area Manager** at Chicago Lakeshore Hospital, 2005 to 2008, **Center Administrator** at Holy Cross Hospital, 2002 to 2005, and **Account Manager/Coordinator of Customer Support** at St. Bernard Hospital, 2000 to 2002. Spent 6 years in clinical behavioral health roles at Chicago Beth Israel Medical Center, St. Vincent's Hospital, and Northwestern Memorial Hospital.

EDUCATION & CERTIFICATIONS

Northwestern University, Evanston, IL | **MS,** Health Systems Management, 1997 & **MSW,** School of Social Work, 1998
Kendall College, Chicago, IL | **BA,** Psychology/Business, 1994

University of Chicago, Chicago, IL | Health Informatics for Innovation Value & Enrichment Certificate, 2021
Loyola University, Chicago, IL | Practice Leader in Medical Home Development Certificate, 2016

TRICIA MAXWELL

Award-Winning Sales Executive

Winston, FL 33815 | 313-575-1519 | tricia.maxwell@yahoo.com

www.linkedin.com/in/triciamaxwell

*"Tricia relocated as Regional Sales Manager to take over an underperforming region … and delivered the **largest revenue growth** and the highest performance to quota, **exceeding quota every month**."*

– Tyrone Williams, *prior supervisor, Records Management Company*

Tenacious revenue generator, #1 in the nation 2 years in a row by aggressively developing a continual pipeline of new clients and quickly surpassing sales targets. Talented negotiator with the gift of assessing client needs and offering viable solutions to secure the sale. Well versed in Salesforce, Word, PowerPoint, and Excel.

Strategic Relationship Building | Situational Fluency | Business Development
Market Expansion | Territory Development | Account Management

Career Highlights and Awards

Records Management Company	*Maximum Corp., Inc.*
Ranked #1 sales producer in US.	**Boosted sales from zero to $1.2M in 18 months.**
Built client base valued at $19.7M.	**8-time President's Club Winner.**
Counted in top third of company sales metrics.	**Sales Excellence Award Recipient.**

Career Progression

Director of Sales | Records Management Company, Miami, FL (2021 – 2023)

Managed team of 5 Account Managers and Sales Agents promoting multiple product lines, including data protection support, records management, and shredding services, across regional territory spanning Virginia to Florida. Persevered through multiple restructurings to instill focus and resilience among team, leading to consistent top results.

- ▶ Acknowledged as **#1** in country among 18 counterparts, 2020 and 2021, by achieving **112%** of goal.
- ▶ Built and maintained a **$9.2M** client portfolio with **2.93%** growth factor in 2022.
- ▶ Captured **$1.4M** in new sales (non-recurring) and **$547K** in recurring new sales revenue in 2022.
- ▶ Recognized as **#6** across the US in 2022 with quota attainment of **111%** and new sales revenue of **$1.9M.**
- ▶ Nurtured client accounts collectively valued at **$19.7M,** yielding a **2.5%** growth factor in 2022.

VP of Sales, Southeast Region | Maximum Corp., Inc., Naples, FL (2008 – 2011)

Coached, led, and supervised 15 staff while identifying effective growth strategies and executing profitable marketing solutions to boost revenue at $150M print service bureau.

- ▶ Produced **$7.1M** in yearly sales, meeting firm goals with no additional staff despite severely shrinking market.
- ▶ Secured **$23M** in retention revenue and earned **#1** position of 5 Regional VPs.
- ▶ Generated **$4.3M** within 1 year, achieving **105%** of corporate objective.
- ▶ Drove sales from zero to **$1.2M** over 18 months by developing and managing new territory *(see adjacent chart).*

Early Career

Progressively promoted with Maximum Corp. from Billing Clerk to Account Executive and Senior Account Manager. Generated **$1.3M** in sales by targeting and capturing key accounts with industry leaders Equifax and South Bank.

Training & Development

Major Account Planning Process, Dale Carnegie Public Speaking, Solution Selling, High-Performance Management, Power Message Training, Challenger Methodology, Situational Fluency

[Read and learn about this resume inside, in the Start with the Wow! chapter.]

Melanie Denny, CPRW, CIPCC • melaniedenny.com

CHAPTER 3:
Put Your Objective in the Driver's Seat

The #1 reason you're creating a resume is to position yourself for your next job. Of course, your work experience, achievements, education, and other qualifications are all critical resume building blocks, but *how* you include your information, *where*, and *why* should all be dictated by your current career goals.

When you know the jobs you want, you know what skills are in demand and what employers value most. That information becomes the foundation upon which you build your entire resume.

For some people, that's easy. If you're a sales representative looking for another sales opportunity, you can showcase your success in increasing sales revenues *(including numbers and percentages)*, capturing key accounts, launching products, building new markets, and all of the other sales functions of your job.

It becomes more challenging, however, when your current career goals don't directly align with your past experience. Let's suppose in your sales job you spent 20% of your time training new sales associates, and now you want to pursue jobs in training and development. That 20% becomes the primary focus of your resume, showcasing all of your relevant experience in training, mentoring, creating training materials, designing training programs, and performing related activities.

The other 80% … of course you'll include some or even most of that information, but it becomes secondary to all training-related experience and qualifications.

Your goal is to paint the picture of yourself that you want someone to see. **You never want to lie; you never want to misrepresent.** What you do want to do is put the focus where it belongs, minimize or omit what doesn't add value, and align your resume with your current career goals and aspirations.

> **PRO TIP: If you're not certain of your career objective, STOP!** To write a powerful and effective resume, you must have some idea of your job targets. Some options for homing in on a target:
>
> - Look at lots of job postings to find those that interest you the most and for which you have some related skills, experience, or educational qualifications.
> - Identify your top skills and interests, then match them to available opportunities.
> - Consult a career coach, who can guide you through career exploration and discovery.
>
> When you've defined your career objective (see page 243 for our Goal-Setting Worksheet in Part VIII— Resources), you can move forward, creating a well-targeted resume to help you achieve that goal.

Following are 3 strategies that will put your objective in the driver's seat:

- **Write to the future … to your next job.** A resume is not an autobiographical retrospective (although it does include some of the same information). Rather, today's modern resume is a marketing tool designed to merchandise you as a strong candidate for the jobs you're pursuing by showcasing your experience, education, achievements, and everything else about your career that directly supports your objective.

- **Reweight your skills and experience.** The sales representative, referenced on the previous page, who wants to transition into training and development is the perfect example of when to reweight skills, qualifications, experience, educational credentials, and anything else you might include in your resume. Put the heaviest emphasis on the things that relate to your objective and the least emphasis on things that do not.

- **Integrate critical keywords.** We address this topic in greater detail in Chapter 9, but it deserves a brief mention here. Keywords are the foundation for all resume-scanning systems (ATS—Applicant Tracking Systems), so it is imperative that your resume contain essential keywords for the jobs and industries you are targeting. If the sales training resume does not have the right training-related keywords, it will simply be passed over by ATS and by hiring managers seeking people with those specific skills.

Summary vs. Objective Statement

The final point in this chapter is a discussion of the use of an Objective in today's modern resume.

Bottom line, we don't recommend Objectives for the vast majority of job seekers. When you include an Objective, you're telling employers what you want from them and, frankly, they don't care.

Rather, the Summary has largely replaced the Objective. In a Summary, you can tell employers what you can do for *them*, the value you bring to their organization, your strongest areas of expertise, and other information that should entice the reader to contact you. Instead of writing "this is what I want," you're communicating "this is what I can do for you"—a message that will immediately resonate with employers.

But we don't dismiss objective statements entirely. In select circumstances they can be helpful, particularly for job seekers whose objectives will not be clear from their work experience, skills, or educational credentials. If that's the case, a clean and well-targeted Objective can add value and clarity to the resume:

Objective: Position in Purchasing & Supply Chain Management

With a glance, employers know what this candidate wants—and that's essential information.

> **PRO TIP: There is NEVER an occasion to use an Objective that says nothing of value.**
>
> *Seeking a challenging opportunity offering growth and long-term career development.*
>
> What's wrong with that Objective? It's not specific—it tells us nothing about what industry or profession the job seeker is targeting. And it's not employer focused—it says nothing about the value that person brings to a company. It's simply a waste of space.

As you'll see from the samples in this book, we believe a Summary is a stronger, more employer-focused way to begin your resume. A Summary allows you to put your job target in the driver's seat by showcasing all that you have to offer in support of your goals. And, as we've stated, your current career objective will impact every decision about every element in your resume.

The following 2 resumes demonstrate these principles very effectively.

Emma Faith Resume—page 30

As a recent graduate with limited related work experience, Emma has created a resume that expertly positions her for a professional opportunity within the music industry. In this case an Objective (here referred to as a Target) is highly beneficial, instantly and clearly communicating the specific positions she is pursuing.

The second paragraph of her Summary showcases relevant keywords, followed by her equally important technology skills. Detailed descriptions of her 3 internships allow her to present rich, relevant content and include many other keywords essential for ATS scanning. The use of a testimonial adds instant and powerful third-party validation of her competencies.

Alex Rodman Resume—page 31

Your first thought when reviewing Alex's resume is that he is an experienced network administrator. Everything in the resume positions him for that specific goal. It is not until you read his Employment, at the very bottom of the page, that you learn he is actually a supply officer in the US Navy.

Everything in the resume is 100% accurate—it simply reweights his network administrator experiences into the most prominent content in the resume, in line with his current career goals. Perfect!

Emma Faith

555.555.5555 § Em.Faith@email.com § LinkedIn Profile

Target: **A&R Coordinator | Creative Manager within the Music Publishing Industry**

Spirited, performance-focused professional able to efficiently manage processes required for the execution of business-impacting initiatives and known for consistently exceeding expectations. Strong interpersonal skills and ability to collaborate with cross-functional teams to support operations and objectives. Innovative, detail-oriented, motivated, and ready to launch into the next career phase, with the creative and practical skills, ambition, confidence, and passion to succeed.

Core Competencies: *Talent Management & Support, Music Promotion, Relationship Building, Publishing Processes, Creative & Administrative Support, Event Planning, Data Entry & Database Management, Tracking & Analysis, Reporting, Project Management*

Software Skills: DISCO, iMaestro, TuneSat, MS Office (Word, Excel & PowerPoint), Google Suite (Calendar, Docs, Drive, Sheets & Slides)

Education

Bachelor of Business Administration (BBA), Music Business—TOWNSEND UNIVERSITY, *Nashville, TN* (2020)
GPA: 3.67 | EARNED DEAN'S LIST

Relevant Courses / *Music Publishing, Survey of Music Business, Survey of Audio Engineering Technology, Record Label Operations, Music Industry Contract Law, Computer Proficiency in Business, Copyright Law, Managing Information Systems in Business*

Associations / Sanford Business Ethics Case Competition § CMA EDU § The Recording Academy § Alpha Gamma Delta, The Marilyn Shepard Initiative & Academic Honor Society § Los Angeles West Program

Professional Experience

Publishing Creative Intern / ELKS GROVE MUSIC PUBLISHING, *Nashville, TN*   Jan 2022–May 2022
Contributed to the song delivery process, including receiving and categorizing audio files and song metadata from rostered songwriters, often up 75 songs per day. Downloaded audio files and organized over 1,000 songs and associated data in DISCO.

- Extracted metadata from song delivery for iMaestro, transcribed lyrics, and filled in gaps of missing files, dates, and details.
- Assisted with calendar management for the Nashville writer roster, tracking and documenting new releases.
- Assembled and collaborated on pitch idea playlists and maintained hold list, cut list, and pitch log.
- Took initiative to learn how to do additional data management and cataloging tasks to increase efficiency of team members and streamline the song delivery process.
- Contributed to event planning efforts for company's Songwriting Camp, including researching and contacting vendors and venues to collect quotes for various services and food and beverage packages.

"…incredibly organized, efficient and diligent … She has a deep understanding of the music industry … She also represented Elks Grove incredibly well at external events and showcases." (Internship Supervisor)

Licensing Intern, Film & TV / ENIGMA MUSIC SERVICES, *Sacramento, CA*   Aug 2021–Jan 2022
Provided operational support to film, TV, and international departments, encompassing licensing, management, and A&R teams. Assisted with the song delivery process and database management, provided administrative and meeting support, assembled and monitored pitch and placement reports, managed complex artist and tour calendars, and aided in planning and execution of a songwriting event at Red Bull Studios in Santa Monica.

Intern / TALENT MANAGEMENT CO., *Nashville, TN*   Feb 2020–May 2020
Assisted with a variety of administrative and artist support responsibilities, including organizing tour itineraries and contracts, attending and assisting with rehearsals and photo shoots, and responding to a broad range of inquiries, both internal and external.

Additional experience in customer service roles, providing personalized support and efficiently executing tasks.

Community Service / Coalition for Women Prisoners § JDRF § St. Jude § Second Harvest § Food Rescue & Recovery

ALEX RODMAN

630-555-5555

arodman@msn.com
www.linked.com/alexrodman

PROFESSIONAL PROFILE

Network Administrator with 10+ years' experience in technical training, project management, computer architecture, and technology operations. Expert in networking, TCP/IP protocol, and network security.

Skilled troubleshooter with attention to detail and ability to work effectively in fast-paced, mission-critical environments. Talented team leader who consistently achieves/surpasses desired results. Top Secret clearance.

TECHNICAL SUMMARY

CERTIFICATIONS
- A+ | Network + | Linux + | LPI | MCSA | CNA
- VMware Certified Professional (VCP)
- Cisco Certified Network Associate, Routing & Switching (CCNA-R&S)

KNOWLEDGE & SKILLS
- Windows 8/10 | Windows 365 | Windows Server 2012 | UNIX | Linux | Exchange Server 2013
- Cisco IOS | TCP/IP | LAN/WAN | BGP | DHCP | DNS | TLS/SSL | Gigabit Ethernet
- VMware vSphere | Data Center & Storage Management Platforms | Cloud Services (SaaS, IaaS, PaaS)

EXPERIENCE HIGHLIGHTS

- **NETWORK ADMINISTRATOR:** Provided workable and proven solutions to maintain various operating environments. Installed, configured, and maintained the network for military training school, achieving zero classroom downtime for more than 3 years. Demonstrated strong diagnostic abilities with attention to detail and ability to work effectively and efficiently in a fast-paced environment.

  Recognized as a competent and credible authority on establishing procedures, conducting tests to verify correct operation of equipment/systems, implementing fault-tolerant procedures for hardware and software failures, and designing audit procedures to test systems integrity and reliability.

- **PROJECT MANAGER:** Managed $3.5M supply inventory and annual budget of $600K. Provided all logistics, including parts issues, contingency purchasing, and emergency field delivery, with no measurable losses.

- **RISK ANALYST:** Identified potential liabilities in computerized military accounting system training program. Analyzed accuracy, usage feasibility, and deficiencies while providing solutions for obstacles.

- **LEADER:** Earned multiple awards for performance excellence. Motivated and inspired organizations ranging in size from 30–400 personnel. Effectively guided and directed associates to achieve their highest potential. Encouraged and supported a teamwork environment that resulted in increased efficiency and productivity.

- **INSTRUCTOR:** Played a major role in design and implementation of self-paced curriculum at military training facility, increasing throughput and retention of more than 150 students per year.

EDUCATION

B.S. Computer Science, Excelsior University, Alameda, CA   2022
A.S. Computer Technology, Empire College, Santa Rosa, CA   2017

EMPLOYMENT

United States Coast Guard   2007–2022
- Supply Officer/Department Head—USCG BOUTWELL (WHEC-719), Alameda, CA, 2017–2022
- Supervisor/Assistant Branch Chief—Maintenance & Logistics Command Pacific, Alameda, CA, 2013–2017
- Instructor—USCG Training Center, Petaluma, CA, 2007–2013

CHAPTER 4:
Write with Meaning & Power

Read these 2 sentences:

> *Responsible for managing the design, development, and marketing of new biomedical equipment that the company had developed. After product launch into the market, helped with sales that exceeded expectations in the first year.*

Now, read this sentence:

> *Championed design, development, and market roll-out of new biomedical equipment that generated $12M in first-year sales—27% above projections.*

Can you tell the difference? Can you *feel* the difference in the strength and impact of the second sentence? Even though both sentences say essentially the same thing, the second one says it with meaning, power, and a real story about that job seeker's performance.

> **PRO TIP: Writing a resume is just like writing any other marketing communication.** You have a product—yourself—to promote, and the more powerfully you can write about it, tell stories about it, share achievements of it, and highlight notable assets, the more enticing you will be.

What are the elements of that second sentence above ("Championed design, development ...") that make it so strong and effective—instantly capturing a reader's attention and interest? How is it an example of writing with meaning and power?

Professional resume writers use the following techniques to make that happen.

Technique #1: Quantify Achievements

Numbers and percentages are always valuable to include in your resume because they're a measurable indicator of your performance. For example:

- **Cut costs 20%** after redesigning administrative and office procedures.
- **Increased yield $10M** with implementation of next-generation manufacturing technology.
- Restructured staffing models for 10 locations and **improved productivity 28%.**

The obvious next question is … what if you don't have quantifiable achievements? A big part of preparation for writing your resume and conducting your job search is recalling your career success stories. It is those successes that are at the root of quantifiable achievements. When you dig deep into each story, you can often generate numbers, dollars, and percentages that will instantly add power and meaning to your resume.

Refer to Dig-Deep Questions, on pages 247–248 in Part VIII—Resources, for a list of idea-inspiring questions to help you uncover your numbers and other specific results.

> **PRO TIP: Not everything is quantifiable**—we know that, and employers know it too. If you can't quantify many of your achievements, pay special attention to the writing techniques in the rest of this chapter so that your resume content is strong, clear, and specific even if not quantified.

Technique #2: Lead with Strong Verbs

One of the first things you'll notice about the 3 bullet points in the previous section is that each begins with a verb—Cut, Increased, Restructured. Verbs convey action and energy—you *did* something. You will increase the energy and intensity of your entire resume by starting each paragraph and each bullet point with a strong verb—even if that paragraph or bullet point is not linked to a quantifiable achievement.

Another good writing technique is to vary the verbs that you use. You will quickly bore your readers if you start many sentences with the same word. Choose verbs that clearly and specifically describe what you did.

For example, if you "increased" sales and "increased" profitability and "increased" customer service scores, think of other diverse and interesting verbs you can use to convey the same valuable information:

- **Built** the #1 sales region in the company, **driving** revenue from $7M to $18M in 2 years.
- **Delivered** profit margins 7% above company average.
- **Reversed** declining service scores and **achieved** double-digit growth in customer satisfaction.

You'll find our very useful list of 440 Resume Writing Verbs on pages 249–250 in Part VIII—Resources. In addition, a thesaurus is a gold mine for identifying a variety of words that convey similar meanings.

Technique #3: Write in First Person … Never in Third Person

First person is the most reader-friendly and the most intimate—you're telling *your* career story. Although it is rare that you would use the word "I" in your resume, it is assumed and understood. For example:

> *[I] direct daily operations for Reynolds' highest-volume manufacturing plant ($18M annual volume, 189 employees, 2K sq. ft. facility).*

Eliminate the "I," capitalize the "d," and you've got a strong and meaningful resume sentence to add to a short paragraph or include as a bullet point within the job description. It even starts with a verb, as we just discussed in Technique #2.

Conversely, writing in third person by adding an "s" to the end of each present-tense verb changes the tone and feel of your resume, and not for the better:

[She] directs daily operations for Reynolds' highest-volume manufacturing plant ($18M annual volume, 189 employees, 2K sq. ft. facility).

Now the focus is on "she"—someone else—and not on you. Instantly, you've lost ownership of your resume and all of the wonderful content. Don't ever let that happen … not even in your Summary, where sometimes it feels more natural to write in third person.

PRO TIP: If you were to write a professional bio to accompany your resume, it can be written in third person, and many of them are. Bios are a different type of career marketing and networking tool, meant as an introduction, an addendum to a business plan, an inclusion in a project portfolio, and for other professional activities—job search related and not. However, first person is best for resumes, LinkedIn profiles, and most other career communications.

Technique #4: Eliminate Words, Phrases, and Introductory Statements You Don't Need

Read through your resume and see how many of these terms you have used:

- Responsible for …
- Duties encompassed …
- Achievements included … (followed by bullet-point achievements)
- Skills included … (followed by a double-column listing of your top professional skills)

Now, ask yourself if those words add any value to your resume. Chances are almost 100% that they do not. Delete them and edit accordingly!

Technique #5: Be Specific

Specifics are much more meaningful and memorable than generalities. To see what we mean, compare these 2 sentences from a job seeker's Summary:

Accomplished retail manager with 10 years of experience and a track record of increasing sales and reducing labor costs.

or

Retail Manager who led 2 different stores to #1 in sales in 20-store Midwest Region while delivering the company's highest profit-per-labor-dollar.

The first sentence is general: It could be written by many retail managers. The second, however, is specific and unique to a single individual. When you write specifics, your resume immediately stands out and you successfully distinguish yourself from other candidates.

While of course you do need to provide some general career details, too many generalities can weigh down your resume—especially today, when we need to capture attention quickly and provide short bites of information to keep readers engaged.

PRO TIP: An added bonus when you write specifics is that you convey essential information. In the example just shown, clearly the retail manager from sentence #2 is "accomplished" and has a great "track record." By telling precisely what he has done, we don't need those over-used words. Instead, we convey that message in a way that's much more powerful, distinctive, and credible.

Technique #6: Add Context to Add Meaning

Synonyms for context are background, situation, and frame of reference. Context helps readers understand and appreciate your achievements—making those achievements even more impressive.

Here's an example of an achievement that, at first glance, seems to be clear and strong:

Increased territory revenue 26%.

Yet consider how much more meaningful and valuable that same accomplishment becomes when we provide a frame of reference:

Increased territory revenue 26%, twice the company average.

You can also add context to your job descriptions by describing why you were hired for the job. For example, rather than simply writing:

Managed a $12M sales territory and supervised 19 independent contractors who provided daily route service to retail accounts.

… you can make that job description much richer with information about the situation that existed when you were hired:

Recruited to reverse declining sales and improve service to retail accounts. In 1 year, grew revenue from $8M to $12M and created a customer-first culture among front-line service team of 19 independent contractors.

Another example of how specifics can work for you has to do with company names—names that are *not* familiar to most people. We all know Apple, IBM, Nike, McDonald's, and AT&T. But what about Reymon Manufacturing, Samuelson Stores, and The Gallery? Those company names mean nothing to a reader.

Sometimes that's okay. If you're not looking for a job in the same industry, it's probably best to omit details that will position you squarely within your past industry. However, if your goal is to work in the same or a related industry, it is vitally important to share specifics about each company. You instantly communicate that you know the industry and, maybe, the market, competition, customer base, products, and more.

Be specific, but be succinct! For example:

Reymon Manufacturing ($32M industrial equipment manufacturer/distributor)

The 2 resumes that we're showcasing in this chapter, for Bernard Henry and Taj Gupta, are both great examples of all 6 of the writing techniques in this chapter. They:

- Have quantifiable achievements.
- Lead with strong verbs.
- Are written in first person.
- Avoid unnecessary words and details.
- Are very specific throughout.
- Include context that adds meaning and impact.

Let's look more closely at each.

Bernard Henry Resume—pages 37–38

Bernard's resume includes:

- A Summary with specific details about his career accomplishments.
- Succinct company descriptions that help us understand his work environment.
- Specific and quantified achievements highlighted in bold numbers and eye-catching graphics.
- Precise verbs and other high-impact language.
- Context information to tell us why he was hired for each job.
- Just enough information to help us understand his career successes without drowning in detail.

Taj Gupta Resume—pages 39–40

Taj's resume showcases:

- Specific industry expertise (online travel) in the Summary, with clear headline and powerful graphic.
- An impressive and one-of-a-kind endorsement.
- Strong verbs that paint a colorful picture of his career and achievements.
- Keywords, action verbs, and other relevant terms that emphasize his broad and deep expertise.
- Concise descriptions of the scope of each position—budget, direct reports, and focus of the job.
- The context around each position—why he was chosen for that job.
- Quantified achievements, with numbers and other results highlighted in bold.

BUSINESS TURNAROUND ➲ CUSTOMER FOCUS ➲ RAPID IMPLEMENTATION

BERNARD M. HENRY

Tulsa, OK 74115 ➲ 918-838-5000 ➲ bhenry@wordright.com

INDUSTRY EXPERTISE   Manufacturing ➲ Supply Chain ➲ Warehouse Management ➲ Shipping

VP | DIRECTOR SUPPLY CHAIN MANAGEMENT ▸▸ VP | DIRECTOR ENTERPRISE RESOURCE PLANNING [ERP]

INFLUENTIAL, TOP-PRODUCING BUSINESS EXECUTIVE, expert in leading rapid implementations, transforming performance, and driving profitability. Recognized for collaboration, teamwork, negotiation, influence, and relationship-building. Dozens of impeccable end-to-end business process conversions completed on time and on budget.

MBA BOSTON UNIVERSITY | APICS AND ICCP CERTIFICATIONS | MULTIPLE INDUSTRY AWARDS

CRITICAL COMPETENCIES

- Process Reengineering | Implementation
- P&L | Capital Investment Decisions
- Business Continuity Planning
- Negotiation and Influence
- JDA | Oracle | Server Technologies

- Proprietary Systems Migration
- Business Intelligence
- Team Development | Mentorship
- WMS | Manufacturing Platforms
- Enterprise Change Management

- Customer Service | Support | Retention
- Product Design | Development | Marketing
- System-Oriented Architecture
- Warehouse and Inventory Management
- Integration Solutions (FTP, EDI, XML)

PROFESSIONAL EXPERIENCE

CHIEF TECHNOLOGY OFFICER   Tele-Enterprises Incorporated   2021 – Present

Cloud-based $67M multi-functional supply chain management software and ERP company with 275 employees.

Reporting to CEO and Owner, recruited to drive sales and product marketing in preparation for the imminent sale of the firm.

- Led product demand-sensing pilot project that led to major contract and product usage expansion with **$12.7M** identified savings.
- Drove winning presales engagements by developing proposals and detailed Statements of Work (SOW) with 3 international Fortune 500 clients.
- Led sales strategy for Force One Global (won **$5M+** contract) and Braxton, Inc. (secured **$2.5M** extension of existing contract).

DEMAND SENSING PROJECT: $12.7M IN SAVINGS OVER 3 QUARTERS

CHIEF INFORMATION OFFICER (CIO)   Public Employee Retirement Plan (PERP)   2018 – 2021

$39B public pension plan formed from American Public Employees' Pension Plan and American Teachers' Retirement Plan.

Recruited by CEO to improve plan performance, transformed it to best-in-class from most poorly performing fund in US history. Reengineered business technology processes, revitalized underperforming teams, and restored accountability, trust, and confidence among governing bodies.

Managed **$88M** budget, 6 direct reports, and 250 total staff in IT, Operations, and System Design.

SPEARHEADED INTEGRATION OF 2 MULTIBILLION-DOLLAR PENSION ADMINISTRATIONS AND CONSTRUCTED WORLD-CLASS IT OPERATIONS.

Maureen Farmer, CHRP, CCMC, CRS, CCS • Word Right Career • wordrightcareer.com

(PERP continued)

- Transformed services-level retirement processing from **77%** late to **80%** on time.

- Decreased costs by **$5M** and increased internet usage from **300K to 16M+** annual views by designing and implementing "Plan Interactive" application that improved web-based client service.

- Negotiated **$110M** technology renewal plan by state Boards of Directors for 4-year industry-standard IT operations strategy to build mission-critical and sustainable technology infrastructure.

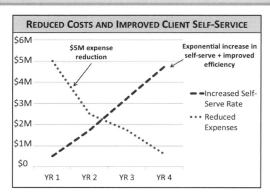

REDUCED COSTS AND IMPROVED CLIENT SELF-SERVICE

CREATED PMO, LEADING 110+ PROJECTS ANNUALLY WITH 88%+ ON-TIME, ON-BUDGET DELIVERY.

- Catapulted APERP to an unqualified audit position and implemented a disaster recovery and business continuity plan, mitigating risk and building organizational capacity and resilience.

- Orchestrated 2-year **$3.5M** data cleanup project to restructure 300,000 member accounts, enabling real-time provision of online retirement calculations and pro-forma statements. Results cleared the path for outsourcing of the 401k pension portion.

SENIOR DIRECTOR	High Volume Technologies, Toledo, OH	2014 – 2018

Global supply chain management software and services company acquired by IMF Software Group in 2015 with a market capitalization of $2.2B and 200 employees.

Reporting to VP Global Sales, directed a team of 39 staff, 7 direct reports, and **$11M P&L**. Company grew from **$4M to $1.1B**. Recruited by CEO for reputation of stellar results at 2 Fortune 100 companies.

Grew product marketing for pharmaceutical, metals, oil and gas, and chemical business units. Implemented business plans and product vision.

- Achieved **$11M** revenue by optimizing productivity and restoring regional divisions to peak performance.

- Drove revenue by **250% to $1.4M** and achieved stretch quota goals from **11%** to **39%** in 2 quarters. Captured **88%** market share for domestic metals industry.

- Coordinated and integrated engineering function, staffing, products, and marketing post-acquisition of Turner Technologies and Ironworks.

- Achieved **$52M** sales quota by generating e-trading sales wins.

- Produced top software-selling region by combining 2 regions, reducing headcount **44%,** and implementing strategies to reach **$15M** sales target.

MARKET- LEADING PERFORMANCE IN SUPPLY CHAIN MANAGEMENT

PRIOR EXPERIENCE

Progressed through supply chain and operations management roles with Ryder Dedicated Logistics and UPS.

EDUCATION, CERTIFICATIONS, AND INDUSTRY AWARDS

Master of Business Administration | New York University
Bachelor of Science in Industrial Management | Wharton School of Management
5 President's Club Honors Awards for Excellence in Leadership | High Volume Technologies

Bernard Henry, Tulsa, OK 74115 ☎ 918-838-5000 ✉ bhenry@wordright.com

Taj Gupta

20 Years of Experience Shaping the Online Travel Industry

Strategic Leader – Executive Director – Online Travel Industry Expert

277-333-6655 – taj.gupta@coldmail.com – www.linkedin.com/tajgupta – Atlanta, GA 30303

"Taj brings expertise in both the online travel industry and executive management that allows our business to be at the forefront of our industry." - CEO, quickbeds.com.

Internationally experienced, **commercially focused Executive Director** positioned to drive responsible progression and authentic results. Depth of experience encapsulates **financial management, strategic leadership,** and **key stakeholder engagement.** Authority in advancing controls and transporting business forward by leveraging emerging technologies.

- Key Value Offerings -

- **Respected Executive** with more than **20 years of experience** leading innovation and setting precedence within the **online travel industry.**

- A passion for **shaping organizations** and **building capabilities** complemented by proven results in **implementing systems**, developing emerging leaders, and driving **cultural change to achieve positive financial growth.**

- Reputed for **outstanding negotiation** skills, **leadership,** and **communication talents** that achieve results in multifunctional teams.

☑ Board Reporting	☑ Financial Management	☑ Risk Management
☑ Change Management	☑ Quality Controls	☑ Strategic Planning
☑ Compliance Controls	☑ Board Reporting	☑ Team Leadership

- Key Career Highlights -

Executive Director, quickbeds.com, Atlanta, GA   2021–Present

Approached to undertake the multifaceted role managing the complete strategic functions of the group. Showcased a commitment to stakeholder engagement and achieved unprecedented buy-in to initiatives while positioning the business as a leader in the industry.

Team: 23 Executive Direct Reports	**Budget:** $10M	**Focus:** Positioning as Industry Leader

Shaping Industry: Leveraged cutting-edge innovations to position the business at the forefront of industry and **awarded National Leader in Emerging Technologies in 2022** by Travel, Inc. This was as a direct result of spearheading the introduction of Virtual Credit Cards to pay suppliers, providing a more efficient process as well as untapped revenue.

Systems Improvements: Spearheaded functional enhancements to reflect the expedited business growth of **20% year on year** and removed dependency on legacy back-office systems.

Asian Regional Growth: Expedited the global direction of the business by **driving 48% growth in the Asian region** as a result of migration to standardized group financial systems.

Business Growth: ⇧ 20%	**Regional Growth:** ⇧ 48%	**Performance Rating:** 5 Star

Kylie Chown, CMRW, CARW • Kylie Chown Consulting • kyliechown.com.au

- Key Career Highlights (Continued) -

Chief Executive Officer, quickbeds.com, Atlanta, GA 2016–2021

Prominent leadership role in a period of significant change. Complete responsibility for the strategic functions of the group. Clarified business model to take the business forward. Demonstrated loyalty and dedication with a commitment to achieving results.

Team: 15 Executive Direct Reports	**Budget**: $9M	**Focus:** Strategic Business Growth

Process Management: Elevated multi-site compliance **from 80% to 95% within 12 months.** Project standardized all financial processes and disciplines of the group and improved internal controls.

Executive Team Leadership: Unified a consistent executive management team over a 24-month period that reduced **attrition rates by 20%.** Mobilized the team in developing organizational capabilities and optimizing the headcount that ensured quality outputs reflective of the changing requirements.

Financial Management: Heightened accuracy and expedited **budget process from 8 hours to 2 hours** by developing an integrated and streamlined budget model.

Business Development: Acquired **20% of new business** as targeted clients. Initiated a hands-on approach towards organic and inorganic growth reflective of long- and short-term strategic objectives.

Risk Management: Lessened critical incidents reported by 20% over 12 months. Consolidated all risk management functions and implemented strategies to mitigate negative impact.

Business Growth: ⇧ 20%	**Compliance:** ⇧ 95%	**Performance Rating**: 5 Star

Operations Director, quickbeds.com, Los Angeles, CA 2015–2016

Identified as a high performer and rapidly promoted to Operations Director to manage the business at a strategic level. Delivered business improvements that increased business performance to unprecedented levels.

Team: 10 Executive Direct Reports	**Budget**: $7M	**Focus:** Improvements and Cost Reduction

Continuous Improvements: Accelerated **increases in turnover by more than 25% in 12 months**. Identified labor-intensive processes that were then retooled for maximum efficiency and reduced costs.

Cost Reductions: Identified opportunity and **renegotiated service contracts for a 74% reduction in cost**.

Best Practices: Maintained 100% compliance to best practices, identified as a competitive advantage. Performed continued business analysis to refine processes and procedures.

Business Growth: ⇧ 22%	**Compliance:** ⇧ 100%	**Performance Rating**: 5 Star

- Education -

MA Economics, University of California, Los Angeles, CA	2016
BS Business, University of Southern California, Los Angeles, CA	2011

 Resume of **Taj Gupta**

CHAPTER 5:
Write Tight, Lean & Clean

Writing tight, lean, and clean refers to techniques that impact every single item on your resume, from minor things like locations and contact information, to major items such as job descriptions, achievement statements, project highlights, educational credentials, professional affiliations … everything.

A modern resume must be powerful not only in its conten; it must also be written so that it's quick and easy to read. Today's modern resume is:

- **Written succinctly to match readers' short attention spans.** Rather than intricate sentences, lengthy lists of bullet points, and long-winded paragraphs, capture that same information in a tighter, more telegraphic writing style and ditch the words that don't matter.

  Ask Yourself: Does every word I've written on my resume mean something and have value?

- **Designed for skimmers rather than readers.** Make sure critical information is noticeable in a glance to quickly capture attention of recruiters, hiring managers, and other key decision makers.

  Ask Yourself: Can someone skim my resume in just a few seconds and immediately understand who I am?

Bottom line … you want to eliminate all unnecessary details and focus on what's most important to prospective employers.

Following are our favorite strategies and techniques to sharpen your writing, tell your career story in half the words, and visually draw the reader's eye to what's most important. In addition, we've included samples that demonstrate how to transition lengthy content into short, concise, easy-to-skim bites while still retaining critical information.

Strategy #1: Transform dense Summary paragraphs into short branding statements.

The most important consideration when writing or tightening your Summary is to keep the information on point and on brand. The easiest way to accomplish that is to identify and then focus on the 2 or 3 things you want readers to instantly know about you.

In this example, we've replaced an entire paragraph of relatively generic information (the traditional version) with 2 sharp lines that highlight this executive's unique value (the modern version).

Example #1: Traditional

Global Corporate Development Executive
Senior Operating Executive / VP, Sales & Marketing

Bilingual (English/Spanish) leader with demonstrated achievement including both top- and bottom-line growth in domestic and international markets. Effective business builder and mentor with a keen insight to solving business problems and creating synergies that drive multimillion-dollar growth regardless of economic environment. Tenacious at identifying new revenue opportunities, securing customer loyalty, and forging solid relationships with external and internal business partners.

Example #1: Modern

Global Corporate Development Executive
Senior Operating Executive / VP, Sales & Marketing

Bilingual (English-Spanish) Business Leader
Delivering Top- & Bottom-Line Growth in Multinational Markets Since 2015

Strategy #2: Transform long bullet-point Summaries into short, easy-to-read paragraphs with a headline as a bonus.

A bullet-point Summary is often a great way to present a lot of different information clearly and concisely. But when the list becomes too long, readers quickly tune out. In this example for a new graduate, we've transformed a long bullet list into a headline, subheading, and simple 2-line paragraph that communicates what's most important.

Example #2: Traditional

- Master of Science in Accounting Student at Baruch College (2023 graduation).
- Bachelor's Degree in International Economics & Trade.
- Strong analytical and mathematical talents. Won national and provincial awards in native China.
- Superior ability to learn and use accounting, statistical, office, and design software.
- Teamwork experience and record of working effectively on both group and individual projects.
- Proven ability to set and achieve goals, adapt to new challenges, devise effective solutions, and support/encourage people of all ages, professionally and personally.

Example #2: Modern

ACCOUNTING & FINANCE PROFESSIONAL
Passion for International Business

MS in Accounting and **BS in International Economics & Trade.** Award-winning analyst with multicultural background, fluency in English and Mandarin, and deep interest in the global economy.

Strategy #3: Trim the fat from company descriptions.

It's important to provide details about the companies where you've worked, but make them brief to keep the focus on you. In this example, the company description went from 3 lines to 1 by eliminating unnecessary detail.

Example #3: Traditional

RYDER DEDICATED LOGISTICS (HQ—Dallas, TX) — 2018–Present
$420 million transportation and dedicated logistics company with 20,000+ customers around the world and 100,000+ employees working in 106 countries throughout North America, South America, Europe, Asia, and Africa.

Example #3: Modern

RYDER DEDICATED LOGISTICS (HQ—Dallas, TX) — 2018–Present
$420M transportation & dedicated logistics company; 20K+ clients; 100K+ employees in 106 countries

Strategy #4: Transform dense job descriptions into 1-line job scope summaries.

When you're writing about your experience, you want to focus attention on your actions and achievements, and not the mundane duties of every job. A modern technique is to replace full sentences and paragraphs with short phrases describing job scope and responsibility.

Example #4: Traditional

Galaxy Air Lines, Houston, TX 2019–2023
Senior Account Manager
Managed $300M territory, servicing Fortune 500 accounts (Dell, Exxon, and Shell) as well as large travel agencies. Used solution-selling approach to drive continuous market share increases in a challenging and competitive environment. Built strong customer relationships based on performance and trust. Presented to and negotiated at all levels, from purchasing agents and travel managers to senior executives. Overcame objections and devised creative strategies to retain business despite severe cost competition.

 (followed by accomplishment bullets)

Example #4: Modern

Galaxy Air Lines, Houston, TX 2019–2023
Senior Account Manager
$300M territory | Solution selling to Fortune 500 (Dell, Exxon, Shell) | C-level presentations & negotiations

 (followed by accomplishment bullets)

Strategy #5: Focus on the big-picture story and results and not day-to-day routine tasks.

Readers are not really interested in reading job descriptions that could be identical for everyone who ever held a similar job. Keep that information to the minimum and focus on what's unique about you and your situation.

Example #5: Traditional

Senior Website Designer • BAY STATE COLLEGE, Boston, MA (2020–Present)

Design websites and manage day-to-day site maintenance. Determine design goals and specifications based on user requirements, marketing input, and comparative research. Prepare schedules and requirements documents; coordinate with marketing, content administrators, programmers, and others to deliver final product. Create mockups, final designs, templates for content developers, Flash timelines, and other special features. Test content for cross-browser compliance. Provide technical support for content providers and end users.

  (followed by accomplishment bullets)

Example #5: Modern

Senior Website Designer • BAY STATE COLLEGE, Boston, MA (2020–Present)

Built award-winning web presence for 25,000-student college. Provide end-to-end site management to ensure maximum functionality, uptime, and responsiveness to changing needs of students, faculty, and administration.

  (followed by accomplishment bullets)

Strategy #6: Sharpen bullet points to make impact and results jump off the page.

In the traditional example below—for that same web designer—it's hard to quickly find and focus on the great results she achieved. The bullet points are long and in many cases the results are hidden at the end of the sentence.

The modern example presents sharp, 1-line bullet points that lead with results and provide only enough detail to create context for the achievement.

Example #6: Traditional

- Redesigned organization's website (www.baystatecollege.edu) and earned customer accolades and recognition by Northeast Education Consortium as "Best College Website" in 2021 and 2022.

- Served as designer on team that delivered project for remake of organization's main, 4000-page website 2 months ahead of schedule; met deadlines on all other projects.

- Enhanced quality of sites through improvements in architecture, elimination of redundancy, and incorporation of user-friendly design; maintained quality and consistency by developing and implementing style guidelines.

- Developed canned procedures for frequently asked questions, thereby increasing productivity of website support services.

Example #6: Modern

- Awarded "Best College Website" by NE Education Consortium (165 universities), 2021 and 2022.
- Designed and delivered—2 months early—a total remake of primary, 4000-page website.
- Improved architecture, eliminated redundancies, and added user-friendly style guidelines.
- Increased staff productivity by creating consistent procedures for FAQs.

Strategy #7: Condense content and tighten presentation.

Even in your Education, you may be able to save space that you can put to good use elsewhere. Beyond saving space, the modern version allows the reader to absorb important information very quickly.

Example #7: Traditional

Bachelor of Science Degree in Finance & Economics, 2022

UNIVERSITY OF VIRGINIA, Charlottesville, VA

Cum Laude Graduate

Dean's List—6 semesters

Example #7: Modern

BS, Finance & Economics, *Cum Laude* — University of Virginia, Charlottesville, VA — 2022

Strategy #8: Put like with like and improve skimmability.

Example #8 shows a hefty list of education, certifications, and other credentials. The information is important, but it's hard to skim.

Simply grouping like items together and adding a bit of white space makes all the difference, as shown in the modern version.

Example #8: Traditional

Master of Business Administration, YALE UNIVERSITY, December 2016

Certified Concierge, AMERICAN CONCIERGE ASSOCIATION, August 2014

Certified Hospitality Manager, AMERICAN HOSPITALITY ASSOCIATION, June 2013

Bachelor of Science in Hospitality Management, VILLANOVA UNIVERSITY, May 2013

Certified Front Desk Manager, AMERICAN HOSPITALITY ASSOCIATION, April 2011

Licensed Private Pilot, AIRCRAFT OWNERS AND PILOTS ASSOCIATION, December 2010

Example #8: Modern

MBA, YALE UNIVERSITY, 2019
BS Hospitality Management, VILLANOVA UNIVERSITY, 2016

Certified Concierge, AMERICAN CONCIERGE ASSOCIATION, 2018
Certified Hospitality Manager, AMERICAN HOSPITALITY ASSOCIATION, 2017
Certified Front Desk Manager, AMERICAN HOSPITALITY ASSOCIATION, 2012

Licensed Private Pilot, AIRCRAFT OWNERS AND PILOTS ASSOCIATION, 2012

Now that we've given you our 8 favorite large-scale writing strategies, let's look at other, smaller-scale techniques to keep resume writing tight, lean, and clean.

Eliminate the Little Words

You'd be amazed at how much space words such as "a," "an," "the," "by," and others take up on a page. Although they might seem insignificant, when you delete them from your resume—unless you feel a particular need to include one in a sentence here or there—all of your sentences, paragraphs, and pages become shorter and tighter.

Ditch the Details that Don't Matter

Although your tendency might be to include everything you did in each of your jobs, don't. Certain details simply don't matter. Ask yourself:

- If you are an office manager and one of your responsibilities is to order paper, is that resume-worthy? (Probably not.)

- If you're a customer service agent, do you need to mention that you interact with customers? (It is understood from your job title.)

- If you're a project manager who performed the same functions for 20+ different projects, do you need to include the same level of detailed information about each project. (No!)

Review your resume very closely to identify where there is too much insignificant detail, and hit delete.

Edit Widow Lines

How many times have you written a paragraph—whether in a resume, marketing brochure, or business correspondence—where the last 1 or 2 words are "widowed" on a line by themselves? Those widow lines are a prime opportunity to shorten content, reduce text density, and diminish paragraph length.

Our best advice for eliminating widow lines—in paragraphs or bullet points—is to carefully edit the entire section, deleting all words that are not critical to the content and meaning. Often just a minor edit will move the widow up to the prior line so the paragraph becomes tighter.

Use Abbreviations

You can easily abbreviate certain words and be confident that everyone will know what those abbreviations stand for. State names are an excellent example. It is passé to write out their full names—even the United States Postal Service (USPS) doesn't do that.

College degrees are also prime areas for abbreviation. There is no need to spell out Associate of Arts, Bachelor of Science, or Master of Business Administration. The abbreviations AA, BS, and MBA are universally known and fully understandable even to robotic resume scanners. If you have a less-known degree, spell everything out so you're certain to communicate important information.

> **PRO TIP: Two key benefits from using abbreviations are that they save space and they stand out on the page** because they are usually written as all capital letters.

Use Digits

You might have noticed that in this book we break one of the writing "rules" learned in grammar school: Instead of spelling out numbers one through ten, we use digits—1 through 10. The same is true in most of the resumes in this book.

Using digits in your resume offers 2 key advantages:

- It saves space. As we've pointed out in this chapter, we recommend making your resume as lean and clean as possible without sacrificing relevant information.

- It makes those all-important numbers stand out. As you glance through the resumes, notice how the numbers—the digits—catch your eye much more than an equivalent text word would do. Your numbers are an important asset that you want future employers to notice. Making them very visible is a great way to accomplish that.

Use Acronyms

The Oxford Dictionary defines an acronym as "an abbreviation formed from the initial letters of other words and pronounced as a word." Using the right acronyms in your resume can save a great deal of space.

Consider these very common acronyms:

- AIDS—Acquired Immunodeficiency Syndrome
- NATO—North Atlantic Treaty Organization
- OPEC—Organization of the Petroleum Exporting Countries
- Scuba—Self-Contained Underwater Breathing Apparatus

Other acronyms are very specific to certain industries and professions. For example, everyone in manufacturing knows that FIFO means First In, First Out; everyone in the medical field knows that JCAHO is the Joint Commission on Accreditation of Healthcare Organizations; everyone in technology knows that FIOS is Fiber-Optic Service.

When writing your resume, always consider your audience when deciding to use acronyms, as these examples illustrate:

- If you're a quality manager looking for other opportunities in manufacturing, you can use the acronym SAP in your resume and feel confident that anyone reading it will know what it means.

- Conversely, if you are making a career shift from quality management into training and development, you'd want to spell out Systems, Applications, and Products because the SAP acronym might not be recognizable to most readers.

A good basic rule: *When in doubt, spell it out!*

If you do spell it out, use the word first, followed by the acronym: *Earnings Before Income Tax (EBIT).*

You can then use the acronym in the rest of your resume, because now everyone knows what it means.

> **PRO TIP: Keyword searches typically include both the acronym and the spelled-out version of the term.** Employers don't want to miss out on good candidates by searching for consumer packaged goods but not its common acronym, CPG. Therefore, you can safely use common acronyms in your resume and still pass the screening scans.

Write & Then Edit

Tight, lean, clean writing requires good editing. Don't expect to produce a masterpiece in a single sitting.

First, use our Career Vault tool on pages 244–246 in Part VIII—Resources to assemble all of the information you will need.

Next, write your resume, capturing all of the details that you think you want to include. This may take several sittings to accomplish, so don't berate yourself for not doing it faster. Resume writing is a multi-step process—even for very experienced professional resume writers!

Then, take time to read it slowly and carefully. What words have you written that don't need to be there? What details don't add value and, in fact, obscure the meaning of more important information? Delete everything you can. Edit freely, without cutting anything that's relevant, important, or distinctive.

If you follow the guidelines in this chapter, you'll produce a resume that is powerful, memorable, and effective. You can see how well that has been done in the 2 samples that follow—both excellent examples of how to write tight, lean, and clean.

Gerald Jackson Resume—page 50

Gerald's resume is a concise 1 page. It begins with a 1-line Summary that touts his record of efficiency in operations and productivity. His branding statement is a single line and so is the line at the end of his Summary. His company description is 1 line. His job descriptions are short paragraphs, and each bullet point is no longer than 2 lines. The last section of his resume combines what might have been 3 separate sections but is much better presented as 3 distinct items within just 1 section.

Charles Martin Resume—pages 51–52

Charles's resume begins with a headline, followed by a subheading that instantly conveys his top 3 qualifications. His company descriptions are 1 line, and each of his job titles is a single line with a short phrase describing his job scope. There are only 2–3 bullets showcasing his greatest achievements in each position, and those bullets are only 1 or 2 lines long. Other sections are easy to identify, and each includes brief, but important, information. The entire 2-page executive resume is easy to skim and read.

GERALD JACKSON

Holiday, FL 34690 • (727) 334-4544 • gjackson@yahoo.com

PRODUCTION MANAGER

Maximize operational efficiency and cost control through exemplary management of people and processes.

Core Strengths

- **Manufacturing / Production:** Experience guiding a wide range of operations, including quality control and improvement, scheduling, distribution / transportation, and shipping / receiving.

- **Innovation / Leadership:** Track record for designing and executing production improvements to optimize resource planning / management. Six Sigma Green Belt with lean manufacturing capabilities.

- **Team Building:** Strong communication skills and ability to supervise and motivate shift crews to perform at high levels through training, mentoring, and setting of clear productivity expectations.

Outstanding performer and colleague with strong listening skills and commitment to helping others succeed.

CAREER HIGHLIGHTS

ABSOLUTE PHARMACEUTICALS, Holiday, FL • 2017–2023
Company that manufactures injectable drug components and delivery systems for distribution globally.

Area Manager • 2020–2023
Ensured high quality and efficient production operations, monitoring various processes for problems and identifying improvements. Proficiently executed full range of supply chain functions, such as shipping / receiving, distribution / transportation, raw material management, and logistics support. Led completion of special projects.

- Strengthened production staffs' performance through stellar supervision, training, and coaching.

- While serving as sole manager on night shift, took initiative to learn full range of production operations, including tool / dye, quality assurance, and machine mechanic processes.

- Gained reputation as a hands-on, highly communicative manager and supervisor, often serving as intermediary between line staff and senior management on HR and work-related issues.

- Earned respect and trust from subordinates by leveraging production experience and active listening / participatory management style.

- Saved company $5K+ through design of Kanban system to avoid over-production of raw materials.

Press Operator • 2017–2020
Operated production machinery in manufacture of medical caps, setting up and monitoring operations to identify and resolve cap defects and minimize waste and downtime. Worked closely with quality assurance staff.

- Performed effectively within press operations team employing 3 staff and 8 presses to manufacture approximately 1M medical caps daily.

- Groomed by senior management to assume role as Area Manager; given opportunity to participate in numerous corporate-sponsored training seminars within high-level leadership and management areas.

EDUCATION / CERTIFICATION / COMPUTER SKILLS

Associate's Degree in Communication, Stephenson University, Irvine CA
Six Sigma Green Belt
Microsoft Office Suite (Word & Excel) and Kronos Scheduling Software

Steven Watson, PhD, CPRW • St. Petersburg Resume Services • stpetersburgresumeservices.com

CHARLES MARTIN

212-730-9168 | charles.martin@gmail.com | linkedin.com/in/charlesmartin | New York Metro

SENIOR EXECUTIVE: CEO / CHANGE MANAGER

Growth Catalyst | Turnaround Architect | MBA

Executive repeatedly promoted to lead strategic expansions and turnarounds. Consistently drive revenue growth, transform culture, and improve operations. Bring focus, drive, and energy critical to building businesses. Excel at developing strong teams of top performers while creating and executing marketing and branding strategies.

Strong analytical skills with sharp focus on the bottom line. Responsive. Direct.

EXPERIENCE & ACHIEVEMENTS

Hercules Investment, New York, NY   **2019–2023**
Company invests in small to medium-sized unlisted companies with intent to grow them long-term.
MANAGING DIRECTOR

$600M revenue | 5 portfolio companies | 600 employees

- **Turned around 2 subsidiaries** (Bilbao and Volva).
- Delivered **37% EBITDA** on the portfolio, more than 2X average of the S&P 500.
- Acquired $50M, 50-staff engineering company in 2012 and sold at **73% ROI** in 3 years.

Star Group, Seattle, WA   **2017–2019**
Family-owned grain products business. $850M revenue, 500 employees, 16 production units in USA, Canada, Europe.
MANAGING DIRECTOR, Star Group North America
BOARD MEMBER, Star Group

$600M revenue | 5 companies + subsidiaries | 7 production units

- **Reversed 3 years of sliding performance,** turning around 4 of the 5 companies through assortment analysis, rationalizations, and workforce reductions.
- **Increased North American revenues 28% and profits 35%** in 2 years.

Northern Food Products, Dallas, TX   **2014–2017**
NASDAQ-listed food company. $15B revenue, 5000 employees.
GENERAL MANAGER, Northern Food Retail

$400M business unit | 8 production units | 1400 employees

- **Grew company in stagnant market**, achieving positive results every year and increasing business unit profits **40%.**
- **Launched Northern Food into the burgeoning Fast Casual channel,** striking deals with Panera and Qdoba.
- Led smooth integration of Premier Foods into Northern. Doubled retail business unit from **$200M** to **$400M.**

Venture Corporation, Seattle, WA   **2009–2014**
Leading food company. NASDAQ-listed, $2B revenue, 500 employees.
SALES DIRECTOR, Venture Cheese & Dairy, 2013–2014

$900M revenue | 28 employees

- Member of the management team involved in company-wide strategy setting and decision making.
- **Refocused sales team.** Outlined and implemented key account manager structure, new business programs, and profitability strategies that together led to **18% jump in sales revenue and 34% surge in profits.**

Birgitta Moller, ACRW, MRW • Cvhjälpen • cvhjalpen.nu

MARKETING DIRECTOR, Venture Cheese & Dairy, 2010–2013

$30M marketing budget | 7 employees

- Recruited to build marketing and products organization from ground up when 2 business entities merged.
- **Dethroned market-leading company** and increased market share radically when cutting-edge concept was launched and **became category captain**.
- **Increased brand awareness 6 percentage points.**

MARKETING MANAGER, Venture Food Partner, 2009–2010

$300M revenue | 3–person marketing organization

- **Built and grew** range of products for newly launched partnership.
- **Architected business plan** from scratch covering marketing and branding strategies.

Comida XYZ, Madrid, Spain   **2007–2009**

Group owned by Hola, leading supplier of branded consumer goods. Turnover $34B, 12,5000 employees.

PRODUCT MANAGER

$250M revenue | 1 direct report

- Launched new fast-food concept in Spanish market. **Grew revenue from $0 to $60M in 2 years**.
- Directed process of replacing all equipment and products at 260 units in Europe.
- Created business plan for concept, assortment, branding, and marketing.

Promoted out of Management Development program **in 6 months** and appointed **Comida's** Product Manager in Spain.

BOARD POSITIONS

Chairman of the Board/Acting CEO, Upstart XYZ (Food Technology)	2022–Present
Chairman of the Board, YourHealthNow (Medical Technology)	2021–Present

LANGUAGES

English (native), **Spanish** (fluent), **German** (conversational)

EDUCATION

Executive Master of Business Administration (MBA)	London School of Economics, London, England
Bachelor of Science in Business and Economics	Xavier University, Cincinnati, OH

PART III:
Modernize Your Resume Format

The 4 Principles of Modern Resume Formatting
- Showcase Your Career with the Right Resume Structure
- Follow the Rules of Good Formatting and Select the Font that Fits
- Improve Readability and Skimmability
- Format for Human Readers and Applicant Tracking Systems (ATS)

Format—the structure and layout of your resume—matters, and it matters a lot!

In Part III of this book, we shift our focus from writing great resume content to selecting the resume format that best showcases everything you've written about yourself and your career.

Decades ago, selecting the right resume format was easy. Resumes were basically **chronological** listings of where you worked, what you did, and the dates of your employment. Of course, your education was also included, as well as your personal information.

On occasion, job seekers who faced unique challenges—such as returning to work after years of unemployment or transitioning from military service to the corporate world—used a **functional** resume format to put the focus on their skills and qualifications with just a brief mention of their work experience. Read Part V of this book for detailed discussions and resume samples for these and other situations.

Although much has changed about resume writing and job search over the past few decades, the chronological and functional formats are still the primary foundation for most resumes. In fact, the **chronological** has morphed into what is now referred to as a **combination** resume, capturing the best of both so you can develop a resume format to best showcase your experience and capture the interest of prospective employers.

Beyond actual structure, there are other critical elements to be considered when formatting your resume. Which font is best and why? How can you increase skimmability to engage your readers to keep reading? How do you make your resume compatible with Applicant Tracking Systems (ATS) and other resume scanning technologies?

Read on to answer these critical formatting questions and many others.

CHAPTER 6:
Showcase Your Career with the Right Resume Structure

Which resume format is right for you—Combination or Functional? Let's explore both so you can determine the format that works best to prominently showcase your career—experience, education, qualifications, and more.

Combination Resume

Today's modern resume combines the best of the 2 traditional formats: the structured presentation of your work history and education (the largely now-defunct pure chronological format), along with a strong emphasis on your core skills, qualifications, and achievements (the functional format).

 PRO TIP: 90%+ of all modern resumes are combination resumes.

Combination resumes generally include 3 critical content sections:

- **Summary** (Career Summary; Professional Profile; Qualifications Profile; Core Competencies)
- **Experience** (Work Experience; Professional Experience; Employment Experience)
- **Education** (Education & Professional Credentials; Training & Education; Degrees & Licenses)

 PRO TIP: If you're a young college graduate, Education is your #1 selling point and will probably come before Experience on your resume. For almost all others, Experience comes first.

Other sections that may be appropriate to include in your combination resume, based on your own experiences and career path, include the following:

- Technology Qualifications or Technical Skills
- Professional Credentials
- Professional Affiliations
- Board of Director Appointments
- Community & Civic Memberships

- Languages
- Public Speaking
- Publications

You'll find that the majority of resumes in this book are combination resumes. Why? A combination resume allows you to tell your career story in a way that employers can quickly scan and easily understand. At the same time, it gives you many opportunities to share your specific successes, valuable contributions, and unique qualifications. It offers immense flexibility in an easy-to-follow structure.

> **PRO TIP: Your resume does not have to be 1 page**—that's one of the great myths of resume writing. It needs to be long enough to showcase your qualifications and tell your career story in a readable, attractive format. For some, that takes 1 page; for others, 2 pages are needed—and that's fine!
>
> As a general rule, graduating students and young professionals will have a 1-page resume. More experienced professionals, managers, and executives will often need 2 pages to include all of their relevant information. All of the examples in this book are rich and deep in content, yet well organized and tightly written so that everything fits on 1 or 2 pages—as appropriate for that individual.
>
> With our modern emphasis on lean content and tight writing, we rarely create 3-page resumes, even for very senior executives. But, on rare occasions, the content may warrant a third page.
>
> Botom line, there is no rule. Write the content, edit carefully, format for visual appeal and readability, and make final adjustments for good page layout. Then you'll know if your resume is 1 page or 2.

Goldie Norman Resume—page 57

Goldie's combination resume clearly organizes the information to showcase her experience, achievements, and education.

A few things you'll notice:

- This resume begins with a Headline (Operations Manager) rather than a heading such as the word Summary. Most of the resume samples in this book use the headline technique because it is so powerful. With just a glance, every reader knows *who* this candidate is and *what* she can do. Further, words like Summary aren't necessary. It's obvious it's the Summary.

- After a short paragraph, the Summary continues with a list of core competencies—the all-important keywords that are relevant to Goldie's target positions.

- Employer names, dates of employment, and job titles are clearly shown.

- A short paragraph describes the scope of Goldie's responsibilities, and then 2 to 4 bullet points showcase the most important information in this resume: her unique achievements in each position.

GOLDIE NORMAN

Brooklyn, NY 11230 • LinkedIn.com/in/GoldieNorman
(212) 932-8567 • goldienorman@gmail.com

OPERATIONS MANAGER

Reputation for Delivering Superior Results:
Cutting Costs, Improving Operations & Executing Innovative Solutions

High-impact Senior Operations Leader with 14 years' experience in quality control and business management. Catalyst for building high-performing teams, streamlining operations, and optimizing productivity.

- Inventory Control
- Data Collection & Reporting
- Relationship Management
- Quality Assurance
- Conflict Resolution
- Training & Supervision
- Systems & Controls
- Project Management
- Database Management
- Logistics
- Cost Reduction Measures
- Risk Management

PROFESSIONAL EXPERIENCE

RILEY ENTERPRISES, New York, NY, 2019–Present
Operations & Logistics Manager
Oversee and supervise logistics department, develop and execute onboarding procedures, and establish and manage staff training program.

- Increased **450** customers / **16** direct reports / **14** routes to **1300+** customers / **29** direct reports / **24** routes.
- Saved **$250,000** to date by implementing fuel-tracking program.
- Captured **$40,000** cost reduction by overhauling SOPs, prompting insurance policy revisions.
- Launched company's drug-free workplace (DFW) program, resulting in additional **5%** insurance savings.

WENDELE ENTERPRISES, INC, New York, NY, 2013–2019
Field Operations Manager
Managed 75 direct reports and 15 indirect reports. Oversaw scheduling, performance, and payroll. Directed quality control, corrective action, conflict resolution, hiring, training, and termination.

- Implemented comprehensive quality assurance program that reduced customer complaints **74%**.
- Executed training program to include classroom presentations, field education, and training videos.
- Managed and coordinated all inbound and outbound sales programs and professional development.

GASWIRTH NATIONAL LEASE CORP., New York, NY, 2005–2013
Terminal Manager
Directly supervised 19 commercial tractor-trailer drivers and managed interstate and intrastate dispatch of 30 to 50 commercial drivers for load tracking and emergency response. Administered new hire training, safety inspections, driver surveillance, scheduling, and payroll. Oversaw security concerns for 18 locations.

- Received "Top Performance" awards for 5 consecutive years (2008–2012).
- Reduced security costs more than **65%.** Increased employee performance standards **41%**.

THE SECURITY CORP., New York, NY, 1999–2005
Custom Protection Officer & Supervisor
Handled armed security and supervision of security officer teams for public schools, international airports, state and federal courts, and high-security non-government and government offices.

- Awarded recognition for consistently superior performance and team improvement.
- Lowered security costs **53%** in public sector and **27%** in private sector.

EDUCATION

Bachelor of Science in Business Management – **FIVE TOWNS COLLEGE,** Nassau County, NY

Wendi Weiner, NCRW, CPRW, CCTC, CCM, NCOPE, 360Reach Analyst • The Writing Guru • writingguru.net

Functional Resume

Just like the combination, the functional resume also includes all of your skills, qualifications, achievements, and important and distinguishing information. But it is structured in a way that separates all of that content from when and where it happened.

The advantage to a functional resume is that it can disguise situations such as gaps in employment, an unrelated job history, absences from the workforce, and other challenges faced by some job seekers: career changers, job hoppers, freelancers, people returning to work after caring for family, or people transitioning from military-to-civilian careers. As such, it can be the right format for some. If you fall into any of these categories, read Chapters 14, 15, 16, and 17 for strategies and samples to help you create an outstanding resume.

Because a functional resume makes it hard to determine exactly what you did when and where, many employers prefer the combination resume, which gives them the information they seek in a more predictable format. However, if a combination resume is going to instantly share information that is *not* to your advantage, you may find the functional format a better choice.

PRO TIP: Only about 10% of job seekers need functional resumes. Unless you are faced with a challenging situation, a combination resume is most likely your best option.

A functional resume does include a work experience section, but it's generally at or near the bottom of the resume and includes little or no detail—because all of the valuable information has already been presented earlier in the resume to showcase skills, projects, achievements, and other qualifications.

The functional resume typically includes 4 key sections—the same 3 primary sections found in a combination resume (Summary, Experience, Education), plus one more critically important category that contains the majority of the content.

That fourth section, which showcases your most noteworthy and relevant experience, should have a heading that communicates the value of the information that follows. Here are a few examples of headings that have worked for job seekers in creating effective functional resumes:

- Career Overview
- Key Accomplishments
- Experience Summary
- Experience Highlights
- Skills and Achievements
- Leadership Competencies
- Technology Qualifications
- Core Competencies
- Project Highlights

Or you can create a heading that most closely aligns with your skill sets. For example, Technology Innovation might work well for those in IT, new media, social media, and related professions.

Functional resumes can include additional sections, just like the combination resume, if those sections are relevant to a specific job seeker. As a reminder, those sections include the following:

- Technology Qualifications
- Professional Credentials
- Professional Affiliations
- Board of Director Appointments
- Memberships
- Languages
- Public Speaking
- Publications

Ned Sung Resume—pages 60–61

To see how a functional resume is structured, take a look at Ned's resume. You'll notice:

- It begins with a Headline and a strong Summary paragraph.

- Ned's Leadership and Technical Competencies are positioned in an easy-to-skim format toward the top of the page—a quick reference for hiring managers looking for a specific skill set.

- The third section, Key Accomplishments, is the meatiest and most important part of Ned's resume. His rich experience and strong achievements are explained in some detail, grouped under headings that highlight his key areas of expertise.

- On page 2, Ned's Career History is listed without detail, followed by his Education and Training, with a subheading for his Language skills.

Ned's functional resume clearly positions him for his career goal in information technology (IT) management while minimizing 2 potential negatives: He has never held a formal managerial role, and he has been unemployed for nearly a year. Now you see how well a functional format can work!

Question:	*What piece of your IT Management Team is missing?*
Answer:	NIEN "NED" SUNG
Solution:	Contact Ned at 917.345.8645 or NSung@gmail.com

BUSINESS-FOCUSED IT PROFESSIONAL

Unique blend of **conceptual/visionary thinking** towards improving business processes, **analytical skills** to define objectives, and **hands-on technical acumen.** Able to rapidly comprehend complex environments and communicate effective improvements to both technical and non-technical staff at all levels. Long-standing record of delivering IT projects on time and under budget despite staffing and organizational challenges.

LEADERSHIP AND TECHNICAL COMPETENCIES

- Team Leadership & Motivation
- Project & Program Management
- Process Improvement
- Client Relationship Management
- Vendor Sourcing & Management
- Contract Negotiation & Cost Control
- Demand & Change Management
- Strategic & Tactical Planning
- Business Analysis
- Technology Infrastructure
- Enterprise Application Integration
- Technology Deployment & Evaluation

Skills & Languages:	UML, Data Modeling, XML, XSLT, ESQL, SQL, Java, C, VB, COBOL, EDI X12, SWIFT
Tools:	SalesForce.com, MOSS 2007, Internet Information Services (IIS), WebSphere, MQ, WebSphere Message Broker, WebSphere Business Integrator, WebSphere Transformation Extender, QPasa, ETI*Extract, Business Objects
Databases:	DB2, SQL Server, Oracle
Operating Systems:	Windows Servers, AIX, MVS/TSO
Software:	Microsoft Office Suite (including Vision and Project)
Version Control:	PVCS, Librarian

KEY ACCOMPLISHMENTS

BUSINESS LEADERSHIP

- Identified serious data quality problems in SalesForce CRM system that contributed to unnecessary operational risks. Gained support of business units and presented information to senior management, leading to executive authorization for a cleanup effort across multiple branches.

- Recommended combining database server with web server, ensuring data security and reducing costs by $100K.

- Drove consolidation of cross-department projects, recognizing similar needs and eliminating repetitive work. New application reduced processing time by 50% and could be easily scaled to add new departments.

TEAM LEADERSHIP & STAFF DEVELOPMENT

- Directed team of 2 senior WebSphere MQ engineers managing messaging infrastructure of North American organization, with daily responsibilities for monitoring operational support of 15 production queue managers and 50+ development queue managers on various platforms, including Z/OS, AIX, Solaris, Tandem, and Windows servers.

- Coached, mentored, and motivated underperforming systems officer through weekly one-on-one sessions. Employee became engaged in performance process and empowered to take ownership for expected responsibilities.

PROJECT MANAGEMENT

- Managed e-fax project team with 7 IT staff, 1 telecom vendor (MCI/Verizon), and 3 business people; oversaw $140K budget. Used existing resources and infrastructure to deliver project by 10% below budget.

Michelle Riklan, CPRW, CEIC • Riklan Resources • riklanresources.com

PROJECT MANAGEMENT (CONTINUED)

- Led migration of antiquated intranet to MS SharePoint technology. Obtained buy-in from 25+ business units via internal marketing efforts and proactive communications. Planned and executed project following strict guidelines for vendor management, budget control, development, testing, training, and migration.

- Led technical team to rebuild infrastructure for 4 Internet sites, including cash management and trade finance.

- Assembled and led project team for e-gateway that proved to be a revenue-generating project: $100K in first year.

ARCHITECTURE/DESIGN

- Developed 50+ integrations based on asynchronous message broker architecture, utilizing EAI patterns that included pipes and filters, dynamic routers, splitters, aggregators, request-replies, and canonical data models.

- Created e-gateway application to leverage EDI VAN capabilities for external file transfers. Dynamically routed internal files using WebSphere MQ and the WebSphere Message Broker, providing data transformation services as needed. Designed both the user interface (written in VB6) and messaging architecture.

- Developed e-fax application and outbound fax gateway, replacing legacy system with a high-fail delivery rate. Designed both the web UI (written in C# and ASP.NET 1.1) and messaging architecture well ahead of schedule.

CAREER HISTORY

BANK OF JAPAN, New York, NY   2005 to 2023
Largest bank in Japan, providing a broad range of domestic and international services around the world.

Senior Architect – CRM / Business Intelligence, 2011 to 2023

Project Manager – Web Development / Web Hosting, 2018 to 2021

Manager – WebSphere MQ Administration, 2016 to 2018

Lead Architect – Enterprise Application Integration, 2009 to 2016

Programmer – Comptroller's Group, 2005 to 2009

EDUCATION AND TRAINING

Master of Science, Information Systems Major, New York University, New York, NY
Bachelor of Business Arts, Finance Major, Adelphi University, Garden City, NY

Training: Business Objects Web Intelligence Report Design ▪ Apex and Visualforce Controllers (DEV-501)
SharePoint Technologies Comprehensive Introduction ▪ New Manager Training

Languages: Fluent in Chinese (Cantonese)

CHAPTER 7:
Follow the Rules of Good Formatting

Going beyond the structure of your resume, you must devote the time and attention needed to ensure the integrity of your resume format.

What do we mean by integrity? One definition, particularly relevant to resume writing, is "a sound, unimpaired, or perfect condition," and a synonym is "incorruptibility." Good format integrity makes your resume (and you) appear more professional and more attentive to detail. And it keeps glitches to a minimum on the receiving end—very important when you are emailing or uploading a resume to people who can hire you … or not!

We've compiled 5 guidelines that will help ensure the integrity of your resume format.

Guideline #1: Use the tab function correctly. Most people rely on default settings and simply hit "tab" repeatedly to move text over on the page. But the tab feature is one of the most versatile and useful tools in MS Word. You can use tabs to position text precisely where you want it and know that it will never move even if you change the font, adjust the font size, add new content to a line, or edit existing content.

In a resume, the most valuable use of tab settings is to place dates flush right. Set a right tab at the right margin, hit the tab key once, and, like magic, the dates will all line up perfectly and stay in position.

Tabs are also quite important if you're formatting information in columns. When you create a multi-column list of keywords, for example, you want everyone who reads it to see this:

• *Sales Management*	• *National-Level Profit & Loss*	• *Sales Reporting & Analysis*
• *Negotiation & Sales Closing*	• *Training & Development*	• *Budget Management*

… and not this—a view that can occur on the receiving end when default tab settings are used:

• *Sales Management*	• *National-Level Profit & Loss*	• *Budget Management*
• *Negotiation & Sales Closing*	• *Training & Development*	• *Sales Reporting & Analysis*

If this concept is new to you, Google "how to set tabs in MS Word" to find text and video tutorials that will walk you through the process.

Guideline #2: Be consistent. Consistency of font and font size, spacing between items and sections, placement of columns, use of abbreviations, and other ways that you format certain types of information adds to the professionalism of your resume and aids in reader understanding.

For example, all of your job titles should be formatted identically, in the same font, font size, and font enhancement (e.g., bold, italics, underlining). The same is true for all of your employer names. Section headings should look the same. All of the dates should be positioned in the same way. All like items should look alike.

> **PRO TIP: Consistency provides visual cues** that help readers quickly absorb details in your resume.

Guideline #3: Call attention to the *right* information. When you glance at your finished resume, what stands out? Your format should spotlight the things that are most important and help guide your readers through the document.

Headings should be large and clear and achievements prominent. Your career chronology should be easy to find and skim—unless you want to downplay a choppy work history or period of unemployment. In that case, *don't* call attention to your career chronology and employment dates. Rather, focus on what's most advantageous to you—education, skills, or achievements.

Guideline #4: Proofread very carefully. Sloppy formatting, inconsistent punctuation, grammar mistakes, misspellings, and typographical errors—all send a message of carelessness and lack of attention to detail. Is this representative of the quality of work you're going to produce in the workplace? Many recruiters and employers will nix your resume if they spot a mistake. Proofread … many, many times!

> **PRO TIP: Put periods at the end of bullet-point statements.** Often debated by resume writers and job seekers is whether a bullet point is a sentence and needs a period at the end. Our take: If it's a complete thought, it needs a period—even though it's written in "resume style" that omits the subject (I). Here's an example of resume bullets that need periods at the end:
>
> - Saved $50K in first year of implementing new purchasing guidelines.
> - Increased department productivity 25% by training staff on advanced software functions.
> - Brought major renovation project in on schedule and 8% under budget.
>
> In contrast, you would not use periods at the end of bullets that are simply lists of items, such as a Core Competencies list:
>
> | | | |
> |---|---|---|
> | • CCNA Training | • Operations Analysis | • Troubleshooting |
> | • Data Control Functions | • Diagnostic Procedures | • Customer Service |
> | • Computer Programming | • Installation / Maintenance | • System Evaluation |

Guideline #5: Choose a Font that Fits. You might not think that font selection is a big deal when it comes to the format and appearance of your resume, but that is not true. The font you choose will have a great impact on how the resume looks, how it fits on the page, and how it accommodates the text.

Three factors influence your font selection:
- Universal fonts
- Space considerations
- Image and appearance

Universal Fonts

Recruiters, hiring managers, and other decision makers will look at a digital version of your resume—whether you send by email or upload to a database. Either way, you want to be sure that it is entirely readable and looks just the way you formatted it. You don't want your resume to open with a garbled font, a strange replacement font, or another glitch that affects readability or creates a negative first impression.

The best way to achieve this goal is to use a *universal font*—one that is found on just about every Windows and Mac computer system.

Recommended Universal Fonts

Arial	Bookman	Georgia	Palatino Linotype
Arial Narrow	Calibri	**Impact** (Headings)	Tahoma
Arial Black (Headings)	Cambria	Lucida Sans	Trebuchet
Book Antiqua	Garamond	MS Sans Serif	Verdana

> **PRO TIP: You'll note that Times New Roman is not on the list,** although it is certainly a universal font. In fact, it was MS Word's default font for so many years that it became widely overused. In our opinion, it appears outdated and predictable, so we do not recommend it.

Of course, many more fonts are available, and you may not want to limit yourself to these safe choices. The font you choose has a huge impact on the overall appearance and image that your resume presents, so be sure that it communicates the *right* message about *who* you are and *what* you can do.

A word of caution: If you do use a non-universal font, we recommend saving your resume in PDF format to be sure it transmits properly. In fact, no matter the font, we recommend that you use PDFs whenever emailing or uploading, unless an MS Word file is specifically requested.

> **PRO TIP: For ATS scanning purposes, font is no longer a prime consideration.** When scanning systems were capturing information by physically scanning a page of text, it was important to use a clean, safe font. Now systems read the underlying code rather than text on a page, so your font choice is immaterial.

Space Considerations

Font selection and sizing have a huge impact on not only how your resume looks but also how much information you can fit on a page. Look at the 2 following sentences, both in a 12-point font. The first is in Arial Narrow; the second in Bookman.

- Recruited by Pepsi to capture new customers and build sales volume in the stagnant Midwest region.

- Recruited by Pepsi to capture new customers and build sales volume in the stagnant Midwest region.

Look at the difference in how much space they use. Therein lies your challenge—to find the *right* font that works well with the content you've written while remaining entirely readable.

PRO TIP: If your resume looks crowded or hard to read, try a different font. You might be surprised at how much less space a different font requires—even though it is in the same font size—or how dramatically it changes the overall look of your resume.

The size of your font also has an enormous impact on readability. Because fonts are so variable, we don't have a universal recommendation regarding font size.

In the following examples, we show 4 fonts in the same size. You can see how different they are:

Modernize Your Resume: Get Noticed … Get Hired (9-point Garamond)
Modernize Your Resume: Get Noticed … Get Hired (9-point Calibri)
Modernize Your Resume: Get Noticed … Get Hired (9-point Trebuchet)
Modernize Your Resume: Get Noticed … Get Hired (9-point Verdana)

Above, only Verdana is comfortably readable in 9-point size.

Modernize Your Resume: Get Noticed … Get Hired (11-point Garamond)
Modernize Your Resume: Get Noticed … Get Hired (11-point Calibri)
Modernize Your Resume: Get Noticed … Get Hired (11-point Trebuchet)
Modernize Your Resume: Get Noticed … Get Hired (11-point Verdana)

At 11 point, Garamond is now readable, and both Calibri and Trebuchet would work well. Verdana, however, now appears too large—almost elementary.

Of course, when your resume is read on screen, the reader can enlarge the view if needed. But that is not the case for your printed resume, which still has a significant and important role in your job search—for interviews, networking meetings, and other in-person job search activities.

PRO TIP: Print your resume to be sure that the font selection, font size, and overall presentation are attractive and readable. Do not rely entirely on your computer screen.

Image and Appearance

In many ways, font selection is—and should be—a matter of personal preference. What do you like? What font, in what size, creates a resume that you think looks great and conveys a professional image that is appropriate to your field, function, and role?

Some people find *serif* fonts—such as Bookman and Cambria, with small embellishments to the basic lines of each character—to be more readable. Others feel just the opposite—that *sans serif* fonts such as Tahoma and Arial are more readable. Interestingly, studies have "proven" both statements to be true! You can choose the style that you prefer.

A final consideration in font image and appearance is *contrast*. How much contrast is there between the bold and non-bold type? With some fonts, the difference is extreme:

Tahoma / **Tahoma Bold** • Bookman / **Bookman Bold**

With others, it's less noticeable:

Calibri / **Calibri Bold** • Palatino Linotype / **Palatino Linotype Bold**

If you are using a lot of bold type in your resume, a too-heavy bold may appear overpowering. Conversely, if your resume is relatively text-heavy, use the very bold contrast to improve readability.

> **PRO TIP: Consider using 2 different fonts in your resume:** a primary font for text and a second font for headings. Try Arial or Arial Narrow with Arial Black for headings, or Calibri text with Cambria headings, or another combination that you find adds impact and interest.

Font Enhancements

Bold type is not the only way to enhance a font. When designing your resume, experiment with the many ways you can vary the appearance and impact of your text on the page and on screen.

- ALL CAPS can help you create contrast and send a consistent message—for example, you might put company names in ALL CAPS and job titles in **bold**. Headlines are another great application for all caps. But just as all caps equates to SHOUTING in an email, text, or tweet, the same is true in your resume. Use ALL CAPS for emphasis but not for narrative content.

- SMALL CAPS is a distinguishing younger cousin of ALL CAPS. Similarly, it should be used for consistency and emphasis in titles, headlines, and more, but not for large bodies of text.

- *Italics* are very useful for content that should be understated, such as company descriptions. Avoid using *italics* for large blocks of text or for any material that's really important because it tends to blend in rather than stand out.

- **Colored or shaded fonts**, when used consistently, send a subtle message to readers and help them identify different types of content in a resume. Make certain that any colored text is highly readable on screen and when printed on a black-and-white printer.

Your ultimate objective in choosing a font for your resume is to create a distinctive, professional, appropriate image while conveying all of the information you want to share with prospective employers.

The following 2 resumes showcase strong and consistent formatting. In both, every element has been carefully chosen and presented consistently. Borders, boxes, and shading distinguish different kinds of information and call attention to the most important information. In both, the font selection perfectly supports each job seeker's objective and creates the *right* professional image.

Mark Vandermere Resume—pages 68–69

- Mark's Summary clearly communicates—in the headline, branding statement, bullets, and core competencies—that he is a qualified biomedical engineer.

- Prominent positioning of Education draws instant attention to this new graduate's degree.

- Relevant Coursework & Project Highlights, much like a functional resume, puts a heavy focus on his most important areas of skill and achievement, most of which are related to his Education more than Employment.

- Computer Skills offers a visually brief and easy-to-read presentation of his most valuable software and applications knowledge as it relates to his current search.

- The use of both horizontal and vertical lines adds subtle differentiation and pleasing visual appeal.

- Unique font selection and a small image in the upper left corner quickly capture attention.

Justin Lang Resume—page 70

- The 3 distinctive sections in the Summary demonstrate how to integrate complimentary format styles into one cohesive message.

- Shaded boxes instantly grab readers' attention to the most significant highlight of each of his positions.

- Bold type introducing each bullet point in Experience brings attention to some of the most notable keywords and keywords phrases in this resume.

- Everything is expertly placed within this 1-page resume and nothing competes to overtake another section.

- Bold and italic fonts distinguish the various kinds of information in each section of the resume.

MARK VANDERMERE

Dubuque, IA 52003
563-444-2345
mark.vandermere@email.com

BIOMEDICAL ENGINEER

Enthusiastic recent graduate eager to utilize and expand upon knowledge of microfluidics, bioinstrumentation, nanomedicine, and the engineering design process.

- **Highly motivated professional** with significant interest in drug discovery and delivery as well as strengths in project management, prototype development, and lab-on-a-chip (LOC) technology.

- **Quick study** with solid understanding of technical papers, drawings, and specifications, excellent drafting capabilities, and proficiency in wiring and programming.

- **Valued contributor** to engineering projects through excellent communication and troubleshooting skills, collaborative attitude, and commitment to innovation and process improvement.

Core competencies include:
- Data Analysis
- Mechanical Testing
- Thermal Systems
- Computer-Aided Design (CAD)
- Leadership & Teambuilding
- Report Generation
- Installation & Maintenance
- Recordkeeping

EDUCATION

BS – Biomedical Engineering (Focus in Nanotechnology), University of Iowa, Iowa City, IA (2023)

Honors: Contribution and Enrichment of the Arts Award, Presidential Scholarship

Activity: Treasurer – Biomedical Engineering Society

RELEVANT COURSEWORK & PROJECT HIGHLIGHTS

Biomedical Engineering / Nanotechnology Coursework

Bioinstrumentation ▪ Biosensors, Bio-Microelectromechanical Systems (BioMEMS) & Nanomedicine ▪ Biomedical Thermal Systems ▪ Engineering Physiology ▪ Biomechanics ▪ Biofluid Mechanics ▪ Product Development & Innovation

Robotic Surgery Simulator

Supplied mechanical, electrical, and physiological knowledge to aid in production of simulator to be used for educational purposes to display the advantages/disadvantages of robot-assisted surgery.

- Formulated and installed rotational support system to reduce jitter by 90%.
- Authored future work plan to ensure project completion in organized fashion.
- Delivered presentation at Northeast Bioengineering Conference (NEBEC) in April 2019 and published in subsequent NEBEC article.

Kidney Protection Application

Developed application to calculate risks of kidney stones in patients, using Objective-C to program system to compile information regarding beverage intake and dietary needs.

- Improved accuracy 72% by devising a method that updated the application on continuous basis.

Freddie Rohner, CMRW, CARW, CRS+HR, CRS+AF • iHire • ihire.com

MARK VANDERMERE

563-444-2345 ▪ mark.vandermere@email.com

Project Highlights, continued

Thermo-Modulating Container

Incorporated temperature response system into point-of-care device container to control power to Peltier cooler, using microelectromechanical systems for design of thermo-modulating package.

- Provided valuable leadership throughout group project, spearheading programming of output response to high and low temperature by toggling power of the Peltier cooler.

LOC Detection of Rotavirus in Infants via Saliva

Contributed to team that employed LOC technology to develop rotavirus detection system using microfluidics.

- Created 3 plans in plant design management system (PDMS) to test mixing/separation of particles.
- Constructed and tested device compatible with optical output and fluid transport with centrifuge.

PROFESSIONAL EXPERIENCE

ENG Design, Inc. – Dubuque, IA   2022 to Present

Engineering Supporter

Brought on board to decrease project delays by addressing issues with change processes. Function as central point of contact for several departments, creating/incorporating change orders and investigating critical problems with purchasing, engineering, and production teams as well as vendors. Implement corrective action reports (CARs) and non-conformance reports. Interface with machine shop personnel to re-work current parts in stock as needed.

- Volunteered to complete diverse tasks from several different supervisors to cut release time by 50% (2 months).
- Gained in-depth understanding of ERP system within 1 month and assisted purchasing and engineering departments in preventing duplicate part numbers.
- Work closely with CTO to develop design solutions for new and current product lines; chosen to attend and participate in design review meetings.

ABC Co. – Pleasant Valley, IA   2020, 2021 to 2022

Assistant Design Engineer/Intern (2021 to 2022) ▪ **General Laborer & Polisher** (Summer 2020)

Originally hired for general labor position polishing dandy rolls used for paper machines and assisting with plumbing for waste removal and finishing/installation of dandy rolls. Earned promotion based on knowledge of SolidWorks and received instruction on AutoCAD Inventor, completing drafts needed for key projects within short timeframe.

COMPUTER SKILLS

Autodesk ▪ SolidWorks ▪ ICAPS ▪ Minitab ▪ LabVIEW ▪ MATLAB ▪ Simulink

LibreOffice ▪ MS Office Suite ▪ Windows OS ▪ Linux Mint Cinnamon 17 "Qiana"

JUSTIN LANG

☎ 305-345-1234   ✉ justinlang@gmail.com

MARKETING DIRECTOR
STRATEGIC BUSINESS PLANNING ~ BRAND MANAGEMENT ~ NEW MARKET DEVELOPMENT

Market Share Growth
Positive Earnings Impact
Cost Control/Reduction
Lead Generation
Fiscal Management
Process Improvement
Cross-Team Collaboration

Innovative, profit-oriented leader with demonstrated success increasing market share and earnings, reducing costs, and improving client satisfaction.

Expert in analyzing competitive landscape, conducting market research, and aligning product offerings with customer needs.

Change agent with ability to analyze problems, formulate continuous process improvements, and integrate business system for efficiency and cost management.

Collaborative communicator skilled in building and strengthening relationships across functions to drive cohesive, strategic operations.

CAREER PROGRESSION

PALM BEACH COUNTY MEDICAL ASSOCIATES • Royal Palm Beach, FL

DIRECTOR OF MARKETING — 2019–2023

Spearheaded marketing strategy and programs for 350-physician practice group. Managed 2 Marketing Associates and $4M annual budget.

- **Marketing Strategy.** Refocused marketing toward visibility and relationship building.
- **Event Marketing.** Launched innovative health and wellness fair, attracting 50+ national vendors and 500+ attendees.
- **Social Media.** Added Twitter account, Facebook page, and blog; maintained active schedule of articles and posts, with contributions from 60% of medical staff.
- **Community Presence.** Represented practice on Health and Wellness Committee of Palm Beach Chamber of Commerce.

HIGHLIGHT

Eliminated $500K annual advertising expense while doubling rate of new patient acquisitions.

AUBURN INSURANCE, INC. • Lake Worth, FL

DIRECTOR OF MARKETING — 2017–2019

Recruited as first Director of Marketing for 100-year-old property insurance company.

- **Marketing Strategy.** Created the company's first formal marketing strategy and plan.
- **Program Innovation.** Started radio program dealing with the process of evaluating property claims. Built relationships by featuring local contractors as expert guests.
- **Brand Building.** Uncovered company's core values—customer focus, integrity, and expertise—and built marketing, branding, and advertising campaigns to promote them.

HIGHLIGHT

Built brand recognition through educational marketing on the value of insurance.

WEST PALM DEVELOPMENT CORP. • West Palm Beach, FL — 2014–2017

MARKETING MANAGER

Played a key role in launching new residential development. Assisted buyers in selecting lots, choosing finishes, and completing the process from pre-sale through closing.

- **Marketing.** Developed brochures, print advertisements, and other marketing materials.
- **Event Marketing.** Generated dozens of prospects by creating "Community Confabs" that drew large groups to learn more about homes in a non-sales environment..

HIGHLIGHT

Sold all 37 homes a year ahead of projection.

EDUCATION

BS BUSINESS ADMINISTRATION, University of Florida, Gainesville, FL • 2014

Katrina Brittingham, CPRW • VentureReady LLC • ventureready.net

CHAPTER 8:
Improve Readability & Skimmability

Be wise about how people read today. Whether reading online or on paper, we skim, we glance, we move quickly from item to item, seeking to pick up information quickly.

Make sure that your resume is formatted to reward this reading style. You will keep your readers engaged if you feed them meaningful information in small bites. Specifically:

- **Write short paragraphs**—2 to 4 lines at most. If you have more to say, break your paragraph into 2 or create a paragraph plus bullet list to convey the information.

- **Add white space between paragraphs and bullets.** White space provides "breathing room" for readers to absorb one bite of information before moving on to the next.

- **Limit your bullet lists** to 3 to 5 items in each list. Too many bullets create a large block of text that is very easy for readers to skip over.

- **Use headings and subheadings to segment and introduce information.** This is a great technique to improve the skimmability of your resume and every other document you write.

- **Follow the rules of good page design** in Part IV and the font recommendations in Chapter 7 as you build a resume that is both very readable and pleasing to the eye.

Of course, you don't want to shortchange yourself by omitting valuable information just to keep your content short! Here are 3 techniques that work well when you have too many bulleted achievements.

Technique #1: Divide and Conquer. You've written 7 bulleted items for your current job. All of them are important because they represent your most significant accomplishments over the past 5 years and are relevant to your current goals. When you first write your resume, those bulleted items might look like this:

- Produced $50M+ revenue from previously untapped states and large districts.
- Exceeded revenue target by $16M and attained 97% of margin against plan.
- Boosted market share from 39% to more than 50% of the US.
- Delivered YOY margin improvements since 2019 in a difficult environment; in 2 largest states, beat plan by $6.2M (30%) in 2022.
- Improved win percentage 45% through process changes that enabled team to respond to 25% more bids.
- Secured $145M in key contracts through competitive bids with state agencies in TX and FL.
- Reduced customer-facing errors 25% and liquidated damages $14M within first year of implementing new cross-functional leadership model.

Even though those items are bulleted, it still looks like a large clump of text ... almost like one huge paragraph ... so it's very easy for a reader to simply pass over it.

If you group those achievements under subheadings, see how much cleaner the presentation is and how much easier it is to read. And, by using subheadings that are directly relevant to your job objective, you increase your keyword count and draw further attention to your core areas of expertise and achievement:

Revenue, Profit & Market Growth
- Produced $50M+ revenue from previously untapped states and large districts.
- Exceeded revenue target by $16M and attained 97% of margin against plan.
- Boosted market share from 39% to more than 50% of the US.
- Delivered YOY margin improvements since 2019 in a difficult environment; in 2 largest states, beat plan by $6.2M (30%) in 2022.

Operational Performance
- Improved win percentage 45% through process changes that enabled team to respond to 25% more bids.
- Secured $145M in key contracts through competitive bids with state agencies in TX and FL.
- Reduced customer-facing errors 25% and liquidated damages $14M within first year of implementing new cross-functional leadership model.

Technique #2: Sub-Bullet. Use sub-bullets to break large items into more easily digestible bites.

For example, let's say you have a meaty bullet point that looks like this:
- Revitalized stagnant organization through a fresh look at partnerships, sponsorships, and community initiatives. Grew subscriber base 5% and sponsor/advertiser base more than 15%. Targeted and captured high-profile new sponsors—Pepsi, Subway, KFC, NASCAR, Old Spice. Forged strong, sustainable relationships with partners and affiliates.

By breaking it into a primary bullet with sub-bullets, you instantly make the content more readable:
- Revitalized stagnant organization through a fresh look at partnerships, sponsorships, and community initiatives.
    - ✓ Grew subscriber base 5% and sponsor/advertiser base more than 15%.
    - ✓ Targeted and captured high-profile new sponsors—Pepsi, Subway, KFC, NASCAR, Old Spice.
    - ✓ Forged strong, sustainable relationships with partners and affiliates.

Technique #3: Create Columns. When a bullet list or paragraph contains many short items—such as a skills list—consider using a double- or triple-column format to save space while keeping readability high.

For example, let's look at 3 different approaches for presenting a skills list for a sales manager.

First, we see skills clumped into a single paragraph, which is dense, hard to read, and not recommended:

- Skills include business development, account management, team leadership and supervision, sales prospecting, client sourcing, sales closing, budget development, cost-benefit analysis, ROI forecasting, territory and account management, sales training, contract negotiations, and exceptional customer service.

Second, a double-column bullet list is easier to read but takes up more space on the page:

Professional Skills:

• Business Development	• Account Management
• Team Leadership	• Staff Supervision
• Sales Prospecting	• Client Sourcing
• Sales Closing	• Sales Training
• Budget Development	• Cost-Benefit Analysis
• ROI Forecasting	• Territory and Account Management
• Contract Negotiations	• Exceptional Customer Service

Third, the triple column is efficient, attractive, and easy to peruse:

Professional Qualifications:

• Business Development	• Team Leadership & Supervision	• Account Management
• Client Sourcing	• Sales Prospecting & Closing	• Sales Training
• Budget Development	• Territory & Account Management	• ROI Forecasting
• Contract Negotiations	• Exceptional Customer Service	• Cost-Benefit Analysis

Technique #4: Pop Your Contact Information. The contact information on your resume must jump off the page. In just a line or 2, you let employers know how to reach you and how to find out more about you. Here are 5 guidelines:

- Put your contact information at the top of your resume. While it's possible to position this information at the bottom, on the side, or in the middle of a clever design, we don't recommend it. Your goal is to get a response—an email or a phone call. Make it easy for people to contact you.

- Pop your name. Place your name boldly and distinctly so people know who they are contacting, and to immediately distinguish your resume from all others.

- Use only 1 phone number and 1 email address. No one is going to call multiple phones or send numerous emails in an effort to contact you.

- Use your mobile number, so you're instantly accessible, along with a professional email address (e.g., marysmith@gmail.com and *not* marylovescats@gmail.com).

- Determine whether to include your location. Are you only looking for opportunities in the same city, region, or state that you live in? If so, be sure to include your city, state, and possibly ZIP code.

  Conversely, if you are open to relocation, do not include that information. Share the fact that you're an out-of-state candidate after they're already impressed with your resume and you.

- Include live links to your email address, LinkedIn profile, website (if you have one), and other social media or contact information. You want to make it easy for people to instantly click through to contact you or learn more about you.

Here are 3 sample contact sections that show a variety of ways to present this critical information at the top of your resume so that it is easy to see and easy for employers to connect with you.

Roberto Diaz
212-498-1107 • robdiaz@mac.com
www.linkedin.com/in/robertodiaz • @RobDiaz

LAURIE WILSON

Denver, CO 30039 • lauriewil@mac.com • linkedin.com/in/lauriewilson • 443.629.8362

DANA CASPER

New York Metro
212-604-2910

danacasper@nyc.rr.com
www.danacasper.com

On the next few pages you'll see 2 examples of well-written resumes that are also beautifully formatted for readability and skimmability.

Travis Washington Resume—page 75

Travis's resume, in a sharp-looking 2-column format with a striking and appropriate map graphic, clearly highlights the skills, education, and experience that this new graduate brings to the workplace. The headline and branding statement convey his expertise and his passion. Note how technical skills and activities are succinctly listed under each job title to enhance both content and visual appeal.

Andrea Ponto Resume—pages 76–77

Andrea's resume is a great example of skimmability at its finest. Look quickly at her resume and you'll instantly notice her name, headline, job titles, and a shaded box that highlights the key achievement of each position. Her relevant experience is visually strengthened by bolding metrics, keywords, and other high-value information. In a quick glance, readers instantly know *who* Andrea is and the value she brings to an organization. The expert use of white space further enhances the readability of this resume.

Travis Washington, MGIS

555-555-3455 • travis.washington@gmail.com • Web Portfolio

GIS Specialist • GIS Data Technician • Mapmaker

Merging the art of mapmaking with the science of data management to create solutions that eliminate barriers, form connections, increase human interaction, and solve problems for people and communities.

Education

Master in Geographic Information Science, 2023
PENN STATE UNIVERSITY, State College, PA | GPA: 3.8

Bachelor of Arts in Multimedia Arts and Sciences, 2021
CARNEGIE-MELLON UNIVERSITY, Pittsburgh, PA

- **Emphasis:** 3-D Animation | Minor: Applied Mathematics
- **Capstone:** "Music in Motion," recognized as one of the year's most compelling multimedia pieces

Technical Skills

- **Adobe Suite:** Photoshop, Illustrator, Acrobat, After Effects, Flash, Dreamweaver, Media Encoder
- **ArcGIS Online and Desktop:** Map, App-Builders, Catalog, Database, Globe, Presentation Builders, Server
- **Autodesk:** Maya, AutoCAD, Inventor, Revit, Solidworks
- **GIS Software:** OSM, CartoDB, Java API, SimplyMap, QGIS
- **Google:** Sketchup, Plus, Docs, Sheets, Drive, Keep, Sites
- **GPS:** Trimble, ArcGIS Collector, ArcPad, LIDAR
- **MS Office:** Word, Excel, Publisher, Access, PowerPoint
- **Web:** HTML5, CSS, Javascript, Python

Professional Experience

Web Designer | Social Media Manager | LEISURE INDUSTRIES, INC., Alexandria, VA (Remote) | May 2020–Present

Website Redesign | Website Updates | Social Media | Interactive Application Development | Graphic Design | Document Design | Photography

- Took on increasing levels of responsibility and initiated new projects to support the company's digital presence.
- Conceived idea and created GIS-based interactive site maps for company campgrounds—the foundation for a fully interactive reservation system.

GIS Transportation Intern | PENN STATE TRANSPORTATION SERVICES, State College, PA | May–Dec 2022

Enterprise GIS | Data Curation, Editing & Updating | Database Operations | Map Setup | GPS | Querying | Metadata Documentation

- As lead intern, mentored and tutored 3 interns and served as GIS expert to department heads.
- Created best practices and work flows for handling data and managing all of the university's transportation assets.

GIS Intern | HARRISBURG CITY OFFICES, Harrisburg, PA | May–Dec 2021

Field Data Collection | GPS | Post-Processing | Data Maintenance & Curation | App Development | Parcel Data Updates | 3-D | Spatial Analysis

- Pioneered GPS mapping for Harrisburg, launching the city's first up-to-date and accurate GPS data resource—a critical tool for planning projects, projecting costs, and protecting assets.
- Created an interactive story map and app-based tour of city gardens—melding annual citywide competition into an easily accessible attraction for tourists and citizens. U-Spatial Best Use of Maps award, 2021.
- Developed a customized "base map" for the city, drawing city-specific features and adding detailed information on streets, parks, buildings, wetlands, woods, and other sites.

Interests and Activities

- **Musician** (piano, vocals, percussion)—Penn State Chorale, Select Chorus, and Jazz Bands
- **Volunteer**—Habitat for Humanity, Lutheran Campus Ministries, Community Emergency Services
- **Mapmaker**—GISSO, Maptime, STIF (Students Today Leaders Forever): Planned logistics, mapped, and chronicled 3 annual bus tours bringing students to community service projects across the country.

ANDREA PONTO

Tucson, AZ | 520-654-9087 | aponto@yahoo.com

SENIOR OPERATIONS EXECUTIVE & GLOBAL LEADER

Profitable Growth & Expansion ♦ Business Turnarounds ♦ Operational Transformation
Strategic Planning & Vision ♦ P&L Management ♦ High-Performance Team Leadership

✓ **HIGH-IMPACT EXECUTIVE** with exceptional record of success orchestrating and delivering consistent and measurable breakthroughs in revenue and profit growth, market and customer expansion, and productivity and efficiency gains.

✓ **VISIONARY LEADER** repeatedly recognized for developing and executing strategies that create ongoing value for company, customers, and shareholders. Proven reputation for strong business collaboration and transparency.

✓ **EXPERT** in solving highly complex business problems, turning around stagnant operations and underperforming businesses, and building top-performing teams that produce bottom-line results.

PROFESSIONAL EXPERIENCE

GRANT IGNITION, Cleveland, OH & Phoenix, AZ   2012–Present
Global leader in compression technology, drive technology, and hydraulics with $2.3B revenue and 8,700 employees.

VICE PRESIDENT OF GLOBAL OPERATIONS – DALTRON, LLC ♦ COO, GRANT CONTROL (2019–Present)

Took on new challenge to turn around Daltron, world's leading manufacturer of ignition and control systems for industrial engines while overseeing all operations for global engine division. Manage $150M P&L and 8 direct/350 indirect reports.

➢ **Restored Daltron business to profitability in less than 18 months** through sweeping operational, cultural, and organizational changes. **Transitioned from negative to 30% positive EBITA.** Recognized as most profitable entity among 30+ businesses within company.

➢ **Reinvigorated operations and leadership teams with new energy, vision, and direction.** Built global strategies that streamlined product development process, aligned commercial operations, and standardized margin expectations.

➢ Identified and implemented diverse HR strategies and best practices that **boosted employee engagement scores 35% in 9 months.** Focused on intrinsic motivation, empowerment, bottom-up engagement, and learning and development.

➢ Discovered and resolved significant ERP data quality issues. **Reduced WIP inventory 40% and non-sellable inventory $5M annually,** enabling greater investment in finished goods to lower cycle times and increase customer satisfaction.

➢ Formed internal committee that leveraged Lean Six Sigma techniques to streamline operations and drive efficiency.
  - Reduced overtime 9% (**$1.3M annual savings**).
  - Cut annual rework costs **$700K.**
  - Increased margins **12%.**
  - Decreased production scrap **11% ($340K annually)**.

VICE PRESIDENT OF OPERATIONS – GRANT CONTROL (2016–2019)

Charged with reversing losses and restoring profitability to highly specialized global business unit providing diverse solutions for large reciprocating, natural gas, and dual-fuel engines. Managed $60M P&L and 7 direct/35 indirect reports.

➢ **Generated positive EBIT (16%) after 5 years of losses** by restructuring entire operations team, overhauling cost control and recovery processes, forming project management team, and forging trusted partnerships with suppliers.

GRANT IGNITION, continued

➢ **Realized $4M annual cost savings and added $11M annual revenue stream** by developing leaders' contract management abilities and transforming entire change order process for large turnkey projects.

➢ **Recovered $6M in annual costs and added $600K revenue stream within warranty/repair business.** Created quick, efficient return material authorization process for fuel valves that reduced engine downtime and client inventory.

➢ **Elevated organizational capabilities by fostering culture of collaboration, openness, and teamwork.** Led cross-functional teams in defining process for timely and accurate project handoffs and execution.

➢ **Delivered quick, sustainable results for shareholders.** Participated in sale of business to General Motors.

DIRECTOR OF OPERATIONS – ENGINE CONTROLS (2015–2016)
GLOBAL PRODUCT MANAGER – CONTROLS & INSTRUMENTATION (2012–2015)

Promoted to lead and direct operations for Engine Controls (aftermarket business of Grant Control) while continuing to direct total lifecycle management for control and instrumentation product portfolio. Challenged with driving operational excellence and new revenue and market share growth. Managed $30M P&L and 5 direct/40 indirect reports.

➢ **Increased market share 25% and EBIT 15%** through sharp focus on development and launch of products better aligned with customer and global market demands.

➢ Worked cross-functionally to revamp and enhance product development process, **reducing R&D costs $450K/year.**

➢ **Decreased inventory 29%** by enhancing operational efficiencies and standardizing engineering practices.

➢ Overhauled product design process and introduced new manufacturing methods and technologies, **cutting cycle time 21% and increasing inventory turns from 7 to 11 annually.**

➢ **Lowered headcount 6%** through implementation of Lean manufacturing techniques and 5S system.

PETER BROTHERS (ServiceMaster company), Cleveland, OH   2006–2012
Leading provider of facilities management support and solutions.

ACCOUNT MANAGER / NATIONAL PROJECT SALES ENGINEER (2011–2013) ◆ PROJECT ENGINEER (2007–2011)

Promoted to oversee team of 3 direct/20 indirect reports designing, manufacturing, and selling custom control panels and software systems that reduce energy consumption for large energy users. Captured and managed key accounts across multiple industry sectors (retail, healthcare, government, and others), generating $35M+ annual revenue.

➢ **Generated $12M new revenue** through crucial enhancement of organizational project management capabilities.

➢ **Realized 11% revenue growth and market expansion** by becoming MLC Group Certified Panel Shop.

➢ **Reduced costs and increased margins 6%+** by standardizing core engineering processes and procedures.

EDUCATION & CERTIFICATION

Bachelor of Science, Electrical Engineering – Indiana University

Operations Certificate – Caltech Center for Technology and Management Education (2015)

CHAPTER 9:

Format for Human Readers and Applicant Tracking Systems (ATS)

Is your resume readable for both the human eye and electronic scanners?

Today's modern job search demands that you share your resume through various online and offline channels. The unique requirements of each may call for different formats or small edits to your existing format:

- **Print:** Make sure that the print version of your resume is attractive and highly readable, because you'll need it for interviews and other in-person meetings—and you want it to impress! Print your resume on nice paper (not plain copy paper), and always take multiple copies to an interview.

- **Email:** We recommend that you attach your resume as a Word or PDF file and write your message as an e-note, in the body of the email. An e-note is the modern version of the traditional cover letter.

- **Upload:** When applying to a job online or uploading your resume to a database, read and carefully follow the directions for submitting the preferred format. Word and PDF are the most commonly accepted file formats. As we've stated, we recommend that you use PDF whenever possible.

In previous chapters, we discussed how to make your resume content both highly relevant and highly readable. There's one more consideration—and it's an important one. Because most employers use Applicant Tracking Systems (ATS) for initial resume scanning and sorting, it's essential that your resume be written and structured so that it will be read and understood.

The good news is that modern Applicant Tracking Systems have evolved and can now handle a wide variety of formats, fonts, and structures. You are not limited to a plain-text resume for uploading. But there are a few important considerations.

Integrate All-Important Keywords

First and foremost, understand that **keywords are the backbone of all electronic resume-scanning technologies and ATS.** Nearly all companies and recruiters use keywords as the primary method to identify qualified candidates, and they are *the* words that will help you get found online and make the cut.

To understand how critical keywords are to your search, consider a recruiter seeking a candidate with supply chain experience. Maybe you have all of the core skills—purchasing, logistics, inventory control, and other related activities—but you've never used the exact words "supply chain" in your resume.

When that recruiter does a search using that term ("supply chain") as the #1 keyword, your resume will probably be overlooked even though you have precisely the experience the recruiter seeks. Most recruiters and hiring managers use multiple keywords to identify candidates, but you never know.

> **PRO TIP: In online and database searches, initial candidate selection has evolved into an almost entirely technical function.** Know the keywords for the jobs you are targeting and integrate them throughout your resume.

Now, think beyond just job skills and consider the hiring manager who is recruiting an electrical engineer for a company in Cincinnati. It's easy to do a search for an electrical engineer, but the company only wants local candidates, so Cincinnati becomes a searchable keyword. Zip codes can also be used.

Employers often look to recruit candidates from competitor companies. Some are interested only in graduates from Harvard and Yale. Others might be searching for a rare technical skill. The specificity of a keyword search can be deep, so you *must* focus every word in your resume on the information that matters most.

Keywords and searchable terms have greater range and diversity than you might think. They encompass:

Hard Skills & Facts

Job Titles	Areas of Expertise
Professional Skills	Industry-Specific Language
Technology Qualifications	Project Highlights

Soft Skills

Communications	Interpersonal Relationships
Organization	Collaboration and Teamwork
Prioritization	Personal Traits and Attributes

Educational & Training Credentials

College and University Names	College Degrees, Majors, and Minors
Professional Credentials	Training Programs and Training Organizations
Professional Licenses	Internships and Fellowships

General Information

Company Names	Professional Affiliations
Product Names	Cities, States, and Zip Codes
Foreign Languages	Countries and International Details

If you're currently working in a job that's similar to those you are targeting, you're in luck. The single most valuable resource in identifying keywords for your industry and profession is you! The duties and functions that you perform every day (hard skills) and the manner in which you do your job and the way that you perform (soft skills) are precisely the keywords you will want to feature in your resume.

For others who are seeking roles with greater responsibilities, changing careers, graduating from college, returning to work, or facing other situations, keyword identification might not be quite so easy. Here's a wealth of resources to help you identify your most critical keywords, particularly your hard and soft skills:

- Online job postings
- Company websites (job postings, "About Us," or "Mission")
- LinkedIn Group conversations, job postings, and company pages
- Social media engagement and multimedia sources
- Professional associations (newsletters, meetings, conferences, and networking)
- Formal job descriptions
- Books, trade journals, specialized industry dictionaries, and other online and hard-copy publications

Integrating keywords is a crucial part of modern resume writing. Perhaps the quickest and easiest technique is to create a "key skills" or "core competencies" list of no more than 8–12 items as part of your Summary. Load that list with all of your top keywords to paint a picture of someone who is well qualified for the positions you are targeting. But don't stop there. For maximum effectiveness, keywords must be integrated into all sections of your resume. In essence, you are using the language of your profession to describe your activities and achievements.

When applying to a posted position, take the time to peruse the job description and cross-check your resume to be sure you've included most or all of the keywords that you identify—as appropriate to you and your experience.

Format Your Resume for Applicant Tracking System (ATS) Readability

While modern ATS can read most resume files and formats, there are a few considerations to keep in mind as you create your resume. These guidelines will help ensure that your resume moves smoothly through the system, is read accurately, and credits you with all of your skills, experiences, and accomplishments.

- Use a chronological (combination) format. Functional resumes will not be properly read by ATS because the system cannot match your skills and achievements to specific employment.

- It's fine to use italics, bold, and other enhancements.

- Do not use MS Word's header or footer feature for anything except possibly a page-2 header or footer—with your name and contact information—whose content is not critical to the resume.

- If you use graphics, borders, logos, or charts, understand that they will *not* be read—but they will not affect the readability or scoring of the rest of the document. The ATS will simply pass over them.

- Do *not* use text boxes—i.e., using the "Insert Text Box" command in Word. ATS view text boxes as graphics and, as just mentioned, will not read any of the text inside. Instead, you can mimic the appearance of a text box by using Word's Tab or Table tool.

- You may include your home address, or city/state/zip code, or general metro area, or omit entirely. Location may be a search factor, so you will need to decide if it's better to include or omit.

- Use commonly accepted acronyms, but if in doubt (and for all acronyms that are not well known), spell out the term the first time you mention it and use the acronym thereafter.

If your resume is highly designed—if, for instance, you've used a designer resume template or a tool like Canva to create an infographic or highly visual resume—consider creating a separate plain-text version for uploading to be certain that the contents will be read. Save your beautifully designed resume for emailing and in-person meetings.

As you'll see in the following 2 samples, ATS-friendly does not have to mean plain or boring.

Nicholas Bauman Resume—page 83

Nicholas's resume, written in the universal font Arial, is well designed and attractive. Notice the section headers and structure of the employment listing that promote ATS readability. Also note that Education doesn't contain college or university information but does list his apprenticeship and secondary school (high school) education. Both are appropriate to list for this skilled technician.

Javier Rodriguez Resume—pages 84–85

Javier's resume mixes 2 different fonts to create a distinctive look without adding anything that will compromise ATS readability. Notice the "Skills" section in the Summary, a great addition to beef up those all-important keywords.

Today's Job Search Reality

As you view all of the resume samples in this book, you will notice that many do not strictly follow the ATS guidelines we've just described. That's because we wanted to showcase a wide variety of options for resume content, format, and design to spark your creativity and show you what's possible.

Quite likely, all of the job seekers with highly designed and graphic resumes also have a second, plainer Word version that they use when uploading.

But even more importantly, those job seekers are not relying on passing a keyword scan as their primary strategy for finding their next job. They understand the reality of today's job search—where keyword-scanning systems are everywhere but are *not* the only nor the best method for you to find a job,

If that surprises you, you're not alone. After all, you keep hearing how important it is for you to write and design your resume to make it through the scanning systems. Yes, it's important—and we've just told you how to do that. But even more important is understanding how most people find jobs and how most jobs get filled.

Consider this:

- When you apply to jobs online, you are one of many. The average number of resumes per job has been reported to be anywhere from 115 to 240.

- Your uploaded resume must rise to the very top based on keyword match, specific qualifications, and other factors. Only 2% to 3% of those 115+ resumes are selected from all of the uploads, and only those candidates—the top handful—are invited to interview.

How, then, do most people find jobs? For the majority, the most effective method is to get a referral to the hiring company or hiring manager. When you become a referred candidate (e.g., John refers you to a contact of his who is looking to hire a new staff accountant), rather than a faceless resume in a crowded database, you instantly become a favored candidate!

> **PRO TIP: 100% of referred candidates who have the qualifications will get an interview,** according to one of our most reliable sources, Gerry Crispin of CareerXRoads.

The best method to become a referred candidate is to launch a well-targeted networking campaign. Reach out to people you know—or can get to know through one of your existing contacts. Ask for their advice and assistance. Be ready with a brief explanation of what you're looking for and how you will add value in that position. Your outreach will not only position you as a referred candidate for specific jobs you're targeting; it will also open you to other opportunities as your network expands.

Based on these job search truths, we don't want you to obsess about keyword matching and ATS scanning.

Yes, you should have a version of your resume that is suitable for uploading and scanning. Yes, you should peruse job postings and apply when appropriate. But don't think of that as your *only* avenue or your *best* method for finding a job. It is quick and easy, but for many people it is not very effective.

Clearly, you will get the best results if you spend most of your time seeking referrals to hiring managers at your target companies instead of simply uploading resumes in response to job postings. A targeted search, with networking as its core component, is the time-tested and effective job search method that produces the most leads, interviews, and job offers.

Nicholas Bauman

514-345-8610   nickbauman@gmail.com

Heavy Duty Equipment Technician

Fluent French and German | Proficient English

Physically Fit | Able to Lift 100 Pounds | Prefer Working Outdoors

Ten+ years of diverse experience, mainly with diesel engines, forestry equipment, large agricultural machinery, and construction vehicles. Forklift certification.

Exceptional mechanical inclination and up-to-date knowledge of changing technologies through courses and independent study. Experience and knowledge in:

- Fuel injection systems, lubrication systems, installation and alignment of engines and machinery
- Mechanical and hydraulic transmissions, hydraulic-operated working attachments, and winches
- Troubleshooting and equipment inspection, detecting malfunctions, and determining repairs
- Mechanical and electrical repairs

PROFESSIONAL EXPERIENCE

Grand Mechanic, Montreal, QC
Heavy Machinery Mechanic and Machine Operator (2016 – current)
Work as both a mechanic (40% of the time) and machine operator (60% of the time).

- Operate a CAT digger, working mainly outdoors on construction sites.
- Repair equipment onsite, completing contracts that last from 2 days to 5 weeks.
- Attend safety meetings held for all equipment operators. Maintain excellent safety record.

Garage de l'Excellence, Quebec City, QC
Auto Mechanic (2013 – 2016)
Held responsible role with well-established garage that repairs all makes of cars, automatic and standard.

- Performed service and repairs for domestic and imported cars, small trucks, and large equipment.
- Assigned major engine rebuilds and complex machine repairs; used computerized diagnostics.

Ultimate AG, Zug, Switzerland
Service Technician (2010 – 2013)
Travelled to conduct on-site service and repairs of bulldozers, excavators, and other Caterpillar machinery associated with new road construction and gravel pits.

- Acquired comprehensive theoretical and practical training to carry out contracted service work.

Gut Brands, Zug, Switzerland
Technician, Demonstrator, and Sales Associate (2008 – 2010)
Employer is main Swiss importer of Kawasaki ATVs and sells cranes and cable winches for forestry.

- Completed sales training and while demonstrating machinery also conducted sales.
- Built newly purchased machines according to customized orders.

EDUCATION

Apprenticeship: 3.5 years Agricultural Machine Mechanic, Reinhardt & Cie., Zug
Secondary Schooling: Swiss educational system

Javier Rodriguez

Atlanta Metro Region

404-654-3210 • javier.rodriguez@att.net • LinkedIn

Regional Sales Manager – International Business
Bilingual Spanish / English

Sales Leader and Army Veteran with 20+ years of sales results, business management experience, and expertise in forecasting customer, business, and industry trends.

Performance Highlights

- Delivered double-digit sales increases year after year in intensely competitive markets.
- Successfully introduced products into Latin America, Europe, and Hispanic markets in the US.
- Led region to $4M growth by adding 100+ new distributors over 5 years.
- Formulated a market-entry strategy for Latin America and negotiated exclusive agreements in 3 countries.

Skills

- Sales Management
- Solution Selling
- International Expansion
- National-Level Profit & Loss
- Training & Development
- Financial Management
- Sales Reporting & Analysis
- Deal Negotiation
- Customer Relationship Management

PROFESSIONAL EXPERIENCE

Daisy Foods USA – Atlanta, GA

National Food Service Sales Manager   2021–Present

Craft and execute strategic roadmap for the food service and retail markets, establishing new products and enhancing current product sales. Collaborate with customers – top retailers and major restaurant chains – on product marketing, promotions, and advertising. Lead a team of 7 Regional Managers.

- Grew year-over-year (YOY) sales **18%** despite intense market competition; projecting **40%** growth in 2023.
- Led corporate initiative to penetrate food service and retail markets with new premium ice cream products. Introduced **2** new brands to distributors and **10** new SKUs to large grocery store chains. Generated **$2.6M** in new product sales in less than a year.
- Developed plan for unified and consistent messaging for all marketing and advertising materials.

Summer Edibles, Inc. – Roswell, GA

Food Services Sales Manager / Regional Sales Manager   2017–2021

Developed and directed sales in food service sector, creating sales and marketing strategies to drive brand growth. Led and coached sales team and oversaw a network of food brokers, distributors, and supermarket chains. Negotiated and implemented marketing programs. Created budgets, forecasts, and financial projections.

- Drove **25%** increase in YOY sales by promoting both brand and product quality to customers.
- Managed **35%** of the company's annual revenue and increased Southeast region's revenue by **15%.**
- Propelled **11%** sales expansion by focusing on incremental sales of new core products.
- Gained **9%** in sales in the Southeast region by adding core brand with a Hispanic distributor.

Javier Rodriguez • Page 2   404-654-3210 • javier.rodriguez@att.net • LinkedIn

Dynamic Marketing – Atlanta, GA

Director of Sales & Marketing   2012–2017

Brought on board to lead sales and marketing for young imported foods company poised for growth. Implemented direct and indirect sales plans, established product pricing policies, and trained and mentored business partners and distributors. Added staff to support growth, ultimately supervising 5 sales and marketing employees.

- Focused on distributor channel to drive rapid growth. Quickly added 100+ new distributors, leading to **$4M** sales growth in 5 years.
- Expanded international footprint and increased total sales **15%** by recruiting 12 new affiliates in 7 nations.
- Increased revenue **9%** through an innovative private-label program for dessert manufacturing company.

Globe Corporation – Atlanta, GA

International Sales Manager   2008–2012

Directed worldwide promotion of military footwear. Facilitated sales distribution, advised representatives and distributors, and devised marketing strategies.

- Grew annual sales revenue by **$2M** in 3.5 years.
- Created a brand image program that resulted in international recognition built around the company's reputation as the main provider of military footwear to the US Department of Defense.
- Formulated and led market entry strategy for Latin America. Negotiated exclusive agreements in 3 countries and established the company's entire Latin American presence.
- Discovered and pursued a new product channel in Europe in response to an emerging fashion trend, an innovative approach and strategic repositioning that led to a **10%** increase in overall sales.

EDUCATION

BS Business Administration (International Business specialization), 2008

Emory University, Atlanta, GA

MILITARY

US Army, 1996–2005

Honorable Discharge

COMMUNITY ENGAGEMENT

Wounded Warrior Project

Boys & Girls Clubs of Metro Atlanta

PART IV:
Modernize Your Resume Design

The 4 Principles of Modern Resume Design
- Capture Attention in a Flash
- Follow the Practices of Good Page Design
- Match Design Elements to Your Industry, Profession & Career Story
- Be Distinctive & Embrace Color & Graphics

What design elements will add visual punch to your resume? How can you create an engaging visual presentation that is closely aligned with your profession and industry—and will instantly attract the right people and hiring decision makers?

Here are some of our favorite design elements to give your resume even more visual appeal.

Charts, Graphs, and Call-outs

Visuals that communicate specific messages add powerful and immediate impact to your resume. A chart (shown left) instantly conveys growth and success. A call-out (shown right) draws attention to impressive achievements that can be explained more fully in a bullet point.

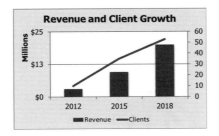

Lines, Borders & Boxes

Here's a small sampling of the variety of lines you can apply using MS Word's Borders feature—the easiest and most reliable method for adding lines to your resume. Alternatively, borders and boxes can be added as graphic files if you prefer that method.

| Boxes—either text boxes or table cells—are another great option. | Shading draws attention to boxed content. |

Images, Graphics & Illustrations

As you will see in many of the resumes we share in this book, visual enhancements like these get noticed.

Monograms

An interesting, attractive way to differentiate your resume is to position a monogram (your initials) at the top of the page—along with your full name, of course.

In the following 4 chapters, we'll demonstrate and discuss how to use the above design elements and others, when color is a great addition, and other visuals that can enhance your resume's appeal. Use these techniques wisely to apply the perfect finishing polish to your new, modern resume.

CHAPTER 10:
Capture Attention in a Flash

The visual presentation of your resume matters … a lot! Before they read a single word, people notice visual cues and form an immediate impression. Make that impression positive and make it count.

A huge part of getting your resume noticed is to capture attention instantly. If your resume doesn't do that, readers move on to the next candidate. Seconds matter. Consider these all-important questions for creating attention-grabbing resumes:

- **Is capturing attention all about using bold designs?** Maybe … for the right candidates in the right industries and professions.

- **Are images, illustrations, and other graphics an important addition to your resume?** Possibly … if you're in an industry or profession where those design elements amp up your presentation.

- **Do tables, graphs, and charts add value to resume design?** Maybe … if you're in an industry or profession where you can measure and quantify your performance.

- **Should you use company and product logos and images?** Perhaps … if those elements add value in terms of positioning you for your next career move.

- **Does every resume have to be filled with design elements?** Of course not! A minimally designed resume will serve you better than one that's so over-designed it creates a negative impression.

- **Does color make your resume stand out?** The answer to that question is a resounding yes. In today's world of job search, where color printers are commonplace and many people will be viewing your resume online or on screen, color adds a rich enhancement and punch.

  Because this book is in black and white, you can't see the wide range of colors used on most of the sample resumes. Of course, even in black and white they look sharp and they engage the reader. But color adds distinction and, when used well, is appropriate for just about any job seeker.

Use Design Elements Appropriately

Design should be used judiciously with an emphasis on including elements that boost your credibility, visibility, and professional brand.

If you're a 62-year-old finance executive with a steady career in the insurance industry, a resume filled with multiple design elements would be inappropriate and off-brand. Anything more than a few tasteful design additions would not be right for you, your industry, or your profession.

Conversely, if you're a 28-year-old graphic artist, your resume is your canvas! You can use color, images, icons, illustrations, and original art to create a resume that actually shows what you can do. The flexibility of modern resumes provides you with a wealth of opportunities to visually demonstrate what you know.

> **PRO TIP: If your resume is filled with design elements, prepare a simplified Word version for Applicant Tracking Systems (ATS).** The design that makes your resume so attractive to people may cause problems when scanned by ATS. When emailing to human contacts, send the PDF version, but when uploading to a job board or employment site, have the less-designed Word version ready to go.

Techniques for Capturing Attention in a Flash

Following are 5 of our favorite methods for capturing attention quickly. They are illustrated—very effectively—in the 2 resumes that follow.

Jason Herrigan Resume—pages 91–92
Aiden Wells Resume—page 93

- **Add a design element at the very top of your resume.** A good example is the distinctive "JH" monogram that sits to the left of Jason's name. On Aiden's resume, his name is enhanced with a different font/font size—a simple touch that immediately distinguishes his resume from others.

- **Use a branding statement.** Aiden doesn't want you to miss the fact that he has "14 straight years of exceeding goals in a multimillion-dollar territory." Jason wants you to know that he is a "tenacious problem solver who brings innovative digital communication solutions from inception to content production." Both of these powerful statements are positioned immediately beneath the Headlines for maximum impact.

- **Introduce colorful and appropriate graphics.** Although you can't see the colors that were used, you can see the logos of major media companies on both pages of Jason's resume and the intersecting circles on Aiden's. They're attractive, distinctive, and, most importantly, appropriate.

- **Enhance with links.** In addition to the traditional links to email and LinkedIn, notice how Jason incorporates video links—and accompanying snapshots—at the bottom of the page. Aiden has linked the names of his company and the community organizations he serves.

- **Highlight achievements.** This technique applies to both the *content* of your resume and the *design*. Of course, you should include all of your relevant achievements, quantified if possible, as discussed throughout Part II—Modernize Your Resume Content. To capture attention in a flash, don't hide those achievements in small type or dense text; rather, let them shine with the right design, as both of these resumes so effectively demonstrate.

JASON HERRIGAN

jason.herrigan@gmail.com | Northbrook, IL 60062
773-847-5555 | www.jhstudio.com

Multimedia Director | Digital Media Strategist

Tenacious problem solver who brings innovative digital communication solutions from inception to content production.

Create high-performing teams: Built 3 departments at 3 different companies from inception to content production.

Anticipate trends: Increased web traffic 500% by introducing new techniques to improve viewer interactivity.

Streamline processes: Cut production time 50% by improving back-end content management workflow.

PROFESSIONAL EXPERIENCE

Chicago Tribune, Chicago, IL   2017–Present

MULTIMEDIA PRODUCER & MANAGER

Elevate organization's communications in a way that effectively immerses audience to gain a deeper connection with the brand.
***Reports:** 15 (max) • **Projects:** 400+ annually*

SITUATION:

Challenged with creating digital communications strategies that increase web presence and grow brand visibility.

STRATEGIES:

Collaboration – Led cross-functional teams to take raw content and translate it into effective digital communications.

Innovation – Introduced new ways to present media and implemented processes to improve production time.

Production – Orchestrated construction and design of 2 $600K studios to support 5 different publications.

Editing Workflow – Developed editorial processes to capture most compelling story elements.

Team Leadership – Grew team from 1 to 7; managed up to 10 freelance photographers, videographers, and designers; mentored 10+ interns.

RESULTS:

- Increased page views 500% for flagship product.
- Gained 3M+ views on YouTube for Transformers 3 Filming video as part of social media strategy.
- Optimized budget by outsourcing specialized multimedia talent.
- Expanded advertising opportunities by strategizing with sales team on promotion to sell space on videos.

PORTFOLIO HIGHLIGHTS:

Shedd Aquarium   40 Under 40   Transformers 3

CAREER SNAPSHOT

AWARDS

ILLINOIS PRESS PHOTOGRAPHERS ASSOCIATION
2022: 2nd Place for Best of Multimedia

NATIONAL PRESS PHOTOGRAPHER'S ASSOCIATION
2021: 1st Place - Video

THE NEAL AWARDS
2020: Best use of video

PETER LISAGOR AWARDS
2020: Best use of online video

THE SOCIETY OF AMERICAN BUSINESS EDITORS AND WRITERS AWARDS
2020: Best use of video
2018: Best in Business Online Audio/Video
2016: Best in Business Online Audio/Video

THE ALLIANCE OF AREA BUSINESS PUBLICATIONS AWARDS
2021: Gold: Best Multimedia Story/Feature
2020: Online Gold: Best Multimedia Story
2018: Gold: Best Multimedia Story/Feature

HUGO AWARDS
2017: Commitment to Excellence Award

EMMY NOMINATION
2016: Best Documentary – Inside 9/11

NY FESTIVAL
2016: Best Documentary – Inside 9/11

See full details of awards at
www.linkedin.com/in/jasonherrigan

ADVISORY BOARDS

Chicago Media Arts Academy
Improve film and broadcast curriculum.

Columbia College
Provide professional insight on curriculum, new trends in multimedia, and new teaching methodologies.

JASON HERRIGAN jason.herrigan@gmail.com | 773-847-5555 | 2 of 2

TriCom Media Inc., Chicago, IL   2014–2017

FINISHING EDITOR | OFFLINE EDITOR

Promoted within 1 year to Finishing Editor for exceeding expectations and learning new skills quickly.

***Projects:** 50+ shows*

- Implemented first detailed training manual to onboard new associate editors faster and more efficiently.
- Earned an Emmy nomination for work on Inside 9/11 documentary.

CLIENT SNAPSHOT:

National Geographic, A&E Network, The History Channel, PBS, NBC

J.H. Studio, Chicago, IL   2012–2014

PHOTOGRAPHER | VIDEO EDITOR | DESIGNER | FOUNDER

Directed creative teams in producing digital and multimedia content.

- Improved website production efficiencies 20% by hiring up to 7-person teams that included developers, designers, and writers.
- Established reputation through grassroots marketing efforts and built business from 0 to 20 clients in 2 years.

CLIENT SNAPSHOT:

Boeing, Starbucks, Dreyer's Ice Cream, Holland America, Windstar Cruises

Travel Channel, San Francisco, CA   2009–2012

MULTIMEDIA & DESIGN MANAGER

Established first-ever 17-person web design and multimedia department.

- Streamlined and built new infrastructure to support everything from shooting videos and photos to publishing them on the website.
- Grew sales 15% by authoring and developing multimedia-viewing module with e-commerce capabilities.
- Increased website views 30% and doubled ticket sales through strategic partnership alliances and customized content.

CNN, Atlanta, GA   2006–2009

MULTIMEDIA PRODUCER

Pioneered role of multimedia producer to integrate photos, videos, 360° images, and audio clips to create immersive experience for viewers.

- Led multimedia production of all worldwide news events and major headline stories.
- Developed new processes to produce multimedia and trained others.

CLIENT SNAPSHOT

SKILLS

Social Media
YouTube, Google+, Instagram, Facebook, Twitter, LinkedIn, Vimeo

Software
Analytics (Google Analytics, Omniture, SiteCatalyst)

Adobe Creative Suite (Photoshop, Illustrator, InDesign, Premiere Pro, After Effects, Bridge, LightRoom, Audition)

Final Cut Pro (Motion, Final Cut, Sound Track Pro, Aperture)

Avid (Nitris Symphony and Adrenaline)

Broadcast Pix Switcher, EditShare, Saxotech, RAMP, Brightcove

Hardware
Field/ENG video equipment, Video Switchers, Audio Mixers, Greenscreen, Lighting

EDUCATION

New York University, New York, NY
Continuing Education in Project Management and Film Studies

Art Institute of Chicago, Chicago, IL
Continuing Education in Video Production, Video Lighting, and Audio Engineering

Indiana University, Bloomington, IN
B.A. in Mass Communications
Emphasis in Journalism & Photography

AIDEN WELLS

(205) 555-1212 ☐ aidenwells1992@imax.com

SALES REPRESENTATIVE

14 straight years of exceeding goals in a multimillion-dollar territory

New Business Development – Profit Margin Optimization – Creative Solutions
Corporate Relationship Prospecting – New Sales Closing – Client Needs Assessment

☐ **Business Development:** Added 6 figures to monthly revenue with a single new-account win.

☐ **Crisis Management:** Preserved business by rapidly resolving costly equipment malfunction for key customer.

☐ **Connecting with People:** Consistently become a trusted member of customers' teams by understanding their business goals and providing solutions to their needs.

SIGNATURE SALES SKILLS

Business Partnerships	Values & Integrity
Customer Service Focus	Current Product & Market Knowledge
Internal & External Communication	Budgeting & Sales Projections
Persistence & Reliability	Innate Work Ethic

PROFESSIONAL EXPERIENCE

SALES REPRESENTATIVE   2008 to present
Infinite Paper, Birmingham, AL
A top wholesale distributor in the Southeastern U.S.; 32 distribution centers and 22 stores in 12 states

Sell fine printing papers and press-room supplies and equipment in a 70-account multimillion-dollar territory. Apply supply chain logistics knowledge to build relationships with key stakeholders and expand business opportunities within customer accounts.

☐ Tackled a challenging North Alabama territory, successfully penetrating large accounts such as the University of Alabama at Birmingham (UAB) and UnderArmour.

☐ Outperformed quota *every year* and averaged 112% of margin goal for 14 consecutive years.

☐ Acknowledged as "Outstanding Salesperson" in multiple divisions of the Infinite Paper Professional Sales Club.

☐ Became known as a problem solver, cementing strong business relationships with customers.

EDUCATION

Bachelor's Degree in Business Administration
Auburn University, Auburn, AL

COMMUNITY INVOLVEMENT

Advisory Boards, Birmingham Metro Chamber of Commerce and Liberty Park Golf and Country Club
President, Birmingham Kiwanis

Alexia Scott, CPRW • A-Winning-Resume

CHAPTER 11:
Follow the Practices of Good Page Design

Good page design is important no matter what the page—resume, cover letter, business correspondence, project proposal, advertisement, marketing flyer, book, or magazine. But before you can begin to design great pages, you must understand the practical basics and structural fundamentals of page design.

 PRO TIP: Good design practices are relevant to *all* job seekers, not just those in creative industries and professions. They are the underlying foundation upon which your own resume will be built.

Focal Point

Readers have many competing demands for their visual attention. When they see your resume for the first time, be sure that their eyes fall first on something important.

Good options for focal point include:

- Your name—personalizing your resume instantly.

- A headline—announcing *who* you are as it relates directly to your job target. This immediately causes readers to start thinking about you in the framework of that profession or industry.

- A chart, graphic, or other image that sends a quick message about you and your capabilities.

- Subheadings that introduce bullet points—reinforcing your primary keywords and giving readers clues about what's in the bullet points.

- Highlights of one or a few impressive accomplishments, for a quick jolt of positive information.

Even as you strive to draw your readers' attention to the important things, work just as hard to draw their attention away from things that aren't that important (e.g., job duties, locations). Or, if you're changing industries, do not draw attention to or include lots of information about your current employer and industry, because they don't align with where you're headed. Your #1 challenge is to demonstrate that your experience does align with the company's needs and that you are a valuable candidate.

Balance

Your resume should be well balanced on the page and on the screen. You don't want it to be top-heavy or pushed to the right or otherwise create an image that will diminish the visual presentation. Use these tips to create a balanced page:

- Set equal margins all around. We recommend a minimum of .5 inch and a maximum of 1 inch. Adjust as needed to fit your content.

- Adjust spacing so that your resume fills the page nicely, with no big gaps at the top or bottom.

- Be certain that the spacing is consistent between sections, between job titles and job descriptions, between sections of bullet points … consistency everywhere.

- If your resume is 2 pages long, you do *not* need to fill page 2 completely to the bottom. Don't add in lots of blank lines and extra space just to fill the page. If it's a half page, that's fine. If it's a third of a page or less, edit or redesign to see if you can fit it onto 1 page without compromising readability.

Proportion

When elements are in proportion, the most significant are the most prominent. Proportion might refer to:

- Size—*larger* draws more attention.
- Emphasis—**bolder** is eye-catching.
- Contrast—anything *different* gets noticed.

Use this principle wisely so that you are calling attention to what you want readers to see.

For example, in many resumes the employer names are larger and bolder than job titles. That's great *if* the employer name is what you want your readers to notice first. More often than not, however, your job titles are more important—and therefore should be more visually prominent—because they tell your career story and quickly identify your professional expertise. Design your resume accordingly.

White Space

White space is not simply blank space on the page. To the contrary, it performs several important functions:

- Indicates the end/beginning of different items and sections in the resume.
- Sets off discrete items such as headings and subheadings so they can be scanned quickly.
- Allows readers to pause and absorb information before moving on to learn more.
- Adds readability to text-rich documents such as a resume.

You can finitely adjust white space in your resume to promote balance, improve readability, and increase visual appeal. Add blank lines or use the Paragraph feature in MS Word for precise spacing control. Above all, be sure to break up any large clumps of text or lengthy bullet lists that readers are likely to skip over.

Consistency

Why does it matter that similar elements in your resume are designed in the same way? Quite simply, consistency aids in reader understanding.

When readers see a job title formatted a certain way, for example, they expect to see *all* job titles formatted that same way. If they don't, there's a disconnect that causes them to pause and shift focus from what they're reading to a "what's wrong with this picture" distraction.

Consistency gives readers clues about the kinds of information they are processing. And consistency gives your resume a polished and professional look.

MS Word has 2 features that will help you create consistent documents:

- Use Styles to build and apply specific formats for different parts of your resume—from the basic paragraph style to headings, subheadings, tables, hyperlinks, and other design elements.

- Our favorite, the Format Painter tool, allows you to quickly copy the format of any one word or paragraph to any other in your resume. We find this to be one of the most useful tools in Word because you can zip through the document and format or reformat in a flash.

Placement

Where will you place each element of your resume—your name and contact information, headlines and headings, design elements, graphics, and all of the text?

Placement is related to several design principles we've already discussed—Focal Point, Balance, White Space. But the more design elements you introduce, the more choices you have regarding what goes where and why.

As you are placing elements on the page, keep these points in mind:

- The top third of page 1 of your resume is prime real estate. Whatever you place there should be of paramount importance. This includes your name and contact information, followed by a Summary that might include a headline, branding statement, notable achievements and other distinguishing details and perhaps a graphic.

- Because readers typically read top to bottom, left to right, it makes sense to left-justify your section headings, such as Professional Experience and Education. That is most typical and what we recommend. However, you can try centered headings (a classic presentation), or even right-justified headings, to see how that affects readability and overall appearance of your resume.

- If you are using graphics or charts, you will need to place them so that they support the relevant text but don't interfere with its readability.

- Think about economy and efficiency in placing different elements on the page. For example, do you need multiple lines for job titles and company names, or for college degrees and universities, or can you fit that information on 1 line? When it works, that can be a huge space saver.

- Where will you place your employment dates? The knee-jerk reaction would be, "at the right margin." Indeed, that's where you'll find the dates on most resumes. That placement certainly makes it easy for employers to scan your employment history, and it's the right choice for many.

  But you do *not* want a spotlight on dates if you have gaps in employment, many short-term jobs, are currently unemployed, or are trying to bring older experience to the forefront to support a career change. In those situations, move your dates elsewhere so that they are not a focal point.

Images, Graphics, Tables, Charts & Other Visuals

We live in a visual world, and print material in all forms—from traditional newspapers to advertisements, brochures, billboards, and even books—now includes more images and fewer large blocks of text.

Studies have shown that online content with images draws many more viewers and keeps them on the page longer, as compared to content only. We think this is true for printed pages as well.

If you decide to use images in your resume, keep these rules in mind:

- Choose an image that supports the content of your resume and relates to either your industry or your profession. A random graphic or image is not going to add value.

- Be sure the image looks great on screen and reproduces well in black and white, because you can't be sure that everyone who receives your resume will have a color printer—and if they will even print your resume.

- Don't allow images to overshadow the all-important content. An exception would be an infographic resume, where the image *is* the message. See Chapter 12 for additional discussion and an example of an infographic resume.

Now, let's see all of these design principles at work.

Andrea North Resume—pages 98–99

The most notable design elements you'll find in Andrea's resume are:
- Attractive black, gray, and white color scheme.
- Use of shaded boxes to segment and call attention to important information—creating multiple focal points for her name, Summary, core skills, and a great endorsement.
- Nicely balanced pages with centered headings.
- Ample white space between bullets.
- Consistent treatment of employer names, job titles, dates, and other fundamental details.
- Interesting and attractive bullet shapes.

Ellen Colbert Resume—pages 100–102

When you review Ellen's resume, the standout design features that you'll immediately note are:
- Two eye-catching charts that instantly convey a career punctuated by growth and success.
- A headline that clearly states her expertise, followed by a subheading that further identifies her most valuable strengths.
- Four 1-line bullet points in the Summary that capture her most impressive performance results.
- Consistent presentation of company names, company information, and job titles.
- Succinct text, with most bullet points 1 or 2 lines and paragraphs no longer than 4 lines.
- Tables on page 2 that quickly illustrate performance above expectations.
- Sufficient white space to ensure readability.

ANDREA NORTH

Boston, MA 02134 | 617-553-1234 | andreanorth@mac.com

COMMUNICATION SPECIALIST

Influencing the hearts and minds of target audiences through …

Clear, precise storytelling and reporting, applying AP style
Exceptional speechwriting, integrating each presenter's natural speaking style
Passionate communication of a brand's story, as an in-person host/media spokesperson

CORE SKILLS

Public Relations
Communication Management
Writing & Editing
Presentations & Speechwriting
Research & News Reporting
Media Relations / Press Releases
Multimedia Communication
Brand Communication
Marketing Collateral
Relationship Building

✧ Charismatic and creative communication director, PR strategist, and journalist with a track record of delivering messages that make a positive impact.

✧ Forward-thinking strategist who formulates targeted communication plans to support internal organizational programs and external PR efforts.

✧ Well-traveled reporter who has journeyed to nearly all continents, including Africa, Asia, and Europe, to pursue journalistic opportunities.

✧ Passionate executive speechwriter who designs cogent discourse that engages audiences and gives presenters a competitive edge.

"Andrea is such a breath of fresh air! Her creativity and natural writing talents shine in everything she does. City Charity has seen a massive increase in public donations over the past few years, and Andrea has been a big reason why." – Simon Smith, VP, City Charity

SPOTLIGHTED SUCCESSES

PR/COMMUNICATION IMPROVEMENT

Elevated the quantity and quality of content produced by City Charity's communication department through a presentation to the Board of Directors, encouraging the engagement of highly qualified PR specialists and journalists to design compelling messages rather than relying on inexperienced volunteers.

PERSUASIVE WRITING

Secured national press coverage for City Charity on NPR, brought attention to the charity's international efforts to combat childhood hunger, and boosted donations 150% in just 3 months by researching and developing a detailed case for a 3-part news series showcasing the charity's Children First program.

PROFESSIONAL EXPERIENCE

CITY CHARITY, Boston, MA ✧ 2017 – Present

ASSISTANT COMMUNICATION DIRECTOR FOR NEWS

Author, edit, and produce persuasive, high-quality content for City Charity Network (CCN). Oversee editorial team of writers and photographers covering global programs. Coordinate news releases and serve as media spokesperson. Orchestrate media events, researching and developing scripts for speakers.

✧ Improved the quality of internal writing and editing by overhauling the CCN style guide.

✧ Transformed CCN into a world-class charitable news service by introducing op-eds, leading the creation of a weekly email news bulletin, and facilitating hands-on training for communication department staff.

✧ Recruited, mentored, and directed a talented team of reporters, photographers, and volunteers for the charity's annual Giving Back Gala, a 7-day conference attended by 2,000 officials from other charities nationwide.

Andrew Pearl, CPRW, CEIP, CERM • Precision Resumes, Inc. • precision-resumes.com

ANDREA NORTH

Page 2 of 2
617-553-1234 | andreanorth@mac.com

ASSISTANT COMMUNICATION DIRECTOR FOR NEWS (CONTINUED)

◇ Promoted financial transparency, strengthening member and public confidence in the organization, by initiating an annual budget news feature to apprise readers of key financial matters.

◇ Gained 500,000 readers by authoring amusing feature stories about the world travels of volunteers working within the charity's 3 main global programs: Children First, Operation Education, and Heal the Earth. Earned the attention of, and special features in, the *Boston Globe*.

RECOGNITION FROM COLLEAGUES AND PROGRAM LEADERS

NEWS SERVICE TRANSFORMATION: "You have certainly made us proud, Andrea! What a fantastic accomplishment to gain attention for City Charity in the *Globe*. Your creative writing is really grabbing the interest of the public and giving us a lot of momentum to move forward with our programs around the world. Thank you!" – Allan Smith, Program Director

GIVING BACK GALA PR TEAM LEADERSHIP: "We just wanted to thank you for giving us the guidance—and freedom—needed to succeed during the gala. It's clear you know how to manage PR, and you've proven that you can bring diverse talent together to support an organization's communication goals." – Jill Smith, Senior Vice President of Special Events

SUBURBAN TIMES, Waltham, MA ◇ 2015 – 2017
STAFF REPORTER

Engaged to produce news features for this growing suburb with a population of 300,000 (at that time). Attended and covered city government meetings. Authored and edited reports on municipal organizations and city personalities.

COMMUNITY CHARITY, Boston, MA ◇ 2011– 2015
EDITORIAL ASSISTANT (2012 – 2015) ◇ **COMMUNICATIONS INTERN** (2011 – 2012)

Hired immediately following internship for responsible role writing and editing news and feature stories for Community Charity publications. Assisted editor with projects and copyedited all materials, including television scripts, news stories, and marketing brochures.

◇ Created a streamlined, straightforward concept for a full-page ad that was selected by Community Charity leadership for placement in the *Boston Globe* to apprise the American public of a major health crisis in Africa.

◇ Authored and revised features for Community Charity's website, traveling to report on stories and representing the organization at trade shows. Developed creative fundraising letters and coordinated a fundraising concert.

EDUCATION

Master of Arts in Journalism & Mass Communication, 2013
University of Massachusetts, Boston, MA

Bachelor of Arts in Communication, 2011
Boston University, Boston, MA

AFFILIATIONS

Public Relations Society of America | American Society of Journalists

Ellen Colbert

ellen.colbert@gmail.com | **617-555-1710** | linkedin.com/in/ellencolbert

Business Development Executive: Technology & Telecommunications

Revenue Growth Driver • Fortune 50 & SMB Relationship Builder • Deal Closer & Negotiator

Proven leader who has spent the last 12 years identifying, defining, and penetrating nascent markets while leading exponential revenue growth across diverse industries. *Career highlights:*

- Expanded customer base 12-fold in 1 year for TechStars.com.
- Generated $10M+ recurring annual revenue to elevate Cranford Group to one of America's fastest-growing firms.
- Averaged 134% of annual sales goal for Whiz Business Services.
- Rose to #1 in region, #7 nationwide in sales for XTeam.

Professional Experience

TechStars.com | Cambridge, MA • 2021–2023

Privately held technology and services firm with a proprietary platform (MyMortgageDocs) and a national network of industry-compliant notaries and signing agents who facilitate loan closings for clients.

VP BUSINESS DEVELOPMENT

Recruited to lead turnaround and expansion for niche player in the mortgage refinance market. Brought on originally as a consultant and quickly hired as chief operations and business development officer for company dealing with multiple challenges: aging technology, inefficient operations, and a single anchor client in an industry sharply affected by changing conditions in the mortgage refinance market. Directed 15 staff.

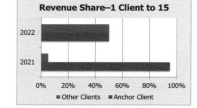

- Recruited talented CTO and worked closely to plan and launch new technology platform in first 6 months.
- Grew client base from 1 account to 15, reducing anchor client's share of revenue from >95% to <50%.
- Revamped organizational structure and workflow, created new company policies, automated processes, and delivered operational improvements – e.g., slashed A/R reconciliation from 4 days/4 departments to half a day.
- Identified untapped opportunity for newly developed technology with large potential in expanding industries.

Cranford Group | Boston, MA • 2017–2021

Privately held market niche leader providing technology/communications solutions to large financial institutions.

VP SALES, 2020–2021 • **DIRECTOR OF SALES**, 2018–2020 • **SENIOR SALES CONSULTANT,** 2017–2018

Primary revenue driver for new division, spurring >5X growth in total company revenue and personally delivering more than 50% of new business. Brought on board to rapidly grow sales for outsourcing division that had stalled in its first year. Transformed sales approach from high-level concept discussions to practical solutions delivery and built division to more than $20M annual revenue.

Promoted 2X in 3 years to lead sales and business development for the expanding business. Generated and managed $10M+ personal book of business and maintained relationships with all key accounts while developing overall sales strategy and directing 5-member project team.

- Invigorated and expanded division from a handful of clients to 50+ of the nation's leading foreclosure attorneys.
- Negotiated and sold long-term multimillion-dollar contracts to marquee clients: GMAC, Citigroup, Fidelity, Chase/Washington Mutual, and others.
- Drove record revenue growth, earning status as one of the country's fastest-growing private firms, as recognized by multiple benchmarking organizations (Inc. 500, Deloitte Technology Fast 500, Software 500).

Whiz Business Services   Burlington, MA • 2015–2017
Provider of advanced voice, data, and video products.
SENIOR SALES CONSULTANT

Consistently outperformed goals, selling integrated solutions to Fortune 1000. Performed full range of sales prospecting, qualifying, needs assessment, data gathering, and presentation to director and C-level executives. Developed proposals and negotiated pricing, multi-year contract terms, and SLAs for an eclectic range of WAN, IP, disaster recovery, managed security services, VoIP, MPLS, equipment, and hosting solutions.

	2015	2016
Performance to Goal	118%	150%

- Landed 60% of new business through referrals from existing clients.
- Developed methodical processes for consistent follow-up with clients both during and after the sale.
- Steadily expanded business contacts through active involvement in regional networking events and trade shows.

XTeam Communications   Boston, MA • 2011–2015
$150M B2B provider of integrated broadband data and voice communication services.
MAJOR ACCOUNT MANAGER, 2013–2015

One of 10 hand-picked from 130 account managers to lead strategic, intensified focus on major accounts. Exceeded all sales goals and landed 2 of the company's top 5 accounts. Hunted new business every month, identifying needs and selling comprehensive communications solutions to targeted businesses.

	2013	2014
Performance to Goal	122%	107%

- Ranked #7 out of 130 reps in the company, #1 in Boston office, 2013.
- Landed company's #1 client ($100K/month) and a second top-5 account at 30X company average.
- Built a powerful network, developing and maintaining relationships with business owners, controllers, VPs, vendors, and networking groups throughout Northeast US.

ACCOUNT MANAGER, 2011–2013

In 3 months, learned technology-based product/service line and ramped up to 100% of quota performance. Developed new business month after month, targeting small to medium-sized businesses and proposing integrated solutions to meet their telecommunications needs.

- Developed exceptional customer relationships built on integrity, trust, and solutions focus.
- More than doubled revenue ($6K to $14.5K monthly) at 1 account without adding services.

Education

MBA, Northeastern University – D'Amore-McKim School of Business	2016
BS, University of Hartford – Barnard School of Business – Business Administration/Marketing	2011

CHAPTER 12:

Match Design Elements to Your Industry, Profession, and Career Story

Does your resume design communicate an enticing message to the industry and profession that you are targeting? From the design elements you've used, can readers instantly recognize that you're a web designer, business leader, sales producer, or theater stage manager?

Choose your design elements to create that much-needed alignment so that, with just a glance, people can see that you belong in the industry or profession that you're targeting. Start by thinking about what matters most for the companies and positions to which you are applying.

Here are a few examples:

- **Sales.** In sales professions, what matters most is delivering the numbers: exceeding sales quotas, capturing new clients, closing deals, and growing sales revenues. Charts with rising columns and upward arrows are a great design match.

- **Hospitality and Retail.** Major brands in these industries are instantly recognizable and impressive, so adding corporate logos can both dress up your resume and quickly communicate the right industry message.

- **Health and Wellness.** Depending on your niche within this industry, you might choose to include images identified with fields that are traditional, such as medicine or pharmacy, or nontraditional, such as massage or yoga.

- **Business and Executive Leadership.** Business leaders have specific goals: typically to grow the business and increase profits. Charts, tables, and graphs can quickly illustrate your success in doing just that, again with rising columns and other visual indicators of upward performance. If appropriate, you can also add in the logos of blue-chip companies where you've worked.

- **Nonprofit.** You might enhance your resume with images that align with the mission of the organizations where you've worked or your specific niche. For example, if you work to improve literacy, a book graphic would be appropriate.

Does your resume design integrate any visual components that are unique to your career story? Just as important as visually communicating that you're a part of the industry or profession you are targeting, your career story can also be an important focus of your resume design. Career stories are unique to each individual and, therefore, give you the opportunity to integrate design elements that focus on you.

The most important consideration to visually communicate your unique career story is to send a powerful message of *who* you are, *what* you do, and *how* well you do it by choosing design elements that help readers understand:

- Where you've been—your prior jobs and employers—and how all of that leads to your next role.
- Your greatest career successes—related to the trajectory of your career.
- Why you have been successful—the intangible qualities you've illustrated throughout your career that will be instrumental in your next position.

As you'll see in the samples that follow, creative presentations are not confined to creative fields. A nurse can very effectively and professionally include graphics, while a technology sales manager can use unusual fonts and eye-catching design elements to capture attention.

The key is to keep your target audience in mind and create something that expresses *you* while simultaneously appealing to *them* because, ultimately, your resume is—and should be—all about what you can do for your next employer.

Infographic Resumes

With regard to career story designs, we would be remiss if we did not mention the trend of infographic resumes. An infographic ("information graphic") is a translation of data into a graphic format, and an infographic resume is a pictorial representation of someone's career.

We do not recommend infographic resumes for most job seekers for 2 specific reasons:

- Because they are primarily graphics rather than text, these resumes include a very limited amount of information. They do not allow job seekers to share all that they know and all that they have done to position themselves for appropriate opportunities. Yes, we want you to *write tight, lean, and clean,* but we do want you to write powerful, informative, and achievement-driven content.
- They don't work well in today's world of online job search. Infographic resumes cannot be scanned by digital readers, they typically include few keywords, and many of the fundamentals—job titles, employers, degrees—are either excluded or presented in such a manner that they are overlooked.

As with everything related to resume writing, there are no rules, and infographic resumes can work for some job seekers in some professions. Review **John Smith's** infographic resume on the next page and then determine whether this type of presentation is right for you.

Note the placement of John's Experience and Education, which he communicates in a unique visual presentation that allows readers to instantly absorb a lot of information with just a glance. Even more distinguishing, on the bottom half of the page John clearly identifies his 4 key areas of expertise—as they relate to his current career objectives—and strengthens each with 2 or 3 very short achievement statements.

John Smith

Senior Technology Executive
CTO / CIO / CISO

LinkedIn Profile
www.linkedin.com/in/smithj

Phone
+1-585-678-1218

Email
hello@jsmith.com

Experience Summary

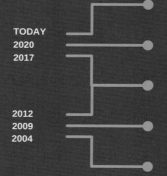

Acquire Services Group
IT Executive / CIO & IT Operations GM

TODAY
2020
2017

Miramar Media Group
Director, Digital Product Management
& Sales Engineering

Salesforce.com
Sales Engineer / Client Engagement
Manager

2012
2009
2004

Bank of America
Scrum Consultant & Product Owner
CRM & ITSM Systems Engineer

Education & Training

M.B.A. Degree
*University of Maryland, Smith
School of Business*

B.A., Leadership Studies
Wheaton College

CISM - Certified Information Security
Manager

CGEIT - Certified in the Governance
of Enterprise IT

Agile, Scrum, DevOps, DevSecOps,
GDPR, Strategy, M&A, Lean UX
Design, TDD, Financial Modeling

Technology Executive with 20+ years of experience in:

Product

Developed four commercially viable
Cloud/SaaS/Digital products

Drove sustained 49% CAGR

Leveraged Agile, Scrum, Lean UX,
DevOps, DevSecOps, and more

Ops

Elevated the user experience (CSAT) at
17 facilities

Cut global R&M IT spend by ~20%

Transformed the culture of IT and the
cyber security practices

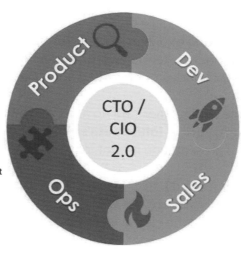

Development

Delivered global product with zero
security breaches

Designed and implemented secure,
100% color-accurate HD streaming at
ultra-high bit rates to 25+ global sites

Sales

Negotiated and closed more than
$30M in recurring annual revenue for
IT services with Fortune 500 clients

Turned around the relationship with
at-risk accounts, saving $5M in
annual recurring revenue

Stephen Van Vreede, CPRW, ACRW, MCS, OPNS, Phello Certified Career Networking Expert • ITtechExec • ittechexec.com

PRO TIP: An infographic resume can be a great supplement to your traditional resume. As mentioned, it's tough to tell your whole career story in a few words and graphics, and we do not recommend infographics as a primary resume for most. But as an adjunct, a well-done infographic can be a great attention-getter and conversation piece.

Add a link at the top of your resume to a website where you have posted your infographic resume, share it on LinkedIn, and send it before or after interviews. It will help you stand out.

In the 2 resumes that follow, notice how all of the design elements align with each individual's industry and profession, and how they work together harmoniously to tell an effective career story. Both of these resumes are readily distinguishable from others, giving these job seekers an immediate advantage.

Ida Davis Resume—page 106

Ida's resume clearly demonstrates how to integrate industry (healthcare), profession (nursing), and career story (distinguishing academic credentials, portfolio of job-specific keywords, and a record of progressively responsible positions). The heart-shaped stethoscope at the top of her resume instantly communicates those messages. Additionally, she has highlighted several impressive rewards with star-shaped bullets that call out evidence of her nursing skill and compassionate manner.

Denise Reynolds Resume—pages 107–108

Denise uses shading, tables, charts, and other graphics to provide a cohesive story of her success in sales. Notice that the actual text of this resume is quite slim—there is a lot of white space and great use of graphics to balance the clean and lean content. The font is unique and the logo is distinctive, and isn't sales all about getting noticed in the crowd? Again, this resume is the perfect balance for integrating the 3 distinct industry, profession, and career story components into appropriate design elements.

IDA DAVIS, RN, BSN

Melville, NY 11747 ▪ 631.555.7777 ▪ IDRN@gmail.com

CAREER TARGET: DIRECTOR OF NURSING—ELDER CARE

ASSISTANT DIRECTOR | NURSE MANAGER | WELLNESS NURSE

Confident and compassionate healthcare provider with proven hands-on experience and a genuine passion for geriatrics.

Maintain an excellent balance of empathy and authority to ease resident and family stressors. Easily establish positive and productive rapport with geriatric population; sensitive and responsive to meeting diverse needs in varied situations. Remain calm and professional throughout critical incidents.

EDUCATION AND PROFESSIONAL CERTIFICATION

Bachelor of Science in Nursing, Adelphi University of Nursing, Garden City, NY
Associate of Science in Nursing, Nassau Community College, Hempstead, NY

State of New York Registered Professional Nurse
State of New Jersey Registered Professional Nurse

New York Department of Health and Senior Services, RN Instructor - Certified Medication Aide
BLS Certification ▪ IV Certification ▪ Telemetry Certification

KEY SKILLS / AREAS OF EXPERTISE

Cardiac ▪ Care Planning ▪ Client Relations ▪ Customer Service ▪ Dementia ▪ Geriatric & Assisted Living ▪ HIPPA ▪ Leadership & Management ▪ Needs Assessment ▪ Patient Advocacy ▪ Patient Education ▪ Quality Improvement ▪ Problem Solving ▪ Rapport Building ▪ Social Service ▪ Staff Education ▪ Team Building ▪ Team Supervision & Mentoring ▪ Workforce Planning

CAREER HISTORY

First Care Senior Services, Port Washington, NY   **2021 to Present**
Provider of private-pay home care services.

REGISTERED NURSE CARE MANAGER

★ Recipient, Key Contributor Award, 2022 ★

Hired to develop an education program for direct-care staff and to ensure compliance with state regulations. Assist with corporate mission to become a preferred provider for the State of New York.

- Assumed newly created role of staff liaison; respond to employee issues and concerns.

- Serve as Clinical Coordinator for clients and families. Perform home visits to address and re-assess needs. Recommend/assist calling physicians as needed. Gain and maintain positive rapport to work with clients and families for determining best level of care.

- Educate and supervise direct-care staff (Home Companions and Certified Home Health Aides). Ensure caregivers are properly prepared and educated on best practices for on-boarding new clients and have full understanding of expectations and responsibilities.

- Assess/re-assess nursing needs for clients and families, develop individualized care plans for each client, and educate caregivers on plans.

Michelle Riklan, ACRW, CPRW, CEIC, CJSS ▪ Riklan Resources ▪ riklanresources.com

denise reynolds

AUSTIN, TX • 490.528.7033 • DREYNOLDS7@GMAIL.COM

SENIOR TECHNOLOGY SALES MANAGER

ACHIEVED 16 STRAIGHT YEARS OF DOUBLE-DIGIT YOY SALES

LEADERSHIP STYLE:

↗ Drove unprecedented triple-percentage sales gains, catapulting US sales from 28% to 76% of HP's business. Fueled above-and-beyond team performance by harnessing talent and empowering emerging leaders.

BEST-IN-CLASS MARKETING:

↗ Capitalized on new marketing initiatives to drive +12% profits, +13% market share, and +24% consumer awareness.

↗ Pioneered social blogging outreach recognized by *Computing Magazine* for boosting brand visibility 53%.

SALES & MARKETING RESULTS:

↗ Strengthened cash flow by slashing advertising budget $143M (44%) and lowering company inventory 52%.

↗ Restructured divisional field structure to trim headcount 23% and lowered promotional spending from $212M.

OUTPACED SALES GOALS UP TO 130%			
YEAR	TARGET	SALES	% TO PLAN
2022	$184M	$214M	130%
2021	$172M	$201M	128%
2020	$156M	$198M	125%
2019	$76M	$97M	123%
2018	$58M	$69M	120%
2017	$22M	$27M	118%

CORE COMPETENCIES:

- ATTAINING BREAKTHROUGH SALES
- DOMINATING RETAIL CHANNELS
- MAXIMIZING VERTICAL SALES
- SUSTAINING MARKET SHARE
- TURNING AROUND PROFITABILITY
- REBUILDING SALES TEAMS
- OVER-PRODUCING REVENUE TARGETS
- INCREASING DIGITAL LEADS
- REVAMPING SALES COMP PLANS

SENIOR SALES LEADERSHIP EXPERIENCE

HEWLETT PACKARD   2005 – Present
NORTH AMERICAN VP OF SALES [2016 – Present]

Promoted to reverse declining national sales growth, rebuild product development, and regain market dominance. Direct $46M divisional P&L with 325 staff, 300 agency personnel, and 4.2K US channel partners. Lead $27M in domestic advertising.

TURNED AROUND US SALES:

↗ Halted hemorrhaging sales, regained growth, and pushed revenue from $28M to $46M. Revamped national sales team and compensation strategies around rebranded products.

↗ Improved printer revenue 28% ($21M) by deepening brand-level margins. Cut costs $14M and decreased spending 19%.

$21M SINGLE-YEAR SALES GAIN

REVITALIZED PRODUCT DEVELOPMENT:

↗ Championed "test-and-learn" strategy to reinvigorate innovation, restructured talent development, and revamped product line leadership. Streamlined new product rollout cycle from 18 to 3 months.

↗ Transformed product positioning through realignment of brands with profit targets. Consolidated 12 product lines to 3 and rewrote web marketing playbook while strengthening channel partner training and product knowledge.

Cheryl Simpson, CMRW, ACRW, COPNS, Certified G3 Coach • Executive Resume Rescue • executiveresumerescue.com

SENIOR SALES LEADERSHIP EXPERIENCE CONTINUE

RECAPTURED MARKET DOMINANCE:

- ↗ Propelled market share from 7.2% to 20.2%, the largest netbook industry boost, employing aggressive advertising benchmarked against key competitor strengths.
- ↗ Fueled 3-place industry ranking rise from #5 to #2 in 2 years by earning #1 Consumer Reports product accolades.

DIVISION GM [2013 – 2015]

Tapped to spearhead market share recapture initiative for a division producing 55% of sales revenue and contribution margin for HP's US business. Directed a team of 227 and 1.4K matrixed personnel with $38M P&L accountability.

DOMINATED RETAIL SALES MARKET:

- ↗ Guided retail sales up 98% over 2014 by designing and steering a 3-phase marketing blitz for the all-new LaserJet brand.

CAPTURED CONSUMER SOCIAL MEDIA FEEDBACK:

- ↗ Upgraded market positioning for new product launches, integrating social media into consumer research. Increased social media participation >74%.

NORTHEAST REGIONAL GM [2011 – 2013]

Positioned region for next-level sales performance, strategizing and leading organizational realignment impacting 373 employees and 1.7K channel partners in 14 states. Enhanced marketing and incentives; managed $26M P&L.

SALES & PARTNER TURNAROUNDS:

- ↗ Surpassed sales contribution margin $70M above forecast. Gained 1.5 market share points in ultra-competitive market.
- ↗ Reorganized field sales force into 4-region structure while boosting pre-owned sales from 73% to 141% – the highest level industry-wide.

SET NEW INDUSTRY SALES BENCHMARK

VP OF SALES – HP PRINTERS [2008 – 2011]

Produced the highest US annual sales in 53 years and propelled profit margin 32%. Drove national sales operations, from partner management and distribution to sales training and incentives, with a 278-member team and a $17M P&L.

NORTHEAST REGIONAL SALES MANAGER [2005 – 2008]

Improved partner development 34% in 28 Northeastern markets.

ADDITIONAL HP EXPERIENCE: Promoted rapidly through 7 territory and district management promotions spanning sales and business development in NJ, OH, MI, IL, and NY.

EDUCATIONAL CREDENTIALS

Executive Development Program • WHARTON SCHOOL OF BUSINESS
MBA in Sales & Marketing • COLUMBIA UNIVERSITY
BA in Economics with a Minor in Business Administration • UNIVERSITY OF SOUTHERN CALIFORNIA

=

CHAPTER 13:
Be Distinctive

How can you stand out when a recruiter or hiring manager has an in-box full of 200+ resumes to review? His goal is to eliminate as many as possible and reduce the stack to a manageable pile of potential candidates whose resumes he will review more closely.

That is why first impressions are so vital to your success in the job search process. Your goal is to make certain that your resume gets at least a second look—every time—based on the strength of its visual presentation. You can accomplish that by giving it a unique, memorable, and distinctive *look and feel* that lets you stand out from the crowd.

Here are some practical steps to make that happen:

- **Introduce yourself boldly.** Position your name so that it pops off the page, using a font that is large and clear. Don't be overly creative in the placement of your name. People expect to see your name at the top of your resume and that's where it should go, whether flush left, centered, or flush right.

- **Don't be afraid to stand out.** You want to be different … instantaneously noticeable … distinctive from the crowd of other candidates. Don't go over the top or get too carried away, as your resume is *not* an art project. However, there are so many things that you can do to stand out—from simple font enhancements to major design elements and many things in between.

  Just be wise and appropriate about your decisions, always considering who your audience is and what matters most to them.

- **Don't look like everyone else.** If you use a resume template or simply follow the crowd, you'll create a resume that is difficult to distinguish from anyone else's. Even a single element—such as your name in a very large or unusual font, or a colored page border, or a tasteful graphic—will make a difference and keep your resume (and you) from blending into the background.

- **Exude professionalism.** You've invested a lot of time and effort in creating your resume. Employers know that, and they expect it to be an example of your best work. Make sure it doesn't disappoint!

  From the content to the format to the final design, every element must be done well—correctly, professionally, neatly, and with attention to detail and care for the finished product. Not every job seeker is as meticulous as you'll be, and that gives you a great advantage—a resume that stands out simply because of its polished presentation.

- **Brand yourself.** In Chapter 1 we discussed the importance of expressing your personal brand in your resume. One element of branding is consistency across all online and offline search platforms.

  When you choose design elements for your resume, use those same themes, fonts, colors, and graphics for your personal website, business card, professional bio, and any other marketing materials that you create. Every message and every image that a recruiter or employer sees will continuously reinforce your brand.

Embrace Color and Graphics

We believe that color and graphics are valuable additions to most any modern resume. However, the extent to which you use them depends a great deal on your industry and profession. What may work for a graphic designer's resume will definitely not work for a finance executive's resume.

Although resumes and job search have changed dramatically over the years, at its core the resume is a business document, and those receiving it expect to see a fairly traditional presentation. A wild and crazy design is generally not appropriate and can be counterproductive.

This is especially true for people in traditional and conservative professions. It is rare that a boldly creative resume for an accountant, manufacturing manager, actuary, attorney, or insurance claims adjuster would be appropriate, because it sends mixed messages … like the infamous mullet haircut that was "business in the front and party in the back"!

That certainly doesn't mean resumes for traditional professions have to be staid, boring, or cookie-cutter. Tasteful and appropriate images, charts and graphs, and a professional touch of color can be added to just about any resume to give it a distinctive appearance while still remaining professionally conservative.

For those of you in creative professions, you have much greater flexibility in integrating more distinctive design elements because they match your profession. If you're a theater director, multimedia specialist, website designer, or any one of hundreds of other creative types, then let your creativity shine through in all that you do with your resume.

We encourage all of you, whether in traditional or non-traditional careers, to embrace the use of color and graphics in your resume as it is appropriate. Consider these possibilities for adding visual impact, along with ideas for when and how to use them:

- **Tables** are useful for presenting several specific pieces of information—perhaps a list of technical competencies or core skills—in a way that keeps each item separate for easy skimming. Tables can also be used to display relevant numbers and can incorporate color across rows, down columns, or in headings.

  Tables are a standard feature of MS Word and other word processors.

- **Charts and Graphs.** As we've shown in prior chapters, charts and graphs communicate an instant message and add pizzazz to a text-rich resume. A chart or graph can quickly show upward or downward movement. It's perfect for illustrating sales or revenue growth, cost or error reduction, productivity or efficiency gains, and other points of measurement and comparison.

  When creating a chart, be certain the visual display sends the right message. If you've had a lot of up-and-down sales years, you would be better off highlighting total sales growth over a period of years rather than showing a graph with numbers that veer wildly from good (up) to bad (down).

Charts and graphs can be created in Word or in a spreadsheet program and imported into the Word document (resume).

- **Boxes.** A simple box—shaded and colored or not—is an easy technique for setting off important information in your resume. We recommend that you use Word's "Borders and Shading" tool to create a box, rather than the "Insert Text Box" feature. As mentioned in Chapter 9, the contents of a text box cannot be read by Applicant Tracking Systems, and that has the potential to negatively impact your search results

  Try different styles and widths of borders and different colors of fill and shading to find the right combination that emphasizes important information while keeping the look entirely professional.

- **Borders and Lines.** Horizontal borders are one of the easiest techniques to master and use in your resume. Use Word's "Borders and Shading" tool to create lines across the page, above or below headings, and in other places to create a visual break and to separate sections of your resume. When you look at the resume samples in this book, you will see dozens of border and line treatments that you can imitate and use for your own resume.

  Border lines are also an ideal place to add a dash of color to your resume without compromising readability or going overboard with too many design elements.

- **Logos.** Logos are not commonly used in resumes, but when they are, they can be extremely effective in communicating key points about your experience. Take a look through the sample resumes and you'll find examples where a logo creates instant identification with a company, product, or school.

- **Images.** It's possible to add photographs, drawings, and clip art to your Word document. Examples in this book include a stethoscope for a medical professional, a bulldozer for a construction manager, a pile of money for a finance executive, and—most unusually!—a martini glass for a cocktail waitress. Be certain that any image you add to your resume strengthens the message, is relevant to your current career goals, and is appropriate for your profession and level.

- **Shapes.** Microsoft Word's "Smart Art" feature is a great source of interesting shapes that you can insert into your resume, adding color and distinctiveness while highlighting brief bits of relevant career information. As with any graphic insertion, take care that what you're adding is going to enhance and not distract from the key messages in your resume.

- **Color.** Color helps your resume stand out, sends a more modern message than the traditional black-and-white resume, and garners longer looks from readers—it's been proven in several studies. While it's never necessary to add color, it can be beneficial, and we recommend that you give it a try—remaining appropriate, professional, and tasteful, of course!

Following are 2 examples of resumes filled with distinctive design elements, including color and graphics, that give these job seekers instant recognition and a solid advantage in a competitive job market.

Anthony Tanner Resume—pages 113–114

Anthony's resume uses a combination of design elements—boxes, shading, graphs, reverse white print on black background, and more—to instantly communicate his brand (Healthcare Administrator) and most notable achievements. Pay special attention to:

- A money graphic in the top left corner to reinforce his brand message of generating revenue.

- The dual focus on his most notable achievements, mentioned briefly in the text and then visually represented with 2 different styles of graphs.

- Appropriate use of italics, bold, and underlining to communicate specific messages and visually differentiate specific pieces of information.

- Leadership Competencies (core skills) in a table format with alternately shaded rows.

- Other distinguishing touches that include font choice (Gill Sans), large drop-cap in Summary, and dark-shaded boxes.

Matthew Charles Resume—page 115–116

Matthew's resume is rich with graphic elements that create a unique look and positive impression. Specifically:

- A graphic to the left of his name emphasizes his expertise: Business, Growth, and Success.

- A reverse-type box, directly beneath his name, conveys his personal brand as a "Masterful Relationship Builder" and his professional expertise as a "Business-to-Business Sales Leader."

- Boxes and shading throughout the resume highlight headings and areas of expertise, and banners announce his top sales results.

- Tables on page 1 and page 2 distinguish his most notable achievements in each position.

ANTHONY J. TANNER

Richmond, VA 22932 | 434.555.2623
tony.tanner@gmail.com | linkedin.com/in/tonytannerhealthcare

HEALTH CARE ADMINISTRATOR

Clinical operations leader who articulates vision for the organization, drives strategic execution, and engages direct reports in delivering high-quality results.

Progressive thinker committed to advancing the capacity and capability of a progressive health care system. Socratic, collaborative approach: define objectives, welcome input, and factor in data and insights.

Innovator who's impacted clinical operations, ambulatory care services, freestanding radiation therapy facilities, and partner-based radiation oncology programs to the benefit of the institution and all patients.

> **"EXCELLENT ADMINISTRATIVE LEADER & EXPERT ..."**
>
> "Tony has no comparison in this field when it comes to establishing and growing clinical operations. He is an excellent administrative leader and expert whose unique talent is engaging clinicians so they understand the critical impact of the services they deliver."

LEADERSHIP COMPETENCIES

Health Care Administration	Patient Services	Performance Optimization
Clinical Operations Management	Physical Relations	EMR & Technology Implementation
Clinical Program Development	Partner Engagement	Data Management, Analysis & Intelligence
Ambulatory Services Operations	Staff Recruitment & Leadership	Quality & Standardization Initiatives
Fiscal & Budget Management	Employee Engagement	Outcomes Measurement

PROFESSIONAL EXPERIENCE & SIGNATURE ACHIEVEMENTS

SOUTHERN VIRGINIA HEALTH SYSTEM, Norcross, VA   **2012 to Present**

570-bed hospital comprising NCI-designated Cancer Center, Outpatient Surgery, Children's Medical, and Long-Term Care Centers.

<u>Senior Administrator</u> (2020 to Present): Advanced to this role to strategically direct operations and service delivery for 50 outpatient clinics.

Declared vision of change and transformation to eliminate siloed culture and promote cross-departmental relationships. Rightsized organizational infrastructure. Leveraged and paired managers of clinics providing complementary services. Recruited and installed dynamic team after evaluating candidates for fit with the new culture. Conducted research and delivered national presentations.

- **Led critical initiative** to raise appointment availability. Evaluated utilization data and identified openings to assign patients to providers.
  - Invested $2K in telemedicine technology to schedule appointments previously blocked for grand rounds.
- **Drove year-over-year employee engagement** to 75th percentile. Critical factor was realigning salaries with area market.
- **Built financial snapshot** for medical directors and executive leadership indicating budget, volume, and utilization for 3-year cost reduction and budget-rebalancing initiatives.
- **First of 4 family medicine clinics to gain approval** to operate as officially sanctioned patient-centered medical home.

HIGHLIGHTS OF IMPACT

5.6% Patient Volume Increase

3.9% Cost Per Visit Decrease

2.0% Patient Satisfaction Increase

Professional Experience & Signature Achievements Continued On Page 2

Jewel Bracy DeMaio, CPRW, MRW, ACRW, CEIP • Perfect 10 Resumes • perfect10resumes.com

ANTHONY J. TANNER

434.555.2623 | tony.tanner@gmail.com | linkedin.com/in/tonytannerhealthcare | Page 2

SOUTHERN VIRGINIA HEALTH SYSTEM (CONTINUED)

Medical Center Director (2014 to 2020): Guided operations of radiation oncology and focused ultrasound. Scope encompassed financials and budgeting, clinical care delivery, and patient satisfaction. Promoted change management in the form of telemedicine adoption and technology implementation.

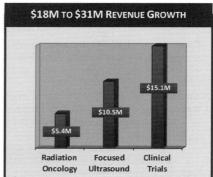

$18M TO $31M REVENUE GROWTH

- **Principally directed series of initiatives** key to increasing gross hospital revenue from $18M to $31M.

  - Markedly increased awareness of clinical trial program and raised trial enrollment 25%, directly leading to $15.1M in new revenue in a single year.

  - Orchestrated opening of focused ultrasound facility, which exceeded projections and generated $10.5M the 1st year.

  - Captured $5.4M annually in highly competitive radiation oncology service and raised patient satisfaction 4.4%.

- **Promoted medical records virtualization** by using Mosaic to capture all manual data and by defining EMR workflow process. Launched chartless environment with Mosiac several years prior to implementing EPIC.

Chief Medical Dosimetrist (2012 to 2014): Recruited to newly created role to provide change management as center capitalized on series of technological advancements and transitioned from 100% paper environment.

Promoted technology adoption and leveraged technology to advance radiation oncology research capabilities. Led QA, data compilation, and process and procedure development regarding IMRT implementation. Oversaw dosimetrists at 3 radiation facilities. Assisted in providing radiation therapy didactic and clinical education.

LOUISVILLE RADIATION ONCOLOGY, Louisville, KY   **2008 to 2012**

Start-up radiation oncology service that progressed to leading status in Louisville metropolitan market.

Administrator: Merited advancement to this role following 4 years as *Medical Dosimetrist*. Directed daily operations and led formulation of calculations to maximize radiation dose to tumor cells while sparing healthy tissue.

EDUCATION

MASTER OF HEALTH SCIENCE ADMINISTRATION
Virginia State University, Petersburg, VA   2020

BACHELOR OF SCIENCE, OCCUPATIONAL TRAINING & DEVELOPMENT
University of Kentucky, Lexington, KY   2009

CERTIFICATE IN MEDICAL DOSIMETRY
Boston Medical Center, Boston, MA   2007

PRESENTATIONS

U.S. Society of Therapeutic Radiation Oncological Practice
"Can Holding Your Breath Be That Important?" (2022)

34th Annual National Panel of Medical Dosimetry Practitioners
"Quest for a Chartless Department in an Academic Medical Center: Lessons Learned" (2021)

MATTHEW CHARLES

BUSINESS-TO-BUSINESS (B2B) SALES LEADER | MASTERFUL RELATIONSHIP BUILDER

206-255-8736 ◆ matthew.charles@gmail.com
Seattle, WA 98136 ◆ LinkedIn.com/in/matthew.charles

SALES MANAGEMENT EXECUTIVE

COMMERCIAL AEROSPACE ◆ ELECTRONICS ◆ DEFENSE ◆ HEALTHCARE ◆ PHARMA/BIOTECH

Champion multimillion-dollar growth in international and domestic market segments, driving sales strategy, key market expansion, channel partner development, and program management.

Deliver consistent year-over-year (YOY) growth. Provide organizational leadership in matrix environments. Inspire teamwork, develop exceptional talent, and achieve sustainable sales results.

PROFESSIONAL EXPERIENCE

Safety Detection Systems, Inc., Tacoma, WA [2017–Present]

Lead efforts to expand market presence in critical infrastructure and emergency response markets for global safety and security technologies, advanced threat detection solutions that safeguard society (civil and military) from chemical, biological, radiological, and nuclear materials (CBRNE) and explosives.

DIRECTOR OF US SALES 2020–Present	DIVISIONAL SALES MANAGER – EAST 2019–2020	REGIONAL SALES MANAGER 2017–2019
130% of Quota	**#1** Sales Performer	↑**92%** Regional Sales
>**$28M** Business Revenue	**101%** of Quota	+**$10M** Exclusive Contract
+**4%** Market Share Gain	**#1** Company Account	**#1** of 16 Sales Representatives

DIRECTOR OF UNITED STATES (US) SALES (2020-Present)

**Lead Development of Scalable Business Strategy and Commercial Plans to Drive National Performance
Outperformed Sales Goals Annually: +28%, 2020 | +30%, 2021 | +31%, 2022**

Sales Leadership – Plan and execute sales strategies for diverse clients (private and governmental agencies, including Department of Defense and Department of Homeland Security) with critical infrastructure. Manage $300K department budget, 12 direct reports.

- Develop sales objectives, analyze key metrics, and evaluate performance of business/product lines.

- Interface with stakeholders across the US, Mexico, Latin America, the Caribbean, Canada, Finland, Germany, and the United Kingdom.

- Exercise profit and loss (P&L) responsibility for achieving revenue and profit targets. Ensure efficiency and effectiveness of US Sales go-to-market activities; manage field sales activities; develop sustainable pipelines.

- Guide strategic development of a comprehensive US Commercial Distributor Program, spanning internationally across key market segments.

- Provide corporate representation within global areas of operation; liaise with key leadership/stakeholders of charitable and civic institutions and professional associations.

Talent Management – Collaborate with sales leadership across divisions. Establish sales force training plans, forecast funnel activity, and reinforce critical sales competencies.

Manage Programs
Align Organization Goals
Conduct Market Research
Perform SWOT Analysis
Expand Market Presence
Engage Clients
Attract Business Partners
Convert Prospects
Improve Market Share
Deliver Net Revenue/Profit
Exceed Growth Targets

– Continued on Page 2 –

Lisa Parker, CERM, CPRW, CEIP • Parker-CPRW • parkercprw.com

MATTHEW CHARLES

DIRECTOR OF UNITED STATES (US) SALES (continued)

Business Development – Develop and implement long-range business plans for the Americas. Manage and grow company revenue, margin, and market share across business segments. Develop strategic partnerships and executive-level networks to support a lucrative client base.

Organizational Leadership – Lead a geographically dispersed sales organization (4 continents); build, cultivate, and empower high-performance teams across a multichannel go-to-market strategy.

Quality Systems Management – Safeguard standardization across functional areas; monitor import/export controls, international procurement, brand management, marketing, professional development, and worldwide security regulations.

EASTERN DIVISION SALES MANAGER (2019–2020)
REGIONAL SALES MANAGER (2017–2019)

Ranked #1 Sales Performer of the Year | Achieved 101% of Annual Quota | Landed Company's #1 New Account

Sales– Consistently exceeded sales goals and earned recognition for sales results: revenue growth, customer relationship management, contract negotiations, business expansion.

- As DSM, captured the company's largest account, negotiating a multiyear, exclusive supplier agreement with a major global transport company. Contract value exceeded $10M. Ranked #1 company-wide in sales.

- Over a 2-year period, grew regional sales by 92% (from $1.3M to >$2.5M). Ranked #1 of 16 in sales.

Capture Planning – Identified business opportunities, analyzed advances in technology, and created pursuit strategies. Led brainstorming sessions to drive key initiatives.

Customer Relationship Management (CRM) – Exceeded customer expectations while promoting sales growth and facilitating product line expansion.

MediSurge Pharma, Seattle, WA [2013–2017]

Presided over sales of neuroscience products, medicines designed to promote health equity and improve health outcomes for patients with depressive disorders, schizophrenia, and bipolar management.

TERRITORY BUSINESS MANAGER

RANKINGS	GROWTH STRATEGIES	ORGANIZATION DEVELOPMENT
#7 – Southeast Region Top **15%** of 365 Nationally **#7** – Race for President's Club	Customized Roadmaps (30, 60, 90 Sales Plans) Proactive Customer Needs Assessment Solution-Oriented Selling	Sales Meeting Leadership Team Training and Mentoring Introduction of Sales Analytics

RECENT TRAINING

Leadership Edge Training, Pinon Group *[2021]* | Mastering the Six Levels of Leadership, Sales Concepts *[2021]*
Sales and Leadership Academy, Safety Detection Systems *[2021]* | Key Account Management, ASLAN *[2021]*
Certified in Radiation Safety, Amboy & Associates *[2020]*

ACADEMIC EDUCATION

Master of Business Administration (MBA)
University of Washington, Seattle, WA [2022]

Bachelor of Business Administration (BBA), Major in Marketing
Oregon State University, Corvallis, OR [2009]

PART V:
Resumes for Challenging & Emerging Situations

Many job seekers are faced with particularly challenging job search situations or are learning how to take advantage of our rapidly changing employment landscape.

You may fall into one of these categories:

- Changing careers
- Engaging in consulting, freelancing, and other "gig" opportunities
- Making a military-to-civilian career transition
- Returning to work after an extended absence

If so, pay special attention to the information and resume samples in Chapters 14, 15, 16, and 17 on the following pages. You'll find clear and concise explanations of each of the 4 categories, along with specific resume writing strategies to position yourself for your targeted career opportunities.

 PRO TIP: When writing a resume in a challenging situation, focus on the things that matter most as related to your current objectives, and downplay the items that are less relevant.

For some job seekers facing challenging circumstances, past work experience will be the most relevant information in their resume. For others, educational credentials will be primary. And for many, at the forefront will be "transferable skills"—expertise that you gained in one field but now want to use in another.

Let's consider the concept of "transferable skills" for a moment. The idea is great—you can transfer skills that you already have from one profession to another. But we recommend that you avoid using that term—"transferable skills"—because it sends a message that you are not familiar with your new field and will have to adapt your skills and knowledge rather than being productive immediately.

In our view, once you have a skill—no matter where you developed it—you own that skill and can prominently position it in your resume as one of your key qualifications. Don't minimize it by referring to it as "transferable" just because you learned it or used it in a different environment. Don't shortchange yourself!

If you are changing careers, transitioning from military service to a civilian career, returning to work after an extended absence, or pursuing emerging freelance, consulting, and gig opportunities, use the resumes in this section to guide your resume writing decisions. However, feel free to use other samples from this book to give you even more ideas on how to present your experience, educational credentials, skills, and all of the other information that makes you a uniquely qualified candidate.

CHAPTER 14:
Resumes for People Changing Careers

This chapter will be relevant to you if you are making a big change in your career and moving from one profession to another or one industry to another. That's what we consider a true career change and the types of resumes that we showcase in this chapter.

When writing a true career-change resume, the focus should be on showcasing the skills and knowledge you have that are most relevant to your new career objective. Often this means separating your skills from the environment (jobs or industries) in which those skills were acquired.

Of course, a "career change" is not always a dramatic transition. People make career changes all the time. They get promoted, they switch industries but retain similar career paths, they move through numerous similar positions with multiple companies, and they transition from for-profit to non-profit and vice versa. For those types of career changes, you'll uncover valuable information in this chapter as well as sample resumes from other chapters throughout the book and, of course, the Resume Portfolio in Part VII.

> **PRO TIP: Begin your resume writing process by identifying the skills, knowledge, and expertise you possess that will be valuable in your new career.** Never belittle those skills or their relevance by thinking of them as "transferable." Of course, you'll be using them in a new environment, but you own those skills, no matter the job, company, or industry where acquired.

As you've read earlier in this book, it is our general recommendation that resumes be written in a combination-chronological style—beginning with a Summary, then showcasing your Experience and career achievements, and ending with Education and any other important information.

That structure is often *not* the best choice for career-change resumes. Many career-change resumes are functional in style, beginning with a detailed Summary of skills, qualifications, experiences, educational credentials, projects, achievements, and other details from your career that align with your current career goals. How you organize that Summary section (or multiple sections) can vary dramatically from resume to resume, as you'll see in the samples in this chapter and in the Resume Portfolio later in this book.

Following the detailed Summary, most functional resumes include a brief listing of Experience (to communicate that you do have work history and to share important details *if* they are relevant or impressive), followed by Education and other information—such as technical skills, languages, testimonials, affiliations, public speaking, and the like—that could be of value.

> **PRO TIP: When writing a functional resume, be certain to follow the content, format, and design rules described in detail throughout this book**—the identical guidelines that we recommend for the modern combination-chronological resume. You'll be arranging the material differently, but you still must create highly readable, powerful, and relevant content to position yourself for your new career.

The very best way to explain how to write a career-change resume is to demonstrate—in detail—how and why the following 2 resumes were written.

Rolf Hoel Resume—page 121

Rolf's entire career has been in Security, but his objective now is a position as a Java Developer. His resume must present him as a qualified Java Developer so that prospective employers can easily understand his value.

Let's explore each component of his 1-page resume—an excellent example of how effective the *right* functional writing strategy, content, and format can be.

- **Headline**—By immediately labeling Rolf as a **Java Developer,** the Headline tells you who he is and communicates the position he is targeting.

- **Summary Bullets**—Each addresses an important skill or attribute for success in Rolf's chosen field.

- **IT Skills**—This section succinctly communicates all of his specific technical qualifications that are critical for the jobs he is seeking.

- **Education**—First, Rolf's recent Java Developer training is included with some detail. Notice that his prior education is listed as "BSc Program" and not "BSc Degree." This is an effective and honest way to present education for someone who has attended college/university but not earned a degree.

- **Professional Skills**—This section highlights Rolf's achievements and areas of responsibility from his previous professional experience that are relevant to his current job goals, directly and indirectly.

- **Experience**—Now, after reading all of the above and perceiving Rolf as a techie, you realize that any technical experience he has was part of his job as a Security Officer. However, he's positioned himself as a truly viable candidate for Java Developer jobs by demonstrating all of the right qualifications.

- **Languages and Kudos**—Languages add another great skill and dimension to this job seeker, and third-party testimonials are always a powerful addition.

END RESULT: Rolf's resume positions him as a qualified Java Developer with an edge over other graduates. Not only does he have the academic credentials, he has real-life work experience, a definite plus.

ROLF HOEL

▶ 0710-497 67 61 ▶ rolf.hoel@gmail.com ▶ linkedin.com/in/rolf-hoel

JAVA DEVELOPER

- **Trained group leader.** Always calm in critical situations. Meticulous, analytical, and persistent.
- **Trusted problem solver.** Handpicked for complex technical solutions requiring security clearance.
- **Company representative,** working directly with customers either on own assignments or in teams/on projects.
- **Reliable partner.** Known for meeting deadlines and understanding customer and production requirements.

IT SKILLS

Languages/Technologies:	Java, UML, SQL (MySQL, phpMyadmin, MS SQL), Java for Android app development, HTML/CSS, JEE, JavaScript, XML, XLS, PHP, Struts, Apache Ant
Development Environments:	Eclipse, NetBeans, Android Studio, Visual Paradigm
Server Environments:	Tomcat, Apache, Orion

EDUCATION

Java Developer, BD Education AS   2017–2023
- Java: Programming, network programming, advanced interface development, and mobile development
- Advanced object orientation with UML ▪ Data structures and algorithms
- Web application development

BSc Program in Data Technology, University of Oslo (UiO), Norway   2010–2012

PROFESSIONAL SKILLS

Troubleshooting/Communication
- Executed all school projects within set timeframes and scored "high pass" or "with honors."
- Contend with daily vacancies and motivate co-workers to carry out assignments. Oversee 6 departments of ≈300 armed security guards and close protection officers.
- Support group leader with technical skills.

Project Management/Teamwork
- Collaborate daily with 8- to 10-member teams. Coach staff on assignments.
- Met 100% of deadlines in all UiO courses by leading work process, setting goals, allocating tasks, and motivating 4–5 team members with diverse backgrounds. Won "high pass" for 90% of projects.

EXPERIENCE

ARMED SECURITY GUARD / TEAM LEADER, Securitas Norway AS   2013–Present
ARMED SECURITY GUARD & SECURITY OFFICER, Royal Security AS   2002–2013

Protect objects with very complex alarm systems, such as buildings, airports, military security shelters, luxury hotels, and high-profile people. Selected to attend numerous industry-specific trainings.

LANGUAGES

English (fluent, completed 1 year at high school in USA), **Norwegian** (native), **Spanish** (conversational)

KUDOS

"You are easily one of the most talented students I have had … you do more than expected!"—*BD Education AS*
"Rolf has demonstrated discretion, responsiveness, customer care, loyalty & professionalism."—*Royal Security AS*

Birgitta Moller, ACRW, MRW • Cvhjälpen • cvhjalpen.nu

Aminah Sarhadi Resume—pages 123–124

Aminah's 2-page resume paints the picture of an accomplished "Multilingual Healthcare Professional"—and she is. To truly understand her career, however, look at the second page of the resume and you'll see that her entire professional career has been in television news and media (except for a 3-month project with a non-profit).

So how do you make a journalist appear as a healthcare professional? For Aminah, the answer is her education, which became the foundation for her new resume. Let's look at each component:

- **Headline—Multilingual Healthcare Professional**—accomplishes the same 2 things as Rolf's headline—it identifies *who* this job seeker is and *what* she wants to do. (Note that this will only work if you have related experience, education, skills, or other qualifications so that the *who* is accurate.)

- **Branding Statement**—The sentence immediately below the headline that starts with "High-performing …" is most frequently referred to as a branding statement—someone's unique value proposition. Aminah's brand very effectively merges her healthcare, media, and related expertise into one statement that positions her as both qualified and with a distinctive skill set.

- **Boxed Bullet Points**—Each of these 3 statements focuses on a different skill—organizational leadership, communications, operations/program management—all of which are important to her current career goals as a Healthcare Administrator (not a care provider).

- **Strengths and Competencies**—This section demonstrates an effective technique for integrating a number of essential keywords into a resume to create a strong match with job descriptions and electronic resume scanning requirements.

- **Languages and Awards**—These unique bits of information add dimension, interest, and third-party validation of Aminah's success, even if they were from the television industry. (Who doesn't want to meet someone who's had 5 Emmy nominations?) It can often be the unusual things—related to nothing about your job target—that most entice people to reach out to you.

- **Education**—Aminah's recent Master of Health Administration (MHA) degree is prominently listed on page 1, along with her other degrees from Columbia and Yale. Even though her prior majors are unrelated to her current goals, those Ivy League names are impressive and communicate a positive message themselves.

- **Healthcare Fieldwork and Research Experience**—Highlighting 2 major projects she did while pursuing her MHA degree, Aminah's experience section looks like "real" jobs. They were "real" experiences and are presented in a typical job format to give them maximum impact.

- **Professional Experience**—Readers don't even know about Aminah's extensive career path in media until they reach page 2. Although not related to healthcare, the few items mentioned for each job are interesting, unique, adventuresome, and worldly, all of which add value to her job search and help to position her as a uniquely qualified healthcare professional who brings much more than just educational credentials.

END RESULT: A dynamic Healthcare Professional resume stands alone on page 1. Add page 2 to create an even more intriguing picture of that same qualified job seeker with a wealth of other, valuable experience.

AMINAH SARHADI

(585) 689-7837 ◆ aminah@georgetown.edu ◆ www.linkedin.com/in/aminahsarhadi ◆ Washington, DC 21789

MULTILINGUAL HEALTHCARE PROFESSIONAL

High-performing, collaborative leader committed to leveraging over a decade of success in global media, PR, program management, and client relations to advance healthcare system viability and patient outcomes.

➤ Thrive in dynamic, deadline-driven, multi-cultural environments; engage stakeholders at all levels; and build relations with health leaders, agencies, donors, physicians, and patients to achieve common goals.

➤ Exercise sophisticated editorial judgement, global perspective, and media savvy to deliver impactful, enterprise-wide communication strategies and compelling, consistent messaging across media platforms.

➤ Drive efficiency across complex operations through strategic program management, competitive benchmarking, and technical innovation while continuing to deliver demanding daily results.

~ Strengths and Competencies ~

Communication Strategy • Media Relations • Press Releases • Public Relations • Research • Public Health
Writing • Editing • Client Relations • Community Advocacy • Program Management • Disaster Preparedness
Benchmarking • Healthcare Marketing • Community Advocacy • Budgeting • Program Management

Languages – English, French, Hindi, Urdu, Dari, and Farsi *Traveled to 30+ Countries*

Awards – Earned **2 Peabody Awards** and **5 Emmy Nominations**

EDUCATION

MHA – Master of Health Administration – GEORGETOWN UNIVERSITY – Washington, DC *(Expected May 2023)*
MS in Broadcast Journalism – COLUMBIA UNIVERSITY – New York, NY
BA in International Relations, Peace and Justice Studies – Magna Cum Laude – YALE UNIVERSITY – New Haven, CT

HEALTHCARE FIELDWORK AND RESEARCH EXPERIENCE

GEORGETOWN UNIVERSITY MASTER OF HEALTH ADMINISTRATION PROGRAM   Aug 2022 – Dec 2022
Healthcare Marketing Simulation, Insurance Expansion Team Leader – New York, NY
Led 6 healthcare professionals in designing a marketing plan to expand insurance coverage across Colorado.
- Established a cohesive brand and compelling multi-cultural marketing message by creating a memorable tag line and color scheme, developing a website, launching a social media campaign, and writing a blog.
- Developed a targeted advertising campaign in English and Spanish through TV, print, and online ads, direct mail, community outreach partnerships, and marketing collateral for hospitals and healthcare providers.

GEORGE WASHINGTON UNIVERSITY HOSPITAL METHADONE TREATMENT CLINIC   Feb 2021 – May 2022
Fieldwork Consultant, Georgetown University Master of Health Administration Program – Washington, DC
Partnered with COO to transform substance abuse clinic serving 6,000 patients across 16 locations from an insolvent entity into an integrated care provider with restored profitability and enhanced patient outcomes.
- Collaborated with 6 MHA students and faculty advisor to develop new business model and org structure.
- Led needs assessment by conducting site visits, staff and patient surveys, and external benchmarking.
- Reduced prescription costs and turnaround time by upgrading health records management system.
- Expanded program reach and comorbidity treatment by bolstering cooperation with healthcare partners.

AMINAH SARHADI

(585) 689-7837 ◆ Page Two

PROFESSIONAL EXPERIENCE

ABC NEWS   Aug 2014 – Present

International Desk Editor and Acting Supervisor – New York, NY

Lead 6 editors in delivering award-winning news on air, print, and the web for world's leading news network.

- Gain a decisive edge in reporting high-stakes breaking news by using social media and in-depth knowledge of world cultures, geography, and political landscapes to secure timely eyewitness accounts and videos.
- Earned 2 **Emmy Nominations** for Syria and Israel-Gaza coverage and won **Peabody Award** for Gulf Oil Spill.
- Coordinate editing, logistics, technical details, and visuals to deliver robust, multi-dimensional stories.
- Prioritize daily global news stories in partnership with the London, Hong Kong, and Abu Dhabi bureaus.
- Provide editorial oversight to the field, research trends, and recommend stories to senior management.

Healthcare and Humanitarian Coverage

- Covered Ebola, H1N1, MERS, Avian Flu, Haiti Earthquake, Japanese Tsunami, and Philippines Typhoon.
- Developed healthcare networks with stakeholders in the WHO, CDC, health ministries, and hospitals to cover infectious disease outbreaks and the health implications of natural disasters, war, and refugee crises.
- Earned an **Emmy Nomination** for extensive coverage of the international Ebola crisis.

ABC International Newsource Affiliate Editor – New York, NY   Jun 2012 – Aug 2014

Managed global video, print, and editorial content platform, 25 international affiliate partners, and daily news gathering and transmission supporting ABC's largest expansion, connecting the resources of 200+ affiliate stations.

- Developed extensive client relations to acquire 12 new global affiliates and extend existing contracts.
- Delivered 24x7 client support and integrated new technology to meet evolving needs while reducing costs.
- Provided field news story editorial oversight and coordinated recruiting and training of affiliate journalists.
- Earned a **Peabody Award** for outstanding coverage of the 2012 United States Presidential Election.

HORIZON NEWS TELEVISION   Jun 2011 – Dec 2011

Writer, News Anchor – Karachi, Pakistan

Wrote, produced, and anchored daily foreign affairs program for Pakistan's first English-language news channel.

- Conducted web research and community outreach to secure interviews and create video news stories.

HOPE HUMANITARIAN ASSISTANCE   Jun 2010 – Aug 2010

Project Officer – Khorog, Tajikistan

Secured funding and managed disaster preparedness projects for developing areas at risk for natural disasters.

- Improved resource utilization via thorough work plans, financial models, cost-benefit analyses, and training.
- Wrote 3 grant proposals and tracked and presented performance status reports to key donor stakeholders.

EARLY CAREER IN PR COMMUNICATIONS AND MEDIA RELATIONS

- **Writer and Editor, The News International Newspaper**: Composed and edited interviews, editorials, and in-house packages on foreign affairs as a 2009 Summer Editor in Karachi for Pakistan's first English newspaper.

- **PR and Media Relations Specialist, Afghanistan Ministry of Foreign Affairs:** Led PR and media relations in 2007, handling media inquiries, releases, and packages for new Minister of Foreign Affairs in Afghanistan.

CHAPTER 15:
Resumes for Consultants, Freelancers & Gig Economy Workers

Over the past decade, the employment landscape has experienced a dramatic transition. Whereas it used to be that the vast majority of people worked *regular* jobs, what we find today is an explosion in the number of people working as consultants, freelancers, and giggers. As workers have changed, so have companies—slowly at first and then rapidly during COVID, which forever altered how many people work and saw companies, from the smallest to global mega corporations, shift their entire business model.

To best understand the role of consultants, freelancers, and giggers, let's look at similarities between them:

- They move from project to project, each lasting a specific period of time that can range from just a few weeks to months and even years.

- Individuals are most often self-employed and file 1099s—but not always, as you'll read below.

- Individuals may prefer to work within this model because of the flexibility, opportunities, and, most importantly, ability to call their own shots and decide which projects they want and which they do not.

- Leveraging the experience acquired through multiple engagements, most individuals will be able to make the transition to corporate employment at a later date if they choose to do so.

Now, let's discuss what makes them different from each other.

Consulting

The consulting profession has been around for decades, and consultants are now best known as solution providers. According to Merriam-Webster, consulting is being "engaged in the business of giving expert advice to people in a professional or technical field." Legal Definitions outlines the top 7 areas of consulting as Strategy, Marketing, Operations, Finance, Human Resources, Compliance, and Technology, although the reach of consulting is vast.

Most of us think of consultants as individuals who own their consulting firms. In these situations, not only are they providing their subject-matter expertise to their clients, they are also marketing their firm, managing its operations and financial affairs, and performing all other business functions required for the company and the consultant to be successful.

Often, consultants are retained by companies—as W2 employees or 1099 contractors—to bring their expertise into an organization, address a specific problem or opportunity, and craft a strategic business plan to achieve the firm's operational, financial, talent, marketing, and other business goals. It is then up to the company and its people to execute that plan.

Still other consultants are full-time employees of large consulting firms. They are the experts brought in to solve problems and sometimes implement solutions for their clients. Typically they are not involved in the business operations of the consulting firm that employs them.

> **PRO TIP: If you've been unemployed for a year or more, should you put consulting on your resume as your current job?** YES, if you truly are a consultant and have engagements to share. NO, if you're just using it as a space filler.

Gigging & Freelancing

As the term "gig economy" has risen in popularity, the term "freelance" has somewhat faded away. In fact, they mean the same thing. Investopedia defines the gig economy as "flexible, temporary, or freelance jobs, often involving connecting with clients or customers through an online platform," although that is definitely not the only way to pick up gigs.

Most freelancers now refer to themselves as giggers, moving from one project to another to the next. It can be an extremely enticing career track by making work more adaptable to the needs of the moment and the demand for flexible lifestyles. Giggers have a unique value proposition that they offer to their client companies, and it's that expertise that attracts companies to them.

There are a large number of giggers who work in technology as well as scores of other industries. Compare a 25-year-old gaming programmer who worked for 8 different companies in just one year with a 52-year-old regulatory compliance specialist who retired from his decades-long corporate career and now takes on occasional projects that call for his expertise. Although the professions and length of careers are quite different, as giggers, they both do the same thing—specific projects for specific companies that need an individual with specific expertise. When the project is complete, the gigger moves on to the next.

It's important to note that some people turn to gigging because it's the career track they wish to pursue. Others might be forced to accept gigs during this period of massive workplace reinvention but have the long-term goal of returning to a corporate position. As with any other resume, keep your goals in mind when you are writing.

Christa Bradley Resume—page 128

Christa's resume beautifully showcases how to write, design, and format a gig economy resume. Although she has positioned herself as a gig worker and is primarily pursuing those types of opportunities, her resume is equally effective if she decides to pursue a full-time, permanent corporate tech position.

- **Technical Certifications**—Immediately below Christa's name are her 3 distinctive technical certifications, which are spelled out in full at the end of her resume just in case a human reader is not familiar those with acronyms.

- **Headline**—Centered and bolded so that it's prominent, Christa's headline instantly communicates her areas of expertise—SQL Server DBA (Database Administrator), Developer, and Data/Warehouse Analyst—all of which tie directly to her objective for gig opportunities in those technical functions.

- **Area of Expertise**—This brief yet important section highlights Christa's full portfolio of technical skills. She also includes some of her general business skills (e.g., Analytical Problem Solving, Verbal & Written Communications) to showcase herself as a well-rounded tech professional.

- **Engagement & Project Highlights**—As it should be, this is the most comprehensive section of her resume. For each gig, she's included her functional job title, name of employer, location, and dates—quite similar to what a typical Professional Experience section would look like. She then includes a brief statement of why she was chosen for the gig, followed by 2 to 3 bullet points showcasing her notable contributions to each client company. It's a powerful combination of "this is why they selected me" and "this is what I delivered."

- **Education & Technical Certifications**—These 2 lines pack a lot of punch, beginning with her BS Degree and followed by her 3 Microsoft certifications. As you'll recall, those same certifications were very briefly mentioned right under her name at the top of the page. Both spelling these out and using the acronym fills the resume with information that will be invaluable in a keyword search.

- **Testimonial**—Strategically placed at the bottom of her resume is a quote touting her abilities and her achievements. Third-party testimonials are always a great addition to any resume, LinkedIn profile, or other career document because someone else is showcasing your success.

END RESULT: This resume clearly positions Christa for her career target: gig opportunities where she can use her technical and project management skills for engagements that last for several months and may ultimately lead to a permanent position … or further build her qualifications for her next gig.

Christa Bradley
MCDBA • MCSE • MCP

(555) 623-1234 • christabradley@mail.com
https://www.linkedin.com/in/christabradley/

SQL Server DBA, Developer & Data/Warehouse Architect

ENTERPRISE SQL SERVER MANAGEMENT • RELATIONAL DATABASE MANAGEMENT • DATA WAREHOUSE ARCHITECTURE

Shaping high-quality, robust SQL server & data strategies that organize, govern, analyze & deploy information assets

Areas of Expertise

Core Programming Languages & Server Technologies: ANSI SQL, Transact SQL, Python, PowerShell, SQL Server (6.5 to 2019)

SQL/T-SQL Development	Technical Leadership & Team Training	Information Technology Roadmaps
OLTP & OLAP Database Patterns	Agile Methodologies	Continuous Process Improvement
Extract, Transform, Load (ETL) Processes	Stakeholder Relationship Management	Business Requirements Gathering
Azure Cloud Technology	Analytical Problem Solving	Large-scale Technology Deployment
Data Warehousing & Architecture	Verbal & Written Communication	Business Intelligence (BI) & Big Data

Engagement and Project Highlights

Senior Database Engineer • Advanced Gaming Technologies, Cambridge, MA   Aug 2022 – Feb 2023

Brought in to lead and work with Database Engineers on analyzing, correcting, and optimizing database and production performance issues by implementing automated processes, multi-factor authentication mechanisms, and BI applications.

- **Prevented significant revenue losses** by refactoring 9 years of Transact SQL legacy code, building new processes totaling 65,000 lines of code, and implementing multi-factor authentication.
- **Strengthened cloud technology experience** by deploying Azure-based CI/CD pipeline and data-tier application to streamline change management through DevOps and source control models.

SQL Server Developer / Database Administrator / Data Architect • Worldwide Logistics, Providence, RI   Apr 2021 – July 2022

Contracted to provide SQL engineering support for global ETL team and execute ERP data migration strategy.

- **Delivered global data design and ETL integration strategy and long-term solutions for future rollouts** for MS D365, Salesforce, and CPQ systems within tight timeline. Oversaw Microsoft D365 instances in Azure for the team.
- Used Git, Visual Studio, Azure DevOps, Python, XML, XQuery, and PowerShell to build code repository and script ETL commands that **automated deployment of SSIS packages,** tracked code changes, and extracted files for import to D365.
- **Promoted best practices** by producing and managing Run Book detailing contingency plans and troubleshooting procedures to start, stop, supervise, and debug systems, handle special requests, and **support continuing operations.**

SQL Developer • Bayshore Technologies, Waltham, MA   Oct 2020 – Apr 2021

Recruited for 6-month assignment providing technical direction to Developers on T-SQL enterprise database project.

- **Delivered increased functionality** after troubleshooting and diagnosing performance issues in SQL Service Broker.
- Built, tested, and implemented enhancements on existing database architecture that addressed new business requirements and **improved performance without compromising existing functionality.**

SQL Server Developer • Modicum Technologies, Boston, MA   Mar 2018 – Sep 2020

Served as resident SQL expert to team of Full-stack Developers in designing, building, testing, and implementing SQL features.

- **Expanded and improved SQL coding standards** in business applications by drawing on XML, extended properties, code formatting, and relational database theory while minimizing operational disruption and **raising team's SQL knowledge.**
- Delivered reduction in time—**3 orders of magnitude**—needed to run annual report by refining T-SQL code and updating, configuring, tuning, and analyzing indexes, underlying data, and schemas.

Education and Technical Certifications

Bachelor of Science (**BS**), **Mechanical Engineering Technology** • Wentworth Institute of Technology, Boston, MA
Microsoft Certified Database Administrator • Microsoft Certified Systems Engineer • Microsoft Certified Professional

"Few people have the opportunity to work with an SQL Developer like Christa who understands SQL language and has the tenacity to solve existing complex problems left behind and the resulting data integrity issues."   **~ Director Systems Integration ~**

Enrique Hernandez —pages 130–131

Enrique has been a successful Healthcare Consultant for 15 years and is now targeting additional consulting and interim executive opportunities. Note that there are many instances, particularly with C-suite and executive management teams, when a consultant is brought on board for an extended period of time to drive a major initiative and then serves as part of the leadership team for the duration of the contract.

- **Business Credentials**—Right next to his name are his 2 Master's Degrees, which instantly communicate a positive message of value.

- **Headline**—Enrique's 2-line Headline provides instant clarity. He tells us *who* he is and follows up with 3 areas of significant expertise—areas that coincide directly with his objectives.

- **Summary**—Read this brief yet powerful summary and you'll immediately understand Enrique's value to another healthcare organization.

- **Professional Experience**—Notice that his experience is presented as a list of projects—precisely the right content for a consultant. When you read it carefully, you'll see that Enrique has consulted with healthcare organizations worldwide on a diverse range of care and business initiatives—patient care, market entry, acquisitions, technology, policy, and more.

- **Education**—Education is short and to the point. Great! He did not include graduation dates because he is a bit older than you might assume from his work experience.

- **Select Presentations & Publications**—This section is packed with power. The perception is that a person who has led major presentations must be well-qualified, and publications add further credibility to Enrique's expertise.

END RESULT: This is a true consultant's resume that combines a strong introductory section that instantly tells the reader *who* he is and *what* he does, job descriptions that are presented as specific projects and business initiatives, and third-party validation with the inclusion of his presentations and publications.

An added value is that the resume follows our Modernize formatting guidelines and is easy to read, draws the eye to the most significant sections, and uses bolding at the beginning of each bullet point in his job descriptions to highlight healthcare and business keywords that will be essential to his search. (Read more about keywords in Chapter 9.)

Enrique Hernandez, MA, MPH

555-234-1221 | enrique.hernandez@gmail.com

www.linkedin.com/in/enrique-hernandez

Healthcare Consultant

Transformational Program Leader | Growth Strategist | Interim Executive

❑ **Strategic and operational advisor:** 15 years of experience conceiving and driving programs that improve individual, hospital, and population health outcomes.

❑ **Champion for change:** Expert analyst and researcher who makes a business case for transformation and builds internal and external buy-in through a compelling narrative, clearly defined outcomes, and measurable results.

Professional Experience

Healthcare Strategy and Operations Consultant   2018–Present

❑ **Built thriving practice providing healthcare expertise to organizations in the U.S. and internationally.**

- **Market Entry:** Teamed with leading expert on medical tourism for in-depth feasibility study at the request of Moldovan Ministry of Health. Created custom data sets to explain supply-and-demand dynamics, examined hospital norms, identified challenges, and presented well-received recommendations and action plan for becoming a medical tourism destination.

- **Due Diligence:** Led due diligence process for orthopedic group seeking expansion options. Benchmarked trends, vetted assumptions, and researched hard-to-find data about orthopedic services and statistics. Developed proposals for service growth and created powerful narrative to appeal to third-party investors.

- **Growth Strategy:** Completed more than half a dozen feasibility studies for Skilled Nursing and Memory Care organizations. Provided rationale for acquisition, market entry, expansion, and/or service enhancement by tying market information to consumer demand.

Healthcare Consultant and Senior Analyst | Argosy Health, Manila, Philippines   2012–2018

❑ **Steered transformative initiatives that improved patient care, operational efficiencies, and financial results** while boosting the reputation and expanding the footprint of Argosy Health, a leading healthcare delivery organization—the first in the Philippines to receive international as well as national accreditation. The system comprises 16 hospitals and clinics throughout the Philippines.

- **Clinical Program Development:** Forged partnership with US Level 1 trauma center to create a pioneering Emergency Medicine residency program. Introduced gold-standard US curriculum, launched program, and built Emergency Medicine into significant revenue generator and reputation builder for the system.
  - Multiplied nearly 6-fold the number of emergency patients seen daily: from an average of 30 to 175, with 50% continuing to revenue-generating ICU or surgery services.
  - Authored first peer-reviewed and published research about local emergency-related disease.
  - Inspired hospital staff to embrace the new EM department and brainstorm better ways to deliver care.
  - Drove physician engagement that improved retention of EM doctors during department transformation.

- **Program Accreditation:** Spearheaded preparation and process for securing national accreditation for new Emergency Medicine program, with curriculum adopted as national prototype.

- **Market Entry:** Created system's first DRGs for new oncology and elective surgery services and competitively positioned in local market.
  - Achieved rapid acceptance and steady growth—oncology services broke even 6 months ahead of schedule.

Louise Kursmark, MRW, CPRW, JCTC, CEIP, CCM • Best Impression Career Services • louisekursmark.com

Enrique Hernandez, MA, MPH

Healthcare Consultant and Senior Analyst | Argosy Health, continued

- **Electronic Health Records:** Championed major upgrade to EHR system and led 2-year program that incorporated best practices for software development, acceptance testing, and training. Executed numerous successful launches with minimal downtime.

- **Operational Efficiency:** Saved $100K in water and cooling expenditure while increasing beds and demand by preparing facility to earn well-established environmental building award.

Healthcare Consultant   2009–2012

❑ **Took on long-term assignments requiring deep expertise in healthcare-specific data analysis and operations.**

- **Policy Management:** Assessed policies, KPIs, and infection control principles related to safe hospital operations, adverse events, and patient satisfaction. Recommended and implemented updates and enhancements. (Desert Hospital, Las Vegas, NV)

- **Process Improvement:** Increased premiums and provided more accurate policy risk ratings by revising undisclosed operator process for automobile policies. (National Insurance Company, Phoenix, AZ)

Health Management Fellow| International Health Alliance, Cusco, Peru   2008–2009

❑ **Accepted invitation to complete MPH practicum in South America,** supporting a partnership between New York Medical Center and Peruvian Ministry of Health.

- **Patient-Focused Health Policy:** Prepared baseline assessment of national health system to document clinical and administrative capabilities. Assessment resulted in realigning national healthcare budget to more closely match health needs of presenting patients.

Education

Master of Public Health (MPH) | NEW YORK UNIVERSITY, New York, NY
Master of Arts, Political Science | NORTHWESTERN UNIVERSITY, Evanston, IL
Bachelor of Science, Biology | UNIVERSITY OF CHICAGO, Chicago, IL

Select Presentations and Publications

Presentations

- "Development of Filipino Emergency Medicine," Medtronic Global Health Meeting, Nashville, TN, USA, 2021.

- "Emergency Medicine Services in the Philippines," Asian Health Care Association, Singapore, 2020.

Publications

- Edwards, R.R., Hernandez, E., Reyes, P.L., Santos, J. (2018). Analysis of acute care needs in a Filipino emergency department. *Global Medical Journal,* (1)4, 118–125.

- Hernandez, E., Smith, P.A., Vindaloo, J.M. (2018). Emergency medical services utilization in 16 Filipino emergency departments. *Emergency Medicine Monthly*, (4)16, 256–262.

CHAPTER 16:
Resumes for Military-to-Civilian Career Transitions

The single most important question to ask yourself when writing a military-to-civilian transition resume is, who is your target audience? As a general rule, you could target 2 distinct groups of companies, agencies, or organizations:

- Option 1: Military, Government, NGO, and Defense Contractors
- Option 2: General Corporations and Organizations (not affiliated with military, government, or defense)

If you are targeting Option 1, your resume writing process will be easier because much of what you've done in your military career will be relevant—to some degree—to your new targeted positions. Common military jargon, abbreviations, acronyms, technologies, ranks, operations, and other details will most likely mean something when your resume lands in a government agency or a company such as Lockheed Martin.

Even more important, these agencies, companies, and organizations often prefer to hire separating military personnel because of their specific expertise, experience, training, security clearances, and record of performance. You want to prominently and proudly display your record of service and be confident that most readers will understand all that you share.

That same information may not make much sense if you're writing to a general corporation that manufactures tires, consumer products, rugs, industrial HVAC units, and the like. It also doesn't seem very relevant to organizations that sell pet supplies, apparel, home improvement products, cars, and more.

Yet, even in those circumstances, you can uncover common denominators—things that you did in the military that can be related to your current objectives. In this situation, your resume writing strategy and structure will be similar to that used by career changers, who work to separate skills and qualifications from the environment in which they were acquired. If you fall into this category, carefully read Chapter 14 (Resumes for People Changing Careers) and follow the principles we've outlined there as well as in this chapter.

To best understand the differing approaches to these distinct audiences, let's look carefully at 2 resumes, one written for a "military-friendly" audience and the other written for a general company.

Montell Wardner Resume—pages 134–135

Montell Wardner had a long and prestigious career with the US Air Force. His goal is to transition his senior-level program management skills into a military, government, or defense-related organization, where his career positions him perfectly for an opportunity.

- **Headline**—Under Montell's name, at the top of his resume, are 3 very important words—Senior Program Manager. You instantly know *who* he is and *what* he does.

- **Summary**—These 2 short paragraphs give a great overview of his experience with the USAF, along with his strong academic credentials, security clearance, and other distinguishing qualifications. The Skill Sets section lists the 5 most important functions of the jobs he has performed—which are precisely the same skills needed for the jobs he is targeting. Finally, in that same section are 4 achievement statements to further strengthen his qualifications and track record of performance.

- **United States Air Force**—Although you could add the section heading "Professional Experience" or "Military Experience," it's not mandatory. We can quickly see that Montell's entire career has been with the USAF. The job descriptions share his overall scope of responsibility and then focus on his most notable achievements, just as you would write for any civilian resume. And, because he is targeting positions in Program and Project Management, he uses those exact words to introduce his achievements in each of the job descriptions. With this technique, he reinforces those strong skills (keywords) that align 100% with his objectives.

- **Education & Training**—This section includes his college degrees and summarizes his extensive military training in 2 short lines. There is no need to mention every training at this point in the job search process. A prospective employer who wants to know will ask for all of the details.

END RESULT: This resume is a perfect presentation for a similar Program Manager position with a company that is closely aligned with the military. Manhours, money, missions, aircraft, and other information is showcased throughout, demonstrating Montell's success in the USAF and the exceptional expertise he brings to a company.

MONTELL SHANE WARDNER

Senior Program Manager

moward1@gmail.com | 816-562-7572

High-achieving, analytically minded Senior Program Manager with MS in Engineering Management plus 8 years of program development and leadership while serving as a top-ranked pilot instructor and officer for the U.S. Air Force.

Ideally suited for process-focused role in Engineering, Production, Logistics, or Technology, having led multimillion-dollar projects in this arena and always found ways to cut costs through Lean Systems Thinking and Six Sigma methods. Top Secret Security Clearance.

SKILL SETS

Program Management
Project Management
Change Management
Operations Improvement
Process Engineering
Team Coordination

⇨ Reputation for building world-class training, compliance, and evaluation programs while concurrently inspiring teams of 15–200 staff to exceed their own expectations.

⇨ Talent for finding and eliminating the root cause of inefficient systems and processes and building solutions with positive cross-functional impact.

⇨ History of impressing high-ranking officials with metric-driven change-management initiatives; record of challenging and winning support from the Pentagon.

⇨ Multi-award-winning instructor pilot held in esteem by supervisors and peers alike.

UNITED STATES AIR FORCE | 2001–PRESENT

Senior Program Director, Aircrew Training (Edwards AFB).. May 2019 – Present
Recruited by past supervisor to plan and lead pilot training at the highest level of authority, on a $250M budget. Managed 3 program supervisors and 25 military and non-military staff driving the training of 1,500 personnel.

Program Management – Training
- Oversee all 8 flight training programs, comprising 59,000 hours of flying time. Maintain 1,300 records and authorize $4.5M in instructor salaries.
- Initiate and lead quarterly and annual training program evaluations, chairing a 17-person review board.
- Coordinate scheduling, training, and compliance documentation of 950 aircrew, completing 9,000 mandatory air and classroom training events in 1 year.

Project Management – Technology Upgrades
- Directed upgrade of $23M simulation system, including requirements/contract approvals and oversight of private-sector consultants.
- Managed implementation of $48M worth of instrumentation in KC-10 aircraft. Benchmarked with federal agencies and orchestrated RFP process with vendors.

> **Process Improvements**
>
> *—Saved $20M/year, integrating 30% of airfield training into flight simulator system.*
>
> *—Revamped task delegation protocol: set up software and defined approval hierarchy.*
>
> *—Introduced cross-training to maintain productivity through 40% RIFs.*

Assistant Operations Officer (Edwards AFB) ....Nov 2014 – May 2019
Developed and supervised aircrews in executing short-notice cargo and air refueling missions all over the world. Supported allied and multiservice agencies as directed by the President and Secretary of Defense. Served as Interim Operations Officer.

Program Management – Training
- Created, organized, and managed more than 20,000 flight and ground training activities for 160 crew.
- Minimized required flights 20% and completed training 33% ahead of schedule by developing a streamlined requalification program that enabled trainees to retain their office positions.

Program Management – Divisional Compliance
- Championed audit process across 18 departments to preempt official inspection. Developed 42-point checklist encompassing 1,100 points of evaluation, ultimately identifying and resolving 27 infractions.
- Attained 100% compliance across Records, Safety, Scheduling, Quality Control, and Logistics units.

Chief of Flight Training (Lemoore Naval Air Station) .... Oct 2011 – Oct 2014
Formalized $400M "weed-out" combat system officer training program, enrolling 350 students per year with a <20% pass rate.

Program Management – Training
- Established and finalized all aspects of training program, from strategic planning through program development, collateral creation, implementation, and evaluation.
- Boosted trainee productivity 25% by innovating the training program evaluation model.

Montell Shane Wardner
moward1@gmail.com

Senior Program Manager
Resume, Page 2 of 2

UNITED STATES AIR FORCE | CONTINUED

Flight Commander / Instructor (Lemoore Naval Air Station)..Oct 2008 – Oct 2011

Turned around a failing combat systems officer training program in Florida, Colorado, and Texas that was riddled with non-compliance issues. Passed inspection and earned Flight Commander of the Year Award for the entire naval station.

Program Management – Training

- Pinpointed every single point of non-compliance for a 4-phase training program, developed remediation strategy, and advised supervisor operations officer and 41 instructors on implementing adjustments.
- Developed metric-driven report showcasing 2 months of data to challenge the Pentagon's proposed timeline for matriculating pilots. Quantified the need for 20% more planes and 33% more pilots to work on existing timeline, resulting in a 3-day extension per class – eliminating trend of late graduation.
- Designed criteria for the inspection team to evaluate this new training program.

Executive Officer / Instructor (Edwards AFB)..............................Jul 2005 – Jul 2009

Won nominations and awards for efficiency, reliability, and commitment to working beyond the job description. Oversaw personnel activities and career development for 175 unit members.

Project Management – Records

- Dedicated 42 hours to processing a backlog of 35 reports that had been outstanding for 6 months. Digitized and catalogued all documentation.

Program Management – Transport Missions

- Planned 5,000 sorties to 50 airfields, transporting 108,000 passengers and 18 million pounds of cargo. Directed crew members in using $88M aircraft.
- Spearheaded high-visibility missions such as humanitarian relief and airlifts for the Secretary of Defense and the President of Afghanistan.

Operations Manager, Mobility Dept (Edwards AFB).................Jul 2002 – Jul 2005

Ensured travel readiness of 200 unit members by keeping meticulous, updated documentation. Served as interim chief for 2 months.

Program Management – Compliance

- Monitored well over 100 qualifying items for each team member, including visas, passports, medical records, firearm knowledge, combat training and credentials, and airport security clearance.
- Designed a Microsoft Access database with "smart" filter that intelligently auto-populated the correct fields on a suite of forms – cutting out hours in the day per person in data entry.

Program Manager, Awards Dept (Edwards AFB).......................Jul 2001 – Jul 2002

Tracked awards for 180 staff, plus flew a mission to clear airspace for the space shuttle launch.

Program Management – Awards & Decorations

- Wrote 200+ award citations and monitored the approval process across 6 levels of leadership.
- Cut outsourcing costs 300% by developing an in-house lithograph production method (used to design awards).

Pilot Instructor Experience

Concurrent with program management work, flew 100+ missions as a pilot.

Earned the highest-level instructor credential – an FTU Instructor Pilot, taking responsibility for teaching unqualified pilots to fly.

Instructed senior aircraft commanders on strategy, effective decision-making, and task management in high-pressure situations.

USAF Leadership Awards

Gold Leader Award
1 of 17 finalists out of 1,000+ nominated leaders

National Noble Airmen
Outstanding leadership at work and in the community

Instructor Pilot of Year
Ranked #1 out of 42 pilots

Commander of Year
Ranked #1 out of 58 CCs

Distinguished Graduate
Ranked in top 10% of class of 311 students.

EDUCATION & TRAINING

MS Engineering Management: Johns Hopkins University, Baltimore, 2017
BS Astronautical Engineering, Minor in Mathematics: U.S. Air Force Academy, Colorado Springs, 2001

Completed numerous leadership and flight training courses in team management, decision-making, strategic planning, pilot instruction, water survival, parachuting/freefalling, combat, and instrumentation.

Jacob Davidson Resume—pages 137–138

In contrast to Montell Wardner, Jacob Davidson is not looking to work for a company that has any connection to the military, so his resume takes an entirely different approach.

Jacob is targeting a position where he can use his extensive experience as an electrician and mechanic, most likely with a builder, manufacturer, or industrial company. The most important thing his resume accomplishes is to eliminate as many references to the military as possible. It's obvious that's been his career, but the strategy here is to downplay the military while showcasing the actual work he performed.

You'll note that the approach to writing and formatting this resume is very similar to that for career-change resumes, as discussed in Chapter 14. Let's explore how it was done.

- **Wire Graphic**—This little graphic instantly communicates electrical, industrial, and other related functions/operations. It distinguishes his resume and is a subtle but effective message.

- **Headline**—As repeated throughout these special chapters and the entire book, a headline is a very effective way to start a resume. With one quick glance, the reader knows *who* you are and *what* you want to do. There's no wasted time trying to figure it out.

- **Summary**—The introductory paragraph, in bold print, gives a quick overview of Jacob's knowledge and capabilities without ever mentioning his military service. This is an excellent example of separating skills from the environment in which they were acquired. For additional value, the 4 bulleted statements that follow focus on the important personal attributes he brings to the workplace.

- **Core Competencies**—An easy-to-skim section presents a host of relevant skills and qualifications for quick review by any reader—human or electronic. These all-important keywords must be integrated somewhere in the resume, whether in a separate section like this, interspersed throughout, or both.

- **Certifications & Licenses**—By sharing this vital information in the top section of his resume, Jacob quickly conveys that he is exceptionally well trained and qualified.

- **Professional Career Experience**—Notice that your eye focuses on the job titles and not the military installation or unit. A brief paragraph of overall responsibility introduces each job, and Key Results showcase his achievements and project highlights. Virtually all of this information is applicable to any company he might approach, so the resume is successful in separating and showcasing his skills and not restricting him to a military-related role or organization.

- **Professional Training**—Although Jacob does not have a college degree, he has a wealth of training that is important to include. Instead of readers instantly thinking "no degree," we want them to think "lots and lots of relevant training."

- **Awards & Honors**—No matter the profession, industry, or situation, earning honors and awards is impressive and validates everything else that's been written in the resume.

END RESULT: This professional resume clearly demonstrates that Jacob is a talented electrician and mechanic with a wealth of certifications, licenses, and training that are applicable in just about any industrial environment. In turn, he has opened himself to countless potential opportunities across numerous different industries. His military career laid the foundation; now, he's ready for a new career.

JACOB DAVIDSON

Seattle, WA | 206-555-1009 | jd2001@gmail.com

ELECTRICIAN | MECHANIC PROFILE

Credentialed and skilled Electrician and Mechanic with 10 years' experience maintaining and repairing generators, HVAC, mechanical equipment, and vehicles for diverse organizations supporting global operations.

- Train and manage skilled technicians in high-stress, fast-paced environments.
- Deliver strategic solutions through effective problem solving.
- Quickly assess, identify, and mitigate risk.
- Support teams and staff as an advisor, mentor, and technical expert.

CORE COMPETENCIES

Leadership & Supervision	Generators & HVAC Equipment	Quality Assurance/Quality Control
Logistics/Strategic Planning	Automotive Mechanics	Regulatory & Safety Compliance
Change Management/Crisis Management	Heavy Vehicle Maintenance	Inspections/Troubleshooting
Personnel Management	Engines & Fuel Systems	Instruction/Training/Briefings
	Utilities Equipment Repair	

CERTIFICATIONS & LICENSES

- ☑ Certified Electrician
- ☑ Certified Mechanic
- ☑ Certified Fuel Specialist
- ☑ Certified Refrigerant: Recovery, Recycling, Reclamation
- ☑ Certified Heavy Vehicle Operator

- ☑ Air Conditioning Specialist
- ☑ Certified MVAC Technician
- ☑ Certified Forklift Operator
- ☑ Licensed Skid Operator
- ☑ HAZMAT Trained
- ☑ Sanitation Knowledge

PROFESSIONAL CAREER EXPERIENCE

SENIOR POWER GENERATION TECHNICIAN   Dec 2020 to Present
Combat Support Hospital (CSH) – Joint Base Fort Lewis-McChord, WA

Senior Power Generation Equipment Repairer for 375-bed hospital. Manage staff of 10 technicians.

Supervise operations and direct personnel performing scheduled and unscheduled maintenance, repair, or service of the generators, air conditioning systems, and heaters. Hold 100% accountability for the serviceability and accountability of $1M in essential equipment.

Selected for superior technical knowledge to serve as Senior Manager in a high-volume, fast-paced maintenance section. Provide quality control of 300+ critical parts.

Key Results:

- Steered first ever *power distribution set-up* of a "concept 40-bed hospital" – *not attempted before* – during critical preparation exercise for deployment.
- Coordinated/supervised 6000 successfully executed job orders – 350 services distributed across 6 units.
- Trained 100 staff on proper installation, monitoring, and maintenance of power generation equipment. Instructed 12 staff on generators and power distribution boxes.
- Ensured 94% operational readiness rate – exceeded expectations.

Kara Varner, CARW, CPRW, CRS-MTC, CEIP • A Platinum Resume • aplatinumresume.com

 **JACOB DAVIDSON**

POWER GENERATION TECHNICIAN Nov 2017 to Dec 2020
South Korea

Power Generation Equipment Repairer for an organization providing direct support maintenance to 5 companies. Supervised and directed 11 staff. Managed and performed maintenance repairs for all power generation equipment, internal combustion engines, and associated equipment.

Key Results:

- Ensured 98% readiness rate by implementing quality control processes for equipment standards.
- Maintained 100% accountability of special tools, test sets, and supplies worth more than $2M.
- Incorporated comprehensive management and safety procedures – resulted in zero accidents/injuries.
- Trained new staff on power generation repair, working during personal time to ensure appropriate skill levels.
- Earned Army Award for Maintenance Excellence.

GENERATOR MECHANIC Jun 2012 to Oct 2017
Fort Hood, TX

Generator Mechanic on largest US Army base with short/no-notice worldwide requirements missions. Expertly performed maintenance and repair services for generators and heavy-wheel vehicles. Conducted scheduled/unscheduled maintenance on more than 90 pieces of rolling stock. Directed 2 staff.

Expert Inspector, performing quality control and assurance inspections. Troubleshot, identified issues, requisitioned repair parts, and resolved problems. Oversaw equipment worth $25K.

Key Results:

- Reduced safety incidents 75% by emphasizing risk management and safety procedures.
- Crossed-trained wheeled vehicle mechanics on generators; increased operational proficiency.

PROFESSIONAL TRAINING

☑ Generator Operations Course	☑ Advanced Leadership Course
☑ Emergency Operations Communications	☑ Leadership Development
☑ HP UNIX System Administration	☑ HAZMAT / Safety

AWARDS & HONORS

Army Commendation Medal (5) ▪ Army Achievement Medal (4) ▪ Army Good Conduct Medal (4)

CHAPTER 17:
Resumes for People Returning to Work

For people returning to work after extended absences, the most critical resume writing challenge is how to mask that they haven't worked in 6 months, a year, 5 years, or 15 years. The reasons for unemployment might include:

- Staying at home to raise children
- Supporting a spouse's military or corporate career with continual relocation
- Returning to work after injury or illness
- Caring for someone else through injury or illness
- Returning to work after earning degree(s) and/or certification(s)
- Returning to work after retirement
- Reentering the workforce after incarceration
- Returning from an extended sabbatical to travel the world or pursue educational opportunities

Many of the career-change strategies in Chapter 14 can also be effective for return-to-work resumes, so be certain to review that chapter and all of those recommendations as well as all information in this chapter.

One of the first questions to consider is whether a combination-chronological or modern functional format will be best to showcase your experience. We've found that combination-chronological formats tend to work the best for people who do have experience related to their current objective. Conversely, if the experience is not related, then follow the guidelines for creating a functional resume just as you would do for any other career change.

Perhaps the greatest challenge when writing a return-to-work resume is whether or not to include dates for Experience and Education, and how. Because there are so many variables, there is no single recommendation regarding dates. Here are 3 distinct options for your own return-to-work resume.

- In the first sample resume, for Padma Singh, the employment dates are visually minimized by their location. Instead of being positioned at the right margin, where they will stand out boldly, they are more subtly placed in the middle of the line that begins with her job title.

- A creative solution for someone who has been out of work for a relatively long period of time is to use number of years at each position rather than specific dates. You'll notice that Lucas Adams' resume states "14 years" instead of the actual span of xxxx to xxxx. Although not always the best solution, this technique can work favorably if the dates will communicate long-term unemployment and/or older age.

- The final recommendation is to delete dates entirely. While we don't use this strategy often, it can be the best solution for someone with lengthy and frequent unemployment.

Bottom line: Consider the message you're sending with dates and their placement on your resume. Many employers are understanding of short gaps and recent unemployment, so don't be unduly concerned if your resume reflects those circumstances. But if your career history reflects lengthy gaps, multiple periods of unemployment, or long-time unemployed status, employers may be leery—so it's best not to give them information that may cause them to reject your candidacy before ever meeting you.

As with all of our suggestions, put your best foot forward when writing and formatting your resume. Save the less-than-favorable specifics for the interview, after your future employers have already met you and are impressed. Then, those items aren't quite as significant.

> **PRO TIP: Do you include the reason you've been out of work on your resume?** Almost never! That's a conversation better had during an interview. However, there are no absolutes. If you spent the last year climbing the tallest mountain peaks in Asia, it might be worth a brief mention on your resume so that you're accounting for the time you weren't recently working and sharing interesting information.

Let's explore the resume samples in this chapter, starting with Padma Singh, who fits into the largest group of people returning to work—moms and dads.

Padma Singh Resume—page 142

- **Headline—Mortgage Lending/Title/Escrow Professional**—Padma has held these jobs before and it's what she is targeting now, so it's the perfect introduction.

- **Summary**—Five concise bullet points highlight specific skills and experience that Padma possesses that relate directly to her targeted positions. Both hard skills and soft skills are included to paint the picture of someone who has all the attributes needed to do the job.

- **Signature Skills and Technical Proficiencies**—As mentioned for other resumes, a separate keyword section is an effective way to integrate a large number of relevant terms into your resume without taking up too much space. Keywords are essential because they are the backbone for online resume scanning and applications. They are the words that will get your resume noticed and get you selected to interview.

- **Real Estate Industry Experience**—Using this heading allows Padma to put her relevant experience front and center, emphasizing that she does have a significant background in the field she's targeting. The job descriptions are well written and highlight her notable responsibilities and achievements. Most important, the dates of employment are visually downplayed. In this resume, the dates are so non-visually prominent that they almost disappear, and that's precisely the point.

- **Current Leadership & Management Experience**—This brief section adds more dimension to the resume and communicates that she's been busy contributing to her family and her community while not working outside the home. Plus, these volunteer experiences have given her new skills to add to her qualifications and make her a more well-rounded candidate.

- **Education**—Her degrees and university are included with no frills—just the facts, which are more than sufficient.

END RESULT: Padma's resume showcases a talented Mortgage Lending professional with the right skills, qualifications, and experiences to qualify her for a variety of opportunities in this industry. The fact that she hasn't worked in years is barely noticeable.

Lucas Adams Resume—page 143

Another interesting return-to-work story is that of Lucas Adams, who was a long-time Shipping and Receiving Manager until a workplace injury left him out of work entirely for 2 years. At that point he had some significant physical limitations and could no longer work in an industrial environment, so he took a desk job for 6 years. Now he's 100% healthy and ready to return to the work that he loves most. How does he handle the fact that he left his related profession more than 8 years ago?

- **Forklift Graphic**—This instantly communicates a message of warehouse work and is perfect for the jobs that Lucas is targeting.

- **Paragraph Summary**—In just 4 lines, this section clearly summarizes the years of experience that this job seeker has in his targeted industry and includes some personal attributes that are vital to top performance in those types of jobs. One of the first things readers learn is that he has 14 years of relevant experience. That instantly eliminates the need to focus on dates.

- **Core Competencies**—Lucas showcases his most relevant skills with just enough detail to demonstrate that he's well qualified.

- **Related Experience**—The Related Experience heading is one of the techniques that professional resume writers use quite often for people returning to work and, sometimes, for career changers. Why does this work? Because it allows you to move your relevant experience to the forefront rather than sticking with a traditional chronological style that would have put this job—his related experience—after his current, unrelated, job.

- **Current Experience**—As mentioned, by reversing the order of presentation of his work experience, the most relevant comes first. However, his current job is also important because it showcases that he has been working full time, albeit in a different profession.

- **Training**—Just a brief mention of his relevant training, with no date of graduation, is all that matters. Although he is a high school graduate, that information is not included because he does have relevant professional training.

END RESULT: Lucas's resume clearly communicates his skills, qualifications, and 14 years of experience that relate to his current objective. Because of the style of presentation, it's almost an afterthought that the relevant experience is not current. And that's precisely the point of using this format and structure.

Padma Singh

padma.singh@mac.com | 555-123-7654

Mortgage Lending — Title — Escrow Professional

- **Multi-Perspective Experience:** Loan Manager, Loan Officer, Loan Originator.
- **Customer Focus:** Trusted resource for first-time home buyers, resulting in exceptional referral rate.
- **Collaboration and Communication:** Natural relationship builder who connects easily with team members, customers, and industry professionals.
- **Process and Detail Orientation:** Project manager with success leading complex initiatives from vision to reality.
- **Technical Acumen:** Quick study in learning new software, systems, and tools; resource and teacher in helping teammates master new technologies.

Signature Skills
- Project Management
- Time Management
- Attention to Detail
- Customer Service
- Teamwork
- Initiative

Technical Proficiencies
MS Office, Databases, Project Management Software, CRM Software

Real Estate Industry Experience

LOAN MANAGER / LOAN ORIGINATOR | 2005–2008 | Acme Mortgage, Des Moines, IA

Built referral business from the ground up, establishing a niche serving first-time buyers and providing a high level of service and support to generate repeat and referral business.

- Applied professional sales, marketing, and business development skills to generate a steady pipeline of new leads.
- Closed a minimum of 10 loans per month, consistently meeting or exceeding performance goal.
- Managed the mortgage process from start to finish:
  - Identified and steered clients toward best mortgage product for their individual needs and circumstances.
  - Guided clients step-by-step through the process, ensuring their complete understanding of terms, requirements, fees, timelines, and other details.
  - Monitored progress through the lending cycle and kept clients informed.
  - Ensured provision of clean title; prepared loan package; secured funding.
  - Strove for 100% customer satisfaction and actively solicited referrals from happy clients.
- Gained a reputation as ideal partner for first-time home buyers. Counseled and guided clients through what can be a complex and overwhelming process.
- After 1 year, promoted to **LOAN MANAGER:**
  - Trained, mentored, supported, and led a team of 5 Loan Originators while continuing to generate new business.
  - Set protocols and expectations for client communication and follow-up.

WHOLESALE LOAN OFFICER | 2004–2005 | Midwest Savings Bank, Ankeny, IA

In B2B sales/relationship management role, represented Midwest Savings Bank mortgage products to loan officers working with individual home-buying clients.

LOAN ORIGINATOR | 2003–2004 | Reliable Loan, Des Moines, IA

Captured new business and served clients throughout the mortgage lending process. Known for clear communication, efficient processes, and excellent customer service.

Current Leadership & Management Experience

ADMINISTRATIVE MANAGER | 2019–Present | Highland Park Community Church Youth Group Program, Des Moines, IA

Restored integrity to member database and trained staff in best practices for data management. Assumed management of email communications; improved email response rate to 80% and click-through registrations to 50%.

DIRECTOR | 2016–2017 | THRIVE Co-Op, Highland Park, IA

Conceived and launched innovative enrichment program for homeschooled children. Negotiated facility lease; secured state licenses and permits. Created marketing strategy and materials and attracted 42 students in first year.

Education

BSBA, Marketing & Management | **MS,** Public Administration | University of Iowa, Iowa City, IA

Louise Kursmark, MRW, CPRW, JCTC, CEIP, CCM • Best Impression Career Services • louisekursmark.com

Lucas Adams

WAREHOUSE SUPERVISOR

Wayne, NJ | 973-555-1111 | ljadams@ymail.com

Offering 14 years of experience in all aspects of material handling and storage; 8 years in management. Unique ability for 3-dimensional thinking with quick recall of numerous and complex material locations within a huge warehouse. Seeking to return to former career where there is a need for a conscientious and well-organized leader willing to go the extra mile to ensure efficient operations.

CORE COMPETENCIES

✓ **Operating and/or repairing:** electrical/mechanical forklifts … hand trucks … pallet jacks … cherry pickers … various automated equipment
✓ **Driving:** box trucks and delivery vans (commercial driver's license)
✓ **Managing inventory:** daily record keeping … monthly cycle counts … yearly audits
✓ **Leading teams:** shipping/receiving … picking/packing … staging … loading/unloading trucks
✓ **Assisting in production area:** setting up machinery for specialized projects

RELATED EXPERIENCE

SHIPPING & RECEIVING MANAGER, 14 years   Holstead Fabricators, Inc., Paterson, NJ
Custom molding and stamping facility using metals and plastics to make products for the medical, automotive, and electronics industries.

- Started as assembler and earned 4 rapid promotions, advancing to comanage a 10,000-sq.-ft. warehouse, formerly operating out of 3 locations. **Impressed superiors with knowledge** of where all pieces were stored.
- Adapted to frequent management changes. Provided department input in bi-weekly meetings and **enforced any new directives to enhance operations.**
- Trained, scheduled, and led team of 5–7 warehouse workers. **Ensured accuracy and timeliness of picking and packing parts** ranging from minuscule clips to assemblies weighing up to 90 lbs.
- Maintained accurate shipment and inventory records in an automated system monitoring 30,000 parts in different locations for easy access when needed. **Researched reasons for over or short quantities** to bring physical inventory in line with books.
- Expedited urgent materials needed before next FedEx pick-up. **Saved truck rental costs** by personally making local deliveries using a 28-foot box truck.

CURRENT EXPERIENCE

DATA CENTER TECHNICIAN, 6 years   BioData Systems, Dover, NJ
Provider of outsourced sleep diagnostic services.

- As sole operator on my shift, process sleep study files received from 30 sites in the Northeast. **Handle an average of 200 transmissions daily** at peak of operations.
- Organize data consisting of 7–12 pages per file to prepare for scoring by doctors. **Achieved 97% accuracy** in typing, formatting, scanning, and manipulating pages in required order.
- Address minor computer problems. **Avoided IT service calls, repeatedly saving half-day system downtime.**
- Overcame challenges in receiving data from some locations to meet strict turnaround deadlines. **Prevented loss of revenue due to late submissions.**

TRAINING

Bergen County Vo-Tech Institute | CNC Machining Technology

Melanie Noonan • Peripheral Pro • peripro1@aol.com

PART VI:
Linked Profiles

A recruiter once told us, "If you're not on LinkedIn, you don't exist."

Those are very wise words for every job seeker, from graduating students and young professionals to senior managers and executives, and everyone in between. Whether actively engaged in a job search or working to build your professional profile for current and/or future opportunities, LinkedIn (LI) is, and will continue to be, a vital component of everyone's search campaign.

At its very foundation, LI is a social network for professionals. It is the business-suited version of Facebook, Instagram, YouTube, TikTok, and other sites that promote interaction, sharing, and self-expression.

When it comes to job search and career management, your LI profile is as important as your resume. That's because millions of people use LinkedIn, it's the go-to resource for recruiters and hiring managers, and it will almost always be the first thing that people find when they search for you online.

Equally important, LI itself is a vast and powerful network. It offers tools and resources that make it easy for you to find and connect with people, broaden your existing web of contacts, and make connections that will allow you to penetrate your target employers.

What's more, LinkedIn is often the first site that people access to find out about *you*—either before or after they've seen your resume or met you in person. It is an opportunity for you to share *more* and *more insightful* information about yourself, your value, and your personal brand.

As recruiters, employers, and job seekers have discovered its value, LI has grown exponentially, from 37 million members in 2009 to 828 million members in 2022. Today a LinkedIn profile is not just nice to have; it's a necessity for professionals who are serious about their careers and—of particular relevance to you—in the job market for new opportunities.

CHAPTER 18:
Writing Powerful & Well-Positioned LinkedIn Profiles

Now that you've written, formatted, and designed a resume to favorably position yourself in the job market, you have one more essential project to undertake—your LinkedIn (LI) profile. Today's job search is heavily digital-based, and LI will most likely be your most important digital asset, so you must dedicate the time to create a profile that will work hand-in-hand with your resume to tell your whole career story.

Why Not Copy and Paste Your Resume?

We've been asked this question many times, and we get it. You've spent a lot of time and effort creating a great resume that sells your value, qualifications, achievements, and more. Why not simply copy that content into the relevant sections of your profile?

Certainly, that's an option, but we don't recommend it. Here's why:

- As mentioned, many readers will view your profile after seeing your resume. If your profile simply reiterates what they already know, they've wasted their time and you've wasted the opportunity to share even more compelling and relevant information.

- LinkedIn is a different medium than a resume, with its traditional structure and page limitations. As you'll read in this chapter, we recommend a different writing style for your profile and the inclusion of different information to help your readers go beyond your resume, learn more about you and your career, and feel a connection to you.

Now that you understand the value of a powerful LI profile, let's explore how to write one. It's important to note that all of the material you uncovered and wrote about in your resume will come into play as the foundation for *what* you write in your profile, *why*, and *how*. Simply put, you're telling your career story in a different way, with different details, and in a different tone and writing style.

> **PRO TIP: LinkedIn gives readers a quick bird's-eye view of you and your career and the option to click to "see more" in any section.** For the text that will automatically display (the first few lines in every section), be sure that you're highlighting the most important things about you and the most interesting and/or notable things about your performance in each position.
>
> Once readers click to see more, they are already interested. You can then share more information that is engaging, interesting, impressive, relevant to your brand, and supportive of your career objectives.

Five Keys to a Winning LinkedIn Profile

As you begin to write your profile, focus on the following 5 key elements. Each is important to create a profile that will attract, interest, and engage your readers.

Keywords

On LinkedIn, perhaps even more so than in your resume, keywords are king. Recruiter and employer searches are keyword-driven, so to be found for appropriate positions, you must include all of the relevant keywords and keyword phrases throughout your profile.

As we've discussed with regard to your resume, keywords are really nothing more than the language of your profession. They describe your knowledge and expertise. They establish that you have worked in particular functions and industries, held specific responsibilities, have a certain education level, and so much more.

There is no magic, one-size-fits-all approach to keyword optimization on LinkedIn. Use your judgment in integrating keywords into the various sections of your profile. When you've finished writing it, you'll find that keywords naturally fall in everywhere.

As well, consider adding a keyword list at the bottom of Summary/About and at the end of each position description in Experience. You'll increase your keyword density and reinforce the *right* terms for each job you've held, as they relate to your current search.

Personality and Insight

Your LI profile is *not* your resume. It can be more personal and less formal. You can share details that don't obviously relate to your professional qualifications but that can help readers understand both your professional style and personality. It's often the extra information that will attract people to you.

Interwoven among all of your professional experiences and qualifications should be information about you, your demeanor, what you're great at, what inspires you, and what others say about you. Let your personality shine through in both *what* you write and *how* you present it.

Not sure where to start or how to do that? Ask yourself a few questions to spark ideas beyond typical resume thinking, and use what you uncover to inject your personality into the content that you create.

- How are you different from other candidates for the same positions?
- How do you approach challenges?
- What gives you the most professional and personal satisfaction?
- What do you enjoy doing—on or off the job?
- How do others (your staff, your bosses, your family and friends) describe you?
- How do you bring your personality to work?
- How can you help readers understand who you are?
- Who or what has influenced you in your life?
- What motivates you and why?

Storytelling

Humans are hard-wired to respond to stories. Stories stir emotions. They activate multiple areas of our brains. And perhaps most importantly, stories are what people remember (over facts and figures).

When you include stories in your career marketing messages—resume and cover letter, interviews, and LI profile—you instantly make yourself more memorable and more distinctive.

As well, you may create positive perceptions of who you are that cannot be ascertained from a resume or straightforward career facts. You can seem more likeable, funnier, wittier, more sympathetic, more human.

To spark your thinking around stories you might include in your profile, ask yourself questions like these:

- How did you get where you are today?
- How did you choose your line of work?
- How has your past led to your present (and future)?
- What is the accomplishment that you're most proud of?
- What was the greatest challenge or obstacle you've overcome and how?
- What excites you most about your current career track?

Then, think about what each story illustrates about you, what themes from your background might connect, and how to help readers see you in your desired future roles. Use the stories that support your current objectives and align with your personal brand.

There are many ways to incorporate stories into your profile. Some stories are brief excerpts that help frame an experience or achievement. Others are complete "origin stories" that take up the entire Summary/About. Still others provide context for your career choices. Because writing is such an organic process, you'll know where your stories fit in best as you write them.

As with all of your career messages, use good judgment in what you share and how you tell your stories. LinkedIn is a *professional* networking site, and everything in your profile, including your stories, should bolster your professional brand and image. But don't be afraid to reveal a bit more about yourself than perhaps you are used to sharing. Authenticity is an important element of your profile, and stories are a great way to exude your genuine self.

Tone and Structure

Just as in your resume, how you write and structure your profile can affect how easily and how often it is read. Keep these guidelines in mind as you are writing, editing, and polishing your profile.

- **Write in first person and use the word "I."** While it's not a hard-and-fast rule that your profile must be in first person, we strongly recommend it. It creates a friendlier and more social tone than writing about yourself in a third-person voice (using "he" or "she" instead of "I") that reads as though you are writing about someone else.

- **Use natural language—not "resume speak."** When we write resumes, we deliberately use a succinct writing style to get quickly to the point. In addition to the word "I," we often omit modifiers such as a, an, the, by, etc. That's fine for a resume—in fact, it's expected. On LI, a more relaxed, conversational style is appropriate. However, relaxed doesn't mean sloppy! Never forget the rules of good grammar, spelling, and punctuation.

- **Write in short bursts of information.** Just as in your resume, keep in mind how people actually read. They skim, they seek to pick up information quickly, and they move on if their attention isn't quickly captured. When writing your profile, break up big chunks of text into multiple short paragraphs or lists of bulleted items. Allow ample white space so that readers can quickly absorb one bite of information and then move on to the next.

- **Feel free to use all of the available space.** LI has strict character allowances for each section of the profile. Some of these allowances are quite expansive. But, as mentioned, readers will see only the first 3 lines of content and then must click to "see more." Give it to them!

- **Capture attention in the first 3 lines.** What can you say to entice readers to want to "see more"? If you don't engage their interest quickly, they may never take the time to learn more about you.

- **Add emphasis the old-fashioned (typewriter) way.** On LI you can't use the font enhancements and design elements that you likely employed in your resume. You can use ALL CAPS, and you can use various symbols to create borders and bullets. We recommend that you do so. They really help to add distinction and readability to your profile. Consider one or more of these:

Photograph

Although you might consider this a minor point, it is not. We strongly recommend that your profile include a photo—a professional-looking headshot. Many viewers see the lack of a photo as a red flag and a sign of inauthenticity. Don't instantly eliminate yourself from consideration.

> **PRO TIP: Build your visibility through active engagement.** Once your profile is complete, you can multiply its effectiveness by increasing your activity. Share updates, publish articles, comment on posts from your network, join groups, follow industry leaders, and otherwise maintain an active presence. Investing just a few minutes a day will build your online image quickly and professionally.

Tips for Writing Major Sections of Your Profile

The best way to demonstrate what makes for a winning LI profile is to showcase few excellent samples. But first we will share best practices for each of the main sections (Headline, Summary/About, and Experience) as well as guidelines for the remainder of your profile.

Headline (220-character limit, including spaces)

Your Headline appears immediately under your name and photo at the top of your profile. The default content is your current or most recent job title, but you can and should change that.

We recommend a Headline that still quickly tells readers *who* you are but goes beyond simply your job title. Consider adding some of the following to your headline if relevant to your career and objectives:

- Areas of interest or influence
- Distinguishing credentials, qualifications, or awards
- A career achievement highlight
- Your personal brand—what you're known for
- Your key areas of expertise

Summary/About (2600-character limit, including spaces)

The default for this section is blank. Yet it may be, and often is, the most important section of your profile because it is one of the very first things that readers see. It is certainly the most read. Your challenge with this section is to give your readers interesting, informative, and engaging information.

There is no single formula for writing the Summary/About, as you'll see in the samples that follow. Here are a few guidelines to get you started:

- Incorporate keywords in your content and possibly in a separate listing at the end of the section.
- Tell a story or stories to give readers insight into *who* you are, *why* you've been successful, *what* motivates and excites you, and the *value* you bring to your next role.
- Mention a few of your most notable career achievements—be specific.
- Consider touching on intangibles such as leadership skills, communication and persuasion skills, public speaking talents, creativity, work ethic, or any others that help readers understand *how* you work, *why* you've been successful, and *why* you'll continue to excel.
- Connect the dots from your past experiences to your current goals/future career. This is extremely helpful, particularly if you are changing careers or industries. What caused that choice? Tell the story so that readers understand the connection.
- If you are still employed, paint the picture of someone who is a top performer in your current position. Certainly, don't say anything about looking for your next job.
- If you are not employed, we still don't recommend that you announce that you are "open to opportunities." Of course, you are—who isn't? Instead, focus on your story and your value.
- Be strategic—be certain that your story line, the achievements you've highlighted, and the insights you've shared are all congruent with your current career objectives.

Experience (2000-character limit, including spaces, for each position)

The challenge in writing Experience is presenting essentially the same information as in your resume but in a different way.

An added complication is that, because LI is a public profile, you may not want to share financial and other potentially sensitive details that may feature prominently in your resume. Yet you do want to give concrete examples of your effectiveness and success.

As you rethink how to present your career story, these prompts may help you come up with a framework that feels fresh and differentiated from your resume.

- Share context around each position. Why did you take the job? What was the challenge or opportunity? What did you do about it?

- Highlight major projects, challenges, and assignments—perhaps similar to your resume, but in a more relaxed, storytelling style.

- Share specific results whenever possible, because specifics are impressive and memorable.

- Connect to or continue themes that you wrote about in your Summary/About. For example, if you talked about being energized by tough challenges, frame each position in the context of a steep challenge, how you conquered it, and what the results were.

- When listing your employer name, use the drop-down list to populate the exact company name whenever possible. Your profile will then feature the company logo, and that can be a strong and instant identifier.

- Consider closing out each position with a list of relevant keywords that describe functions, skills, and technologies specific to that role.

Additional Profile Sections

Most of the remainder of your profile is self-explanatory, but here are a few tips:

- In **Education,** use the drop-down box to select your college or university and, if appropriate, the specific school at which you studied. When you do that, your profile will include the school logo—a nice visual enhancement and a way for fellow alumni to instantly feel a connection to you.

- Don't hesitate to add stories and details to **Education** if you believe they will help you. Let's say you studied at a university for 3 years but never finished your degree. A brief story can overcome a potential objection. For example, "I left school after 3 years when my startup reached $1M in sales and I needed to devote 100% of my time to running, building, and ultimately selling the company."

- Re-order your **Skills and Endorsements** if need be so that the top 3 shown are indeed your most valuable skills as relevant to your current career goals. This is particularly important if you are changing careers, changing industries, or looking for a big step up in responsibility. Many of your contacts may know you and endorse you for "Sales Management," for example, but you would prefer that "Product Design" be the first skill listed. You can move it to the top of the list.

- Do your best to secure several **Recommendations.** These must be written by others—you can't populate that section yourself. You might need to reach out to a few past and/or current colleagues and ask them to write a testimonial for you. Or, ask a close friend or family member who has a strong LI profile and presence themselves to write something that either supports your professional aspirations or demonstrates your personality, style, humanity, and other attributes that align with your career story and goals.

- Write **Recommendations** for others. These recommendations also populate your profile, and writing endorsements for others may prompt them to write one for you. And it's a nice way to initiate some networking outreach.

- In the **Interests** section, choose companies, colleges/universities, and thought leaders to follow. These listings will help populate your daily feed, provide a regular source of business and industry news, and expand your networking opportunities.

LinkedIn Profile Samples

Following are 4 LinkedIn profiles, each one preceded by its companion resume. You can see the wide variety of styles in which the profiles are written and structured to attract attention, provide insight, express personal brand, highlight keywords, and showcase career successes.

Then, look at the resume that accompanies each profile. Note what's similar and what's different, how the 2 documents complement each other, and how they show different facets of the person. Your resume and profile should also work together to tell your story, convey your value, and advance your career.

To best demonstrate the similarities and differences between each sample LI profile and its accompanying resume, we've created "Compare & Contrast" charts. Review them carefully as you're looking at each document to see how each is uniquely written to capture the attention of targeted readers.

Nate Andrews Resume & LI Profile—pages 155–156

Nate Andrews is a recent BS graduate and a current MS student in Aerospace Engineering. He is targeting both a summer internship and then his first professional job in the AE field.

HEADLINE	
Resume	**LinkedIn Profile**
• Clearly communicates both *who* Nate is and *what* opportunities he is pursuing. • Shares his strongest qualifications—technical, computer science, research, communications, and problem solving—all of which are important keywords for the career path he is pursuing. • Identifies the field he is targeting—Aerospace Engineering.	• Uses the same headline as his resume. • Showcases vital keywords from the onset by including both hard-skill keywords (e.g., aerospace engineering, computer science) and soft-skill keywords (e.g., communication, problem solving) at the very beginning of his profile.

SUMMARY/ABOUT

Resume

- Integrates 3 distinct sections to create a cohesive Summary that is rich in content and keywords.

- Highlights his relevant aerospace experience, citing "NASA-funded space weather research and corporate engineering proposal development."

- Clearly communicates his objectives for both a 2023 internship and 2024 full-time position, providing him with flexibility to use the resume for both purposes and to communicate long-term career interests to his internship employer— in hopes of gaining a permanent job offer post-internship!

- Showcases a powerful list of keywords that are an accumulation of his skills and relevant course-work—an excellent way to integrate important keywords when a job seeker does not have those qualifications from on-the-job experience.

LinkedIn Profile

- Demonstrates how effective it can be to write in the first person using the word "I." Readers quickly get a sense of *who* Nate is, personally and professionally.

- Communicates the *who* in the very first sentence and directly links it to the dual internship and full-time professional opportunities he is pursuing.

- Uses all-caps headings to separate each short section and make each an easy-to-read bite of information.

- Addresses Nate's passion for problem solving and his exceptional mathematical abilities (in the STRONG TECHNICAL ACUMEN section) and then uses that information as a springboard to introduce some of the leading-edge work that he's doing for NASA.

- Details some of his essential workplace skills and even touts that he earned Eagle Scout status.

- Concludes with a keyword-rich listing (copied directly from his resume) of essential skills for individuals targeting entry-level professional positions in Aerospace Engineering.

EXPERIENCE

Resume

- Transforms Nate's Research and Internship experiences into a strong Professional Experience and Research section complete with employers, titles, dates, and projects.

- Begins each description with a 2-line overview of responsibilities, followed by bullet points that showcase his contributions—just as with any professional resume.

- Immediately transitions the perception of Nate from "just" a graduating student into an experienced young professional.

LinkedIn Profile

- Uses the same overall strategy as his resume, but shortens the descriptions to showcase his #1 project and/or achievement for each role.

- Injects a bit of personality into the profile through the use of the first-person "I" and words such as "exciting" and "enjoyed."

- Provides a quick and clear overview of all 4 of Nate's positions that directly support his objective.

NATE ANDREWS

(555) 555-5555 ◆ andrews22@cmu.edu
www.linkedin.com/in/andrews22 ◆ Pittsburgh, PA 55201

AEROSPACE ENGINEERING GRADUATE STUDENT → *Leveraging technical, computer science, research, communication, and problem-solving skills to advance aerospace engineering initiatives.*

High-achieving, collaborative aerospace engineer with experience in NASA-funded space weather research and corporate engineering proposal development pursuing 2023 Summer Internship and Jan 2024 full-time position.

Skill, Competencies, and Relevant Coursework

MATLAB ● Spacecraft Design ● Space Weather ● Astro Mechanics ● Orbit Determination ● GPS Theory & Design
Computer Science Logic ● Propulsion Systems ● Thermodynamics ● Aero/Hydrodynamics ● AutoCAD ● Inventor
Research ● Client Proposals ● Presentations ● Interdisciplinary Collaboration ● Technical Writing ● MS Office

EDUCATION AND HONORS

M.S. in Aerospace Engineering – CARNEGIE MELLON UNIVERSITY – *Expected* Dec 2023
GPA: **4.00** ● Accelerated Graduate School Program ● NASA-Funded Research Project Assistant

B.S. in Aerospace Engineering – CARNEGIE MELLON UNIVERSITY – May 2022
GPA: **3.75** ● Honors College ● Dean's List with Distinction ● AIAA Senior Capstone Spacecraft Design Team Leader

Eagle Scout – 2016 ● **AMERICAN INSTITUTE OF AERONAUTICS AND ASTRONAUTICS (AIAA) –** Member Since 2020

PROFESSIONAL EXPERIENCE AND RESEARCH

CARNEGIE MELLON, COLLEGE OF ENGINEERING – *Pittsburgh, PA*

Graduate Research Assistant – NASA-Funded Space Weather Thesis   **Aug 2022–Present**
Analyzing magnetospheric and solar wind data to identify signatures with periods matching atmospheric planetary waves. Compiling relevant characteristic data, interpreting and presenting findings, and preparing for publication.
- Relate planetary waves to space weather waves and how they affect ionosphere where ICON Mission is positioned.
- Confer with NASA engineers and university professor to review project status and determine next steps.

Undergraduate Research Assistant – Orbit Determination with Laser Radar Data   **Aug 2021–May 2022**
Proved use of laser radar data to track unknown satellites and space debris without corner-cube retro-reflectors under specific conditions by coupling laser range data with optically derived angular data. Presented findings to peers.
- Created MATLAB algorithm to track space objects, ascertained initial orbit data, and compared to known location.
- Evaluated satellite laser ranging data to determine true photons reflecting off known spacecraft.

Undergraduate Research Assistant – NASA ICON Mission   **Aug 2020–May 2021**
Developed remote sensing geometry tools (MATLAB Scripts) currently utilized by NASA satellite to aid in validation and collaboration of data collection for interactions between Earth's atmosphere and the space environment.
- Visualized timeline of maneuvers for satellite and used Mighti A and B, FUV, and EUV space weather instruments.
- Identified opportunities for collaboration between ICON satellite, TIMED satellite, and ground stations.

ENGINEERING ASSOCIATES OF MORRISTOWN – *Morristown, NJ*

Engineering Intern – Reported to Head of Architectural Engineering   **May 2020–Aug 2021**
Drafted proposals, conducted field work, and created AutoCAD drawings for NJ Office of Homeland Security and Preparedness, NJ Department of Property Management and Construction, pharmaceuticals firms, and NJ schools.
- Designed secure government rooms and collaborated with mechanical, electrical, civil, and structural engineers.

Julie Wyckoff, M.Ed., CPRW • Custom Career Solutions • customcareersolutions.com

LINKEDIN PROFILE—NATE ANDREWS

HEADLINE
Aerospace Engineering Graduate Student → Leveraging technical, computer science, research, communication, and problem-solving skills to advance aerospace engineering initiatives.

ABOUT
I am a 4.0 GPA GRADUATE STUDENT pursuing my M.S. in AEROSPACE ENGINEERING at Carnegie Mellon excited to contribute to the field of space and aviation as a Summer 2022 intern and full-time engineer in January 2023.

— — — — — — — — —

STRONG TECHNICAL ACUMEN

For as long as I can remember, I have had a passion for problem solving and exceptional mathematical abilities. As a Carnegie Mellon undergraduate and graduate student researcher for the NASA ICON Mission and Orbit Determination Project, I had the privilege of translating real-world situations into MATLAB computer science logic to drive new discovery and aerospace solutions utilized by satellites currently in orbit. My extensive research opportunities have culminated in my NASA-funded Space Weather Research Thesis Project.

— — — — — — — — —

DEMONSTRATED TEAMWORK AND LEADERSHIP SKILLS

Beyond astute technical capabilities, I bring the collaboration skills needed to thrive in both team settings and leadership roles. I have demonstrated and refined my communication skills developing client proposals across engineering disciplines as an intern for a corporate engineering firm and earning my Eagle Scout honor.

— — — — — — — — —

SKILLS, COMPETENCIES, AND RELEVANT COURSEWORK

MATLAB • Spacecraft Design • Astromechanics • Propulsion Systems • GPS Theory & Design • Space Weather • Computer Science Logic • Orbit Determination • Thermodynamics • Aero/Hydrodynamics • AutoCAD • Inventor • Research • Client Proposals • Presentations • Interdisciplinary Collaboration • Technical Writing • MS Office

EXPERIENCE
Graduate Research—Space Weather Senior Thesis Project: Carnegie Mellon, Aug 2022–Present

I am leading a space weather thesis research project analyzing magnetospheric and solar wind data to identify signatures with periods matching atmospheric planetary waves. Key activities are compiling relevant characteristic data, interpreting and presenting findings, and preparing for publication.

— — — — — — — — —

Undergraduate Research—Orbit Determination with Laser Radar Data: Carnegie Mellon, Aug 2021–May 2022

My research validated the use of laser radar data to track unknown satellites and space debris without corner-cube retroreflectors. I created MATLAB algorithm to track space objects and interpreted and presented findings.

— — — — — — — — —

Undergraduate Research—NASA ICON Mission: Carnegie Mellon, Aug 2020–May 2021

In this exciting role, I developed remote sensing geometry tools (MATLAB Scripts) that are currently being used by NASA satellites to aid in validation and collaboration of data collection for interactions between Earth's atmosphere and the space environment.

— — — — — — — — —

Engineering Intern: Engineering Associates of Morristown, May 2020–Aug 2021

Working for the Head of Architectural Engineering, I drafted client proposals, conducted field work, and created AutoCAD drawings for government agencies, pharma companies, and NJ public schools. I enjoyed collaborating with teams across all engineering disciplines—mechanical, electrical, civil, structural, and architectural.

Ahmed Sapra Resume & LI Profile—pages 158-161

Ahmed's 13-year technology career with one of the world's largest banking institutions has been distinguished by a number of promotions to his current position as a Lead Enterprise Architect. His goal now is to secure a higher-level position, and he'll be approaching companies across multiple industries.

HEADLINE

Resume	LinkedIn Profile
• Starts with a bold headline identifying *who* Ahmed is—by using titles that identify jobs he's performed as well as jobs he is targeting. • Highlights 4 areas of expertise in a shaded box. • Shares his personal branding statement, conveying his special talents and unique value.	• Follows a clear job title with areas of technical expertise that represent many vital keywords. • Divides keywords with checkmarks that capture attention and convey positive achievement. • Takes full advantage of LI's character allowance, using 217 of the available 220 characters.

SUMMARY/ABOUT

Resume	LinkedIn Profile
• Follows the strong Headline, subheading, and branding statement with 2 short paragraphs highlighting leadership in enterprise architecture. • Highlights 3 impressive achievements in a separate section headed "Value Creation." • Presents Areas of Expertise and a Technology Snapshot that bring the reader's eye to those all-important qualifications.	• Captures immediate interest with a question, then a brief story of how he chose his profession. • Explains his career progression in a short paragraph that is easy to skim and read. • Transitions to 4 sections with headings that call attention to important information and list vital and relevant skills, strengths, and experiences. • Uses headings, framed by arrows, to create a distinctive and attractive appearance consistent with the Experience section (below).

EXPERIENCE

Resume	LinkedIn Profile
• Shows a total span of employment with his long-term employer, JPMorgan Chase, immediately communicating a path of steady promotion. • Presents job details and achievement bullets very concisely—nothing is longer than 2 lines. • Highlights his #1 achievement in each job in bold. • Lists 8 relevant educational programs along with his Bachelor's and Master's degrees.	• Transforms his resume into less succinct and more personal language, writing in first person using "I." • Tells each job story in short paragraphs to enhance readability. • Follows each job description with a "Key Contributions" section with formatting that brings immediate visual attention to those important accomplishments.

AHMED SAPRA

BS & MS Computer Science | PMP

New York, NY 11234 | 917.237.5555 | ahmedsapra@myisp.com | www.linkedin.com/in/ahmedsapra

FORTUNE 500 ENTERPRISE ARCHITECT EXPERT ➡ DIRECTOR | CHIEF ARCHITECT

Requirements Gathering | IT Strategy | Solution Delivery | Architecture Management

Translate big-picture requirements into technical solutions driving business outcomes at less cost

Strategic thinker, decisive and confident leader of enterprise architecture for multiple business lines with global impact. Nurture team environment where employees are empowered, valued, and supported.

Head of digital transformation and system architecture improvements aimed at best-in-class architecture management, cost savings, and future state readiness and requiring people management of geographically dispersed teams.

VALUE CREATION

- ❑ **Calculated $15M cost savings** over 2 years from rollout of enhanced business architecture.

- ❑ **Aligned architecture strategy for 3 major financial risk areas** to support business goals.

- ❑ **Delivered world-class solutions to diverse stakeholder groups,** aligning IT with business strategy.

AREAS OF EXPERTISE	Enterprise Architecture	Solution Architecture	Risk Management	Technology Governance	Software Development	Business and Technical Requirements	Strategic Roadmaps	Business Process Re-Engineering	Project Management	Basel I – III
TECHNOLOGY SNAPSHOT	Java Programming Languages (J2SE, J2EE)	XML	HTML	C++	WebSphere Application Server	WebSphere MQ	Unix	Windows	IBM iSeries	Eclipse	NetBeans	Google Cloud Platform Professional Architect	TOGAF and Agile Certified

PROFESSIONAL EXPERIENCE

JPMorgan Chase *(#19 on Fortune 500)* | New York, NY   2010–Present

LEAD ARCHITECT   2020–Present

Global Risk Analytics, Retail Credit Risk, and US Risk

Direct Reports: 3 | Indirect Reports: 8 Senior Architects in US, Europe, and Asia

Head current and future-state business architecture, IT governance, and continuous improvement for high-impact banking functions. Develop architecture roadmaps for operational resiliency and cost reduction.

Key project: planning and leading digital transformation of wholesale credit risk, building analytical models for 3 lines of business (commercial banking, institutional banking, and finance) affecting all 64 operating countries.

- ▪ **On track to save $18M+ in 3 years by harmonizing enterprise architecture to technical landscape.**
- ▪ Collaborating on multi-country system architecture project to reduce costs 30%+ and time to market 60%.
- ▪ Serve as lead architect on Brexit, Basel III, and General Data Protection Regulation (GDPR) projects.
- ▪ Consult on enterprise architecture and IT standards to multiple stakeholders in other business lines.

Brenda Collard-Mills, MRW, NCOPE, CRS • Robust Resumes and Resources • robustresumesandresources.com

JPMorgan Chase (continued)

LEAD ARCHITECT   2016–2020

Wholesale Credit Risk and Global Risk Analytics

Structured enterprise architecture to deliver solutions for 2 (often competing) stakeholder groups and architectural programs that align IT with business strategy. Provided enterprise architecture standards and status reports.

Liaised with senior stakeholders to design system solutions based on needs analysis. Provided strategic roadmaps synced to future state. Met or exceeded all architecture management performance goals and deliverables.

- **Saved $175K through software obsolescence and reinvested in IT systems development.**
- Worked within budget by syncing project funding with IT priorities and improving systems design process.
- Cut costs by creating baseline metrics to measure quality of 5 major codebases against IT standards.

SOLUTION ARCHITECT   2012–2016

Wholesale Credit Risk – Limits and Mitigants

Team leadership of local and offshore resources in US and Asia

Handled solution architecture, business analysis, and project management for core commercial lending systems providing real-time credit limit and collateral management across the global organization.

Named technical lead on business lending, credit risk, and Basel II capital allocation projects. Supervised 24-person team engaged in product realization and testing. Controlled IT spend to meet ~$3M P&L mandate.

- **Automated capital calculation risk metric to manage ~$450B in corporate risk-weighted assets.**
- Executed cost-neutral financial management — held costs to within 10% of target spend.

JAVA DEVELOPER   2010–2012

Provided object-oriented software design, programming, and implementation support for main commercial credit application processing systems. Compiled test plans and documentation for commercial lending systems.

- **Deployed cost-efficient lending systems to 70+ countries with minimal rework requests by stakeholders.**

TRAINING AND EDUCATION

Member—Project Management Institute (2012–Present)

Leadership Effectiveness	2021
Google Cloud Platform Certified Professional Architect	2020
Fusion Enhanced Leadership Training	2015
PMI Agile Certified Practitioner	2013
Certified Project Management Professional	2012
The Open Group Architecture Framework (TOGAF) Certification	2008
Sun Certified Java Web Component Developer	2005
Sun Certified Java Programmer	2003

MASTER OF SCIENCE and BACHELOR OF SCIENCE – Computer Science
Cornell University

LINKEDIN PROFILE—AHMED SAPRA

HEADLINE

LEAD ARCHITECT—Enterprise Architecture for Fortune 500 Company ✔ IT Governance ✔ Systems + Software Development ✔ IT Strategy ✔ Strategic Roadmaps ✔ Certified in Project Management, Agile, TOGAF, Google Cloud Platform

ABOUT

How does a medical researcher become an enterprise architect for a major financial institution? Halfway through my PhD studies at Bodine Cancer center, I took a break and used the time to assess my career goals. That assessment led to a pivot to computer science, where I found a degree of experimentation and intellectual rigor that is similar to life sciences but more closely suited to my interests in business and people leadership.

My first tech role was still in the medical sector as a software developer analyzing data for late-phase clinical trials. I was there only a year before making the move to JPMorgan Chase and ultimately advancing to my current role as a lead architect structuring enterprise architecture for multiple lines of business.

► THINGS I DO WELL ◄
➥ See big-picture requirements and devise solutions in a highly regulated environment
➥ Provide leadership to people, processes, and technology with global impact
➥ Structure for best-in-class architecture management and cost savings
➥ Develop and enhance current and future state business architecture
➥ Manage enterprise architecture for business functions with high operational risk
➥ Collaborate on multi-country, multi-year system architecture working groups
➥ Match IT priorities to budget and tightly control for cost-neutral project finance

► INDUSTRY QUALIFICATIONS ◄
➥ Project Management Professional
➥ Former Director of Application Support, PMI New York City
➥ Google Cloud Platform Certified Professional Architect
➥ PMI Agile Certified Practitioner
➥ Certified Project Management Professional
➥ TOGAF Certification
➥ Sun Certified Java Web Component Developer
➥ Sun Certified Java Programmer
➥ BS in Computer Science

► LEADERSHIP ATTRIBUTES ◄
➥ People management of senior architects in US, Europe, and Asia
➥ Leadership effectiveness training
➥ Certified Level 2 Alpine Ski Instructor and Children's Specialist
➥ Known for critical thinking, empathy, and excellent communication

► SIGNATURE STRENGTHS ◄
BUSINESS ➥ Enterprise Architecture, IT Strategy, Requirements Analysis, Solution Delivery, Risk Management, Digital Transformation, Technology Governance, Strategic Roadmaps, Project Management, Basel I, II, III

TECHNOLOGY ➥ Java Programming Languages (J2SE, J2EE), XML, HTML, C++, WebSphere Application Server, WebSphere MQ, Unix, Windows, IBM iSeries, Eclipse, NetBeans

EXPERIENCE

Lead Architect ▶ Enterprise Architecture ▶ Global Risk Analytics, Retail Credit Risk, US Risk
JPMorgan Chase, New York, NY, 2019–Present

I manage the global enterprise architecture for 3 major business lines in 64 countries. I work with business stakeholders and IT management worldwide — a team of senior architects in the US, Europe, and Asia — and on major IT initiatives pertaining to Brexit, Basel III, and GDPR compliance.

I develop and maintain current and future state business architecture and IT governance, and create roadmaps and process efficiencies to drive revenue and reduce operational friction in measuring financial and non-financial risk.

A large ongoing project is a complex multi-year, multi-country redesign of system architecture for 3 large lines of business to extract costs and expedite time to market. My role as lead architect is to build and run the analytical models for those business functions.

▶ KEY CONTRIBUTIONS ◀
➡ Mapped a new strategic architecture estimated to save millions within 3 years of full implementation.
➡ Integrated IT governance into all technical solutions to improve total cost of ownership.

Lead Architect ▶ Architecture Management ▶ Wholesale Credit Risk ▶ Global Risk Analytics
JPMorgan Chase, New York, NY, 2014–2018

I earned lead architect after managing solution architecture for 2 corporate lending systems critical to wholesale credit risk. In this expanded role, I worked with senior stakeholders on requirements analysis to solve their most pressing problems by building software systems synced to business vision.

Performance goals for architecture management and deliverables were met or exceeded; projects were structured for cost neutrality; systems design process was enhanced; and architecture strategy was tied to business strategy, process efficiency, and cost control.

▶ KEY CONTRIBUTIONS ◀
➡ Offset limited budget by flagging redundant software to free up funds for systems development.
➡ Defined baseline metrics to measure codebase quality compared to IT standards.

Solution Architect ▶ Wholesale Credit Risk ▶ Limits and Mitigants
JPMorgan Chase, New York, NY, 2006–2014

I evolved the role into heading solution and enterprise architecture management of 2 core commercial lending systems used globally; served as technical lead on 3 key projects (business lending, credit risk, and Basel II capital location); and led product realization and testing teams in US and India.

Team efforts improved capital allocation (per Basel II) and collateral management enterprise wide.

▶ KEY CONTRIBUTIONS ◀
➡ Delivered credit limit management system 3 months ahead of schedule.
➡ Automated capital risk calculation for $Bs in corporate risk-weighted assets.

Java Developer ▶ Commercial Credit ▶ Commercial Lending
JPMorgan Chase, New York, NY, 2002–2006

My technology career started here — providing object-oriented analysis, design, and implementation of high-quality code and software for commercial credit and commercial lending, ensuring systems met the business requirements and needs of 30,000 users across 70+ countries.

J.D. Cordero Resume & LI Profile—pages 163–166

J.D. has been in sales and business development for more than a decade. His entire career has been spent with companies that produce and sell technical products and systems to customers in heavy industries, such as oil and renewable energy. He's looking for another sales leadership role, but he is open to a variety of industries and thus does not want to over-emphasize his industrial background.

HEADLINE

Resume	LinkedIn Profile
• Leads with a bold headline that immediately proclaims his profession and current job targets.	• Immediately shares *who* he is to give readers an instant framework for the profile that follows.
• Further identifies his expertise selling "highly technical products and integrated solutions."	• Expands on his *who* statement by stating the value that he brings to every role.

SUMMARY/ABOUT

Resume	LinkedIn Profile
• Uses bold type to further identify *who* he is in 3 short paragraphs that are packed with keywords describing all of the primary activities of his job as a sales executive.	• Starts with a story that captures attention, then segues into how he uses his skills on the job now.
• Highlights 4 key accomplishments in a shaded box featuring bullet points that lead with numbers, in bold, to emphasize impressive and diverse results.	• Provides 3 specific examples of challenges he's faced and value he's delivered.
	• Describe 2 things he "loves most about sales," providing insight into his personality.
	• Draws atttention with a bold arrow-shaped bullet.
	• Closes with a concise description of his expertise and an invitation to connect with him by email

EXPERIENCE

Resume	LinkedIn Profile
• Highlights the #1 achievement of each job in bold type in a shaded box just below the job title.	• Begins each position with a "Performance Highlight" that makes the #1 achievement highly visible even if readers don't click to "see more."
• Describes the context of each position in a short paragraph that also includes important details such as number of staff he managed.	• Follows with a "Scope" framework for each job.
• Leads each bullet point with a strong verb, in bold type, to inject the resume with energy and draw attention to his accomplishments.	• Transitions into a conversational, storytelling style.
	• Creates a consistent look and feel with Summary/About by using the same arrow bullet.
• Combines his earliest career experience in 4 short bullets rather than a separate listing for each.	• Closes with a reference to the story that he used to introduce his Summary/About, again creating consistency and coherence from start to finish.

J.D. Cordero

jdcordero@email.com • 701-232-0990 • linkedin.com/in/j-d-cordero

Sales and Business Development Executive
Highly Technical Products and Integrated Solutions

Growth catalyst with a consistent career history of delivering revenue, profit, and market-share gains for companies in technically sophisticated industries.

- **#1** market share for a Drill Technologies product line—a last-to-first transformation
- **$55M** revenue in first-year sales of a new integrated solutions offering
- **21%** surge in profit margins through a pricing structure overhaul
- **70%** expansion of a technology company's customer base, driving **35%** revenue growth in 1 year

Data-guided strategist who applies analytical skills, customer knowledge, and competitive drive to succeed at diverse sales challenges: capturing new business, turning around underperforming sales organizations, retaining and expanding multi-year contracts, resolving customer issues, and identifying new revenue streams.

Motivational leader able to recruit and develop sales talent, establish clear performance measures, and consistently build top-performing sales teams.

Professional Experience

Industrial Technical Solutions, Fargo, ND   2021–2023
DIRECTOR, GLOBAL SALES & STRATEGIC ACCOUNTS

Generated $55M first-year revenue for new business unit, driving both internal and external marketing to build awareness and generate opportunities.

Recruited to lead a new global sales organization promoting integrated solutions to industrial clients worldwide. Led sales and account management team—7 direct reports at peak and up to 50 global resources.

- **Created** new structure for pursuing integrated solutions sales—new global account management matrix, communication protocols, and customer engagement model.
- **Quickly** identified, pursued, and landed first award—an $18M large-scale intervention project.
- **Aligned** sales cycle with project workflow to build internal collaboration and pave the way to larger opportunities.

McCarron Technology, San Jose, CA   2019–2021
GLOBAL SALES DIRECTOR

Grew revenue 35% YOY after driving a 70% expansion of the customer base.

Brought on board to accelerate growth of technology company serving renewable energy companies worldwide. Managed a team of Country Managers, Senior Technical Managers, and Senior Application Engineers.

- **Immediately** tackled key challenge—an extremely limited customer base—by designing and executing growth strategy centered on expanding and diversifying revenue streams.
- **Targeted** strategic accounts, aligned sales talent with top targets, and incentivized sales team to double the customer base.
- **Adjusted** pricing model to drive up margins for high-value solutions.
- **Introduced** a highly profitable insurance product that reduced customer risk and became a popular add-on.
- **Secured** company's first sales in both Costa Rica and Argentina, generating $2M+ in new revenue and establishing a toehold in emerging markets.

Louise Kursmark, MRW, CPRW, JCTC, CEIP, CCM • Best Impression Career Services • louisekursmark.com

J.D. Cordero   Page 2

Drill Technologies, Inc., Fargo, ND   2005–2021
PRODUCT LINE SALES DIRECTOR, 2020–2021
PRODUCT LINE SALES MANAGER, 2016–2020

Transformed unprofitable, market-tailing product line to #1 in market share and 68% CAGR.

Challenged to turn around a failing product line: losing money and last in market share. Designed ambitious 5-year strategic growth plan, hired the right talent, developed strategic customer relationships, and moved aggressively to win key contracts and displace competition.

- **Increased** annual revenue from $25M to $115M in 4 years and rose to #1 in market share.
- **Retained** a critical account and cemented a new $35M agreement by identifying flaws in the proposal process that added unnecessary cost.
- **Captured** a $65M, 5-year award by brokering a deal to bundle multiple product lines for a prime customer.
- **Cultivated** a strategic target and grew the account from $0 to $6.5M in 2 years.
- **Improved** margins 21% YOY by implementing a new pricing structure.

Prior career progression with Drill Technologies   2005–2016

- **TECHNICAL SALES REPRESENTATIVE, North America Sales Region:** Built customer relationships that generated sales both immediately and years into the future—e.g., a relationship with a buyer at a strategic account later led to a 5-year, $10M contract. 2013–2016
- **ACCOUNT MANAGER, North America Sales Region:** Quickly succeeded in first sales role: Stimulated 15% share gain through a Miller-Heiman LAMP (Large Account Management Process)-based account strategy; garnered $6M in new product revenue after identifying a specific technology opportunity. 2010–2013
- **APPLICATIONS ENGINEER, Global Product Line:** Provided in-house technical support for an overseas pressure pumping contract. Created a new tracking database to maximize production, devised new forecasting methods, and reduced inventory carry levels. 2008–2010
- **DISTRICT ENGINEER | I/E TECHNICIAN, Gulf of Mexico Operations:** Gained hands-on experience working on offshore rigs and supporting complex oil and gas operations throughout the Gulf of Mexico. 2005–2008.

Education
MBA • SAN JOSE STATE UNIVERSITY, San Jose, CA
BS • UNIVERSITY OF NORTH DAKOTA, Grand Forks, LA

LINKEDIN PROFILE—J.D. CORDERO

HEADLINE

Sales & Business Development Executive: Delivering revenue, profit, and market-share gains for companies in technically sophisticated industries

ABOUT

Once, on an offshore oil rig, I put out a fire without losing my cool. That's a true story, but it's also a great metaphor for how I've performed in every job in a career that started in technical maintenance and advanced to senior sales leadership.

Every advancement presented new challenges along with new learning opportunities. And every time, I've responded quickly, found a solution, put it into action, and persisted until the fire was out.

The challenges have been diverse, requiring different solutions.

► For a technology company concentrated in a single market with few customers, my first move was to motivate the sales team to aggressively grow our customer base so that we could generate substantial new revenue (+35% over the prior year).

► To stimulate sales for a new business unit selling integrated solutions, I first needed to create the sales structure to bring together different company resources and form a compelling bid. Within a few months, we landed an $18M project.

► When handed a failing product line for one of the world's leading energy service companies, I knew there was no quick fix. I designed a comprehensive 5-year plan (strategy, process, people) to reach #1 market share ... and we met that goal in 4 years.

The two things I love most about sales:
► Listening to customers—taking the time to learn about them, their products, plans, projects, and problems—before framing the solution that will best meet their needs.

► The intricacy of every solution. Success requires technical product knowledge ... understanding of company processes and capabilities ... a deep desire to solve customer problems ... a talent for leading teams and inspiring people ... and, above all, the competitive drive to persist and win.

My expertise is in highly technical products (integrated solutions, energy industry products and services), where my combination of analytical skills, creativity, and customer focus can deliver major contracts and big sales wins. If you share my interests, let's connect for a conversation. jdcordero@email.com

EXPERIENCE

Director, Global Sales & Strategic Accounts—Industrial Technical Solutions, 2021–2023

► Performance Highlight: $55M first-year revenue for new business unit.

► Scope: Leadership of a new global sales organization. Creation of overall strategy, structure, and processes for landing business, managing accounts, and engaging customers.

The opportunity to take on a global leadership role was exciting. It was satisfying to build the organization from the ground up—to establish the how, what, when, and why of our policies and practices—and to lead my team in achieving big goals.

Once the groundwork was laid, we moved quickly to pursue projects. These were complex integrated solutions for energy companies around the globe. Landing our first ($18M) sale within a few months of startup, we set the pace for annual revenues that exceeded goals.

Global Sales Director—McCarron Technology, 2019–2021

► Performance Highlight: 35% YOY revenue growth.

► Scope: Vision, strategy, and execution to achieve ambitious growth goals. Leadership of a team of Country Managers, Senior Technical Managers, and Senior Application Engineers serving renewable energy companies worldwide.

McCarron was a company that was doing well but recognized it had all of its sales eggs in one basket—a select few customers provided the vast majority of revenue. I was recruited to build new "baskets" and generate new revenue in new markets.

I created a plan and directed/motivated my team to pursue strategic accounts in new target areas. Within a year, we had expanded our customer base by 70% and increased revenues 35%.

I also came up with innovative new products/services to make our offerings more appealing without cutting into profit margins. For example, an "insurance policy" was hugely popular with customers because it vastly reduced their risk at very little added cost. My new pricing model also helped boost both sales and profitability.

Product Line Sales Director/Sales Manager—Drill Technologies, Inc., 2016–2021

► Performance Highlight: Worst-to-first transformation, elevating our product line to #1 in market share with 68% compound annual growth.

► Scope: Sales leadership of a $100M+ product line. Sales team recruitment, selection, and leadership. Proposal development. Customer relationship management.

When I was promoted to lead sales for the product line, the challenge was two-fold: First, the product line was losing money and was last in market share. Second, the company was undergoing a transformation from a functional to a geographic structure.

Not only did we need to boost overall performance, I needed to build collaborative relationships internally to bring the right resources to every solution we recommended and sold.

Within 4 years of my 5-year plan, we reached our goal of #1 market share while growing revenues nearly 5-fold.

Prior positions with Drill Technologies—Each one a learning and growth opportunity with the chance to "put out fires" and develop/demonstrate new skills:

Technical Sales Representative, North America
Account Manager, North America
Applications Engineer, Global Product Line
District Engineer, Gulf of Mexico Operations
I/E Technician, Gulf of Mexico Operations

Alex Madison Resume & LI Profile—pages 169–172

Alex Madison created this resume with one objective in mind—a new Board assignment. He is not looking for a new job, no matter the position, the industry, or the opportunity. He's been working for 30+ years, risen to C-suite positions, delivered remarkable value, and retired from his corporate career in 2016. Since then, he has been working in various Board positions—some corporate, some non-profit. Now, he wants to bring those years of Board experience to the forefront and land another seat on a corporate Board.

HEADLINE

Resume	LinkedIn Profile
• Instantly communicates *who* Alex is and *what* he is targeting with just 4 words—Board Director, C-Suite Executive. It's important to include the latter so that readers will know the level of his professional experience. • Uses a shaded subheading to highlight Alex's areas of expertise—which are precisely the qualifications Boards seek in qualified candidates.	• Starts with his *who* statement. • Transforms the 2 lines from the top of the resume into a personal branding statement—"Build corporate wealth, protect shareholder value, drive performance excellence."

SUMMARY/ABOUT

Resume	LinkedIn Profile
• Presents a concise overview of Alex's career while noting in the very first line that his experience has been with a Fortune 100 company—a term that creates a powerful perception in the minds of most readers and draws them in for more details. • Introduces some of his most important qualifications that are applicable to both corporate work and Board assignments. • Includes a few personal attributes and a widely recognized acronym (DEI—Diversity, Equity, and Inclusion) that will be valuable in a Board role.	• Starts with a thought-provoking question: "What makes me a qualified Board of Directors candidate?" that grabs attention and makes his objective crystal-clear. • Answers his own question with the top 3 elements that perfectly illustrate *who* he is and *why* he truly is a well-qualified Board candidate. • Adds an Executive Qualifications section that introduces executive-level keywords that are vital to a successful Board role, cover a wide range of functions, and make Alex an attractive candidate across multiple industries. • Closes with additional qualifications, keywords, and characteristics to give you a glimpse into *who* Alex is and *how* he operates.

EXPERIENCE

Resume	LinkedIn Profile
• Positions his Board experience at the top and gives a great deal of weight and "real estate" to this highly relevant experience—rather than positioning his Board roles at the end of the resume, as is usually the case for corporate job seekers.	• Prominently positions his Board experience at the forefront, consistent with the resume.
• Uses shading and borders to clearly distinguish the different roles he held during his career—spent entirely with one company, CTK-Global Restaurant Corporation, where he advanced from "flipping burgers" to his C-level executive experience.	• Consolidates multiple board positions into a single listing to bring this valuable information to the top without creating multiple short sections.
• Provides job descriptions that are rich with content and achievement.	• Uses section headings to enhance readability and allow readers to skim to the information they are most interested in.
• Includes the scope of responsibility for each leadership position, further impressing readers with roles leading organizations with thousands of operating locations and billions of dollars in revenue.	• Highlights strong and specific achievements in every role.
• Gives significant space to his role as President of West Division that ended more than a decade ago—because he had some amazing successes that are still impressive.	

ALEX MADISON

555-617-7255 * alexmadisonboston@gmail.com * LinkedIn Profile

BOARD DIRECTOR & C-SUITE EXECUTIVE

Dedicated to:

Building Shareholder Value, Developing Top Talent & Leadership Teams, Strengthening Corporate Governance

Twenty-plus years' experience driving strategic planning and nationwide business operations for F100 company. Dynamic leadership skills with ability to assimilate vast amounts of information across multidisciplinary organizations to provide roadmaps to financial and operational success. Innovator with a clear vision for growth. Tenacious, inquisitive, and always-prepared leader with strong communication and interpersonal relationship skills. Trusted advisor. DEI champion.

BOARD ENGAGEMENTS

Board Member & Committee Member – AMEL Corporation (NDAQ: AML)   2019 to Present

Member of the Board of Directors for $15B global facilities management provider to education, healthcare, sports, entertainment, business and government market sectors. Provide broad strategic guidance across all core business disciplines to help guide the continued expansion of corporate brand and global footprint. Evaluate proposed business synergies, market growth, M&A, and capital expenditures.

- **Audit Committee Member.** Collaborate with full BoD in its oversight of AMEL's financial performance, internal audit function, independent auditor performance, and accounting and financial practices (including quality and integrity of financial statements, legal and regulatory requirements, and enterprise risk management). Collaborate on development and implementation of improved business processes and best practices.

- **Finance & Technology Committee Member.** Review, approve, and advise BoD and executive leadership on capital structure and transactions ($35M+). Evaluate technology strategy and infrastructure, including customer-facing initiatives and enterprise solutions. Provide strategy for introduction of advanced cybersecurity solutions.

- **Compensation Committee and Nominating & Governance Committee.** Active participant in these committees to broaden knowledge and leverage extensive HR and operating leadership to meet business goals.

Board Member – PETA – Lincoln, MA   2013 to 2017
Board Chairperson – World Wildlife Fund – Boston, MA   2004 to 2005

Spearheaded diverse portfolio of fundraising, charitable giving, corporate and community outreach, networking, and special events programs. Oversight of multimillion-dollar capital investments for facility expansion/improvement.

Board Member – Global Facilities Association & **Trustee** – Educational Foundation   2009 to 2011

Provided strategic leadership to strengthen performance of Association, expand programming, and increase membership. Coordinated financial outreach and internships for prominent Educational Foundation.

Trustee – Greenview College (HBCU) – Atlanta, GA   2005 to 2007

Proudly served on Power Advisory Board at Alice K. Duncan's Global Diversity & Inclusion Initiative.

PROFESSIONAL EXPERIENCE

CTK-GLOBAL RESTAURANT CORPORATION (NYSE: CTK)

Spectacular career track, from in-store operations to vital member of C-suite and executive leadership teams.

Executive Vice President & Chief Field Officer – USA (2015 to 2016)

Provided strategy and oversight for stewardship of US turnaround plan. Owned performance of US Operations, Franchising, Franchisee Relations, Customer Experience, Legal, and HR for 2800 franchisees and 18K+ restaurants. Led team of 5 executives; reported to US President/CEO.

ALEX MADISON ... 555-617-7255 * alexmadisonboston@gmail.com * LinkedIn Profile   Page 2

CTK-GLOBAL RESTAURANT CORPORATION (continued)

- Business delivered $29B in sales in 2016, accounting for 40%+ of total operating income. Achieved/surpassed aggressive turnaround targets impacting multidisciplinary functions and organizations throughout the company.
- Re-aligned around new asset light business model by leading high-profile re-franchising initiative, a core tenet of turnaround plan, to grow franchisee organizations.
- Re-franchised 2200 corporate-owned restaurants and accelerated growth with top-performing and forward-thinking franchisees across all US regions.

Chief People Officer – USA (2012 to 2012)

Retired from previous role as West Division President and recruited back by new US President/CEO 9 months later to lead the reinvention of end-to-end HR lifecycle for the company and its ~4K staff. Owned strategy and execution of talent acquisition, position alignment, recruitment, talent development, leadership development, performance improvement, succession planning, benefits, compensation, and technology benchmarks.

- Impacted company throughout all core business disciplines as new leadership team launched aggressive financial and operating turnaround plan. Provided organizational vision, strategy, and transformation milestones.
- Leveraged relationship with the American Franchisee Association to elevate restaurant-level brand standards and ensure brand consistency throughout company and franchised operations.
- Partnered with University of Ohio for design/delivery of new executive education programs to address critical development gaps for Field Officers. Witnessed significant gains in Officer competencies and achievements.

President – West Division (2005 to 2012)

Most-senior executive with full operating and P&L responsibility, building the West Division from $6.6B revenue and 3600 restaurants to $23.8B revenue and 6200 restaurants. Steered all divisional and restaurant operations, franchisee relations, market and real estate development, product innovation, and brand development. Tapped to represent the company at major institutional investor meetings with C-Suite team. Member of Global Leadership Initiative and DEI champion. Developed and modeled executive development programs and succession planning.

- Drove revenue increase of 36% and operating income gain of 48% (22% of company's total operating income).
- Facilitated over-arching "Plan to Win" strategy, collaborating with franchisees, suppliers, and company employees to form ongoing partnerships with shared focus and alignment of business platform.
- Identified opportunities and provided strategic vision for growth through product line extensions and innovations for billion-dollar brand categories. Launched portfolio of new products to capture new markets.
- Conceived, piloted, and implemented customer-centric marketing. Introduced Asian and European best practices to modernize brand and provide foundation for CTK's global business strategy.
- Honored with President's Award recognizing top 1% of global employees.
- Won the prestigious Anderson Forum Leadership Award.

Vice President – Strategic Planning & Business Development – Corporate HQ (2003 to 2005)
Vice President & General Manager – Los Angeles, CA (2001 to 2003)
Vice President & Regional Manager – Seattle, WA (1998 to 2001)
Director of Field Service Operations – Seattle, WA (1997 to 1998)

EDUCATION & CREDENTIALS

Member- National Association of Corporate Directors (NACD)
CERT Certificate – Cybersecurity Oversight * National Association of Corporate Directors
Certificate – CEO Perspective Program * Northeastern University – Duncan School of Management
Brand Mastery Class * Northeastern University – Duncan School of Management
Global Leadership Development * CTK-Global Leadership Institute

HEADLINE

BOARD DIRECTOR & C-SUITE EXECUTIVE. Build corporate wealth, protect shareholder value, drive performance excellence.

SUMMARY/ABOUT

What makes me a qualified Board of Directors candidate?

== I currently serve on the BOARD OF DIRECTORS for AMEL CORPORATION and as a member of their Audit, Finance & Technology, Compensation, and Nominating & Governance Committees.

My contributions to the Board have been significant, from evaluating proposed M&A transactions, to strengthening the integrity of financial reporting, to introducing advanced cybersecurity solutions worldwide.

== I served on 4 other boards: Board Chairperson/Board Member of 2 philanthropic organizations, Board Member of nationwide professional association, and Trustee for College Advisory Board's Global Diversity & Inclusion Initiative.

In each role, I provided strategic leadership and oversight of multimillion-dollar capital improvement budgets, corporate outreach programs, educational opportunities, and diversity, equity, and inclusion (DEI) innovations.

== My 20-year career with CTK-Global Corporation was distinguished by rapid promotion from in-store restaurant operations to the EXECUTIVE LEADERSHIP TEAM as PRESIDENT WEST DIVISION ($23.8B revenue), CHIEF PEOPLE OFFICER (~4K+ employees), and EVP/CHIEF FIELD OFFICER (2800 franchisees, 18K+ restaurants).

EXECUTIVE QUALIFICATIONS:
Strategic Planning, Organizational Development, Corporate Finance & Audit, Risk Management, Technology & Cybersecurity, Franchising, HR Leadership, Brand Management, New Product Innovation, Quality Improvement

EXPERIENCE

Board Member & Committee Member, AMEL Corporation, 2019–Present

Nominated to the Board of Directors for this $15B global facilities management provider to the education, healthcare, sports, entertainment, business, and government market sectors.

Provide strategic guidance and leadership for all major business functions to help facilitate the continued expansion of AMEL's corporate brand and global footprint. Work collaboratively with other BoD members to evaluate and recommend action on proposed M&A transactions, business synergies, market growth, and capital expenditures. Provide strategy for the selection and implementation of advanced cybersecurity solutions.

== Appointed to Audit Committee, working in partnership with full BoD in oversight of AMEL's financial performance, internal audit function, independent auditor performance, and accounting and financial practices. Expanded scope to include quality and integrity of financial statements, legal and regulatory requirements, and enterprise risk management. Guided development and implementation of improved business processes and best practices.

== Assumed additional responsibility as a member of Finance & Technology Committee to review and advise BoD and executive leadership team on capital structure and transactions valued at $35M+. Concurrently, evaluated technology strategy and infrastructure with an emphasis on customer-facing and enterprise solutions.

== Served on Compensation Committee and Nominating & Governance Committee to leverage extensive HR and operating leadership experience and successes to meet AMEL's dynamic business objectives.

Board Member / Board Chair / Trustee, Association Boards, Charitable Boards, Educational Boards, 2005–2017

== BOARD CHAIRPERSON – World Wildlife Fund – Boston, MA (1-year tenure)
== BOARD MEMBER – PETA – Lincoln, MA (4-year tenure)
Fundraising, Charitable Giving, Corporate & Community Outreach, Networking, Special Events. Multimillion-Dollar Capital Investments for Facilities Expansion and Improvement.

== BOARD MEMBER – Global Facilities Association (2-year tenure)
Strategic Planning, Member Development, Programming, Financial Outreach, Educational Foundation Internships

== TRUSTEE – Greenview College (2-year tenure)
Power Advisory Board – Global Diversity, Equity & Inclusion Initiative.

Executive Vice President & Chief Field Officer, CTK-Global Corporation, 2015–2016

Promoted by US President/CEO to EVP/Chief Field Officer at corporate HQ as McDonald's continued their multi-year financial and operational turnaround of US Operations, generating $29B in annual sales (40% of company's total operating income). Owned the performance of US Operations, Franchising, Customer Experience, Legal, and HR for 2800 franchisees and 18K+ restaurants nationwide. Developed and led a team of 5 executives.

== Contributed strategic and operational leadership critical to 1.7% revenue gain in just 1 year.

== Led major initiative to re-franchise 2200 corporate restaurants to franchisee management.

== Honored with President's Award recognizing top 1% of all global employees.

Chief People Officer, CTK-Global Corporation, 2012–2015

Recruited back to CTK-Global by new President/CEO 9 months after retiring as West Division President. Reinvented end-to-end HR lifecycle for CTK USA and ~4K staff. Owned strategy, recruitment, talent and leadership development, performance improvement, succession planning, and technology benchmarks.

== Provided organizational vision, strategy, and transformation milestones as company launched massive reorganization and turnaround of operations nationwide.

== Partnered with American Franchisee Association to elevate restaurant-level brand standards and ensure brand consistency across all company and franchised operations.

== Collaborated with University of Ohio for design and delivery of new executive education programs, resulting in significant gains in personnel competencies and performance achievements.

President – East Division, CTK-Global Corporation, 2005–2012

Promoted to most-senior executive with full operating and P&L responsibility. Led operations, franchisee relations, real estate development, product innovation, marketing and business development, and brand development.

== Built West Division from $6.6B revenue and 3800 restaurants to $23.8B and 6200 restaurants.

Vice President / Director, CTK-Global Corporation, 2003–2005

OVERVIEW: Early professional career was highlighted by a path of accelerated promotion based on years of success in defining strategic vision, strengthening field operations, improving financial performance, driving business development innovations, and delivering consistent gains in revenue and profitability. Career track included:

== Vice President – Strategic Planning & Business Development – Corporate HQ
== Vice President & General Manager – Los Angeles, CA
== Vice President & Regional Manager – Seattle, WA
== Director – Field Service Operations

PART VII:
Resume Portfolio

We've already shared more than 50 resume and LinkedIn samples in Parts I through VI … now, here are dozens more!

There's no doubt that the sample resumes and LinkedIn profiles in this book are a very valuable resource. Every resume you'll see was written by a professional resume writer for a unique client with a precise set of circumstances that dictated the content, format, and design.

We provide these resumes not to give you a template or model, but to give you *inspiration* and *ideas* for how to handle your own specific circumstances and challenges; best present your career story, facts, and achievements; write about your profession and your industry, when relevant; and create a modern resume that is sharp, powerful, and effective so that you can *get noticed and get hired!*

As well, we are delighted to share the contact information of all of the resume writers who contributed their very best work. You'll find the writer's name, credentials, and website (or email address) at the bottom of each resume.

While our goal is to give you everything you need to write your own resume, we know that some of you will find the process challenging. Others will lack sufficient time. Still others will simply decide to hire the best to help them with this important endeavor. We know that our contributors *are* the best, so we hope you will call on them for expert assistance should you have the need.

In the meantime, enjoy the samples and be motivated to produce a resume masterpiece and superb LinkedIn profile of your own!

CONNIE WANG

connie.wang@mac.com | 555-765-4321

ADMINISTRATIVE PROFESSIONAL

Diverse experience in high-profile, senior-level administrative support positions with Fortune 500, healthcare, consulting, and distribution organizations

→ **Resourceful problem solver** who takes initiative—often completing tasks before you even know they're needed.

→ **Organization and efficiency expert** skilled at identifying ways to streamline processes, save time, eliminate redundancy, and create operating systems that support the business.

→ **Effective communicator** and contributor individually and as a team member—professional, friendly, self-confident, and focused on solutions and results.

Areas of Proven Expertise

Written & Verbal Communications | Scheduling & Calendar Management | Gatekeeping | Travel Planning
Confidential Records Management | Financial Recordkeeping & Budget Monitoring | Event Planning & Facilitation
Simultaneous Project Management | Research | Process Improvement | Time & Resource Management
MS Office and other software and office equipment

PROFESSIONAL EXPERIENCE

ADMINISTRATIVE ASSISTANT, 2020–Present | OAKLAND HEALTH SERVICES, Oakland, CA

Initiated and led efforts to improve efficiency, automate processes, streamline data collection, and increase capacity for program that is a significant revenue driver for the health system.

Serve as chief assistant to director of program that works to bring new patients into the health system for early identification of health issues. Manage all administrative functions, including patient screening, registration, and detailed data entry. Create event marketing strategies and materials. Collaborate with other departments and team members to execute plans and drive solutions.

- **Identified** need and created solution that reduced time for data entry by 75%, eliminated duplicate entries and errors, and enabled data filtering for risk management and customized communications.

- **Created** a report—the first of its kind for the program—that provides participant data in a central source that can be searched and sorted.

- **Presented** 2 potential solutions for streamlining and automating the scheduling of screening appointments. The selected solution (scheduled for implementation) will increase scheduling efficiency and patient satisfaction.

- **Assumed** additional role as planner and facilitator of regular meetings for a patient support group. Identify and book speakers. Manage virtual meetings via Office Teams; train attendees and speakers unfamiliar with the software.

- **Earned** highest possible performance appraisal ratings—5 points in every one of 13 categories.

Manager Endorsements

Connie is constantly thinking of ways to improve the functioning of our department.

Connie remains respectful and focused even when given simultaneous tasks with equal priority and very short deadlines.

Connie demonstrates consistent application of the highest ethical standards in all her work.

On a consistent basis Connie displays a "can do" attitude.

Her skill set with digital and virtual methods along with her desire to collaborate has resulted in new ways to move

Louise Kursmark, MRW, CPRW, JCTC, CEIP, CCM • Best Impression Career Services • www.louisekursmark.com

Note: Manager endorsements provide third-party validation of Connie's skills. Older experience with Fortune 500 companies is presented on page 2, without dates that would identify Connie's age and a long gap in employment.

CONNIE WANG

our program forward.

ADMINISTRATIVE MANAGER, 2018–2020 | BAY AREA OFFICE GOODS, INC., Oakland, CA

Took on wide range of administrative and operations functions, wearing many hats needed to launch a startup.

- **Set up** office, established filing systems, installed software, and composed correspondence. Tracked and monitored monthly P&L. Trained on Dynamics AX and learned several modules needed to operate the company.
- **Created** marketing campaigns and distributed via social media.
- **Contributed** creative ideas to acquire new customers. Made cold calls and delivered sales presentations. Responded to and resolved all customer concerns.
- **Processed** all sales orders and purchase orders. Ensured accurate record-keeping, arranged transportation of goods to customers, and oversaw receiving and warehousing.

EXECUTIVE ASSISTANT TO VICE PRESIDENT, 2013–2018 | WEALTH PARTNERS, San Francisco, CA

As "right-hand" assistant, provided comprehensive support to VP of financial consulting firm.

- **Scheduled** appointments and coordinated calendar. Composed correspondence for his signature.
- **Compiled** and typeset detailed financial reports for consultants and clients.
- **Planned** meetings, small conferences, and special events. Selected locations and caterers. Negotiated pricing. Supervised smooth running of all event details.

PRIOR: Progressive career in administrative and sales support roles for Fortune 500 corporations.

ADMINISTRATIVE ASSISTANT, CISCO SYSTEMS, INC., San Jose, CA

- **Earned** annual award and bonus for presenting 13 ideas for process improvements that were implemented— saving time, reducing waste, and eliminating errors from duplication of data entry.

EXECUTIVE SECRETARY TO DIRECTOR OF MIS, ORACLE, San Jose, CA

- **Trained** new employees in proprietary software applications. Managed special projects and all administrative activities of the department.

ADMINISTRATIVE SECRETARY, Human Resources Department, APPLE, Cupertino, CA

- **Managed** confidential employee files. Screened candidates for temporary and permanent employment.

EDUCATION AND PROFESSIONAL DEVELOPMENT

A.S., Business—City College of San Francisco
MOS (Microsoft Office Certified) in Word, Excel, Publisher, PowerPoint, Outlook
Microsoft Dynamics AX (ERP software) trained

Cherilyn Randall

cherilyn@gmail.com | Las Vegas, Nevada | (406) 123-4567

Cocktail Server

Resort ... Casino ... Restaurant ... Nightclub ... Winery ... VIP Parties

Playful approach to unsurpassed service and world-class entertainment
BUILD BRAND VALUE AND CUSTOMER LOYALTY THROUGH ATTENTIVE SERVICE

F&B Delivery – Guest Service – Publicity Photos – Product Promotion

Mixed Beverage Knowledge	– Eight years' casino, hotel, winery, bar, and catered event service
Complaint Resolution	– Champagne, wine, liqueur, beer, and specialty cocktail knowledge
Inventory Control	– Creative French pleat, standing fan, and single pocket napkin folds
Up-Selling and Cross-Selling	– Aloha, Squirrel, and Sable POS to convey drink orders to bartenders
High-Volume Sales	– Cash and personal bank controlled, counted, and reconciled accurately
Wine and Food Pairing	– Fun-filled ambiance created through lighthearted guest interaction
Personal Bank Management	– Regulations prohibiting service to minors and intoxicated persons

Work Experience

Cocktail Server
MGM GRAND HOTEL AND CASINO, Las Vegas, Nevada, 2018 – present

— Ensure safe, fast service for large, VIP, and private parties in bars, nightclubs, gambling areas, dance floors, lounges, restaurants, and poolside at Las Vegas' largest destination resort.
— Employ high energy and flexibility to deliver orders throughout the resort and provide prompt room service.
— Check patrons' identifications to ensure compliance with corporate standards and state alcohol regulations.
— Manage refrigeration units, beer taps, draft towers, and dishwashing systems to ensure well-timed service.
— Built strong rapport with bartenders, bar backs, runners, servers, and slots managers through professional service and positive communications.

Server and Tasting Room Manager
DESERT RAT WINERY, Palm Springs, California, 2015 – 2018

— Managed tasting room pouring of award-winning wines from French-American hybrid wine grapes.
— Served wine at high-profile, no-host tasting parties, fundraisers, weddings, and receptions of 10–250 guests.
— Managed sales, deliveries, and invoicing for wholesale, grocery, restaurant, and retail accounts.
— Improved company's competitive position in the fine wine industry by cultivating new business via cold calling that increased sales and wine club sign-ups.

Education

TIPS Alcohol Certification – TAM Alcohol Server Training
College of the Desert General Education Diploma, Palm Desert, California

Cheryl Minnick, M.Ed., Ed.D., NCRW, CCMC • University of Montana-Missoula • www.umt.edu

Note: The graphic instantly tells readers who this job seeker is before they read a word. Content expresses an excellent blend of both professional skills and personalized approach to customer service.

SAMANTHA BAKER

Lakewood, WA | 253-475-5678 | SBaker@gmail.com

EVENT PLANNER | HOSPITALITY PROFESSIONAL

ENERGETIC and **CLIENT-CENTRIC** professional with diverse background across guest services, event management, program management, client relations, and office administration. Proven track record of turning around underperforming programs/departments, tripling revenue, and implementing process improvements that enhance bottom-line results. Calm under pressure. Dependable and highly organized.

SIGNATURE SKILLS

☑ Event Planning / Management	☑ Business / Office Management	☑ Marketing & Advertising
☑ Program Oversight	☑ Strategic Planning / Scheduling	☑ Process Improvements
☑ Quality Control/ Quality Assurance	☑ Staff & Personnel Development	☑ Emotional Intelligence
☑ Sales / Influential Selling	☑ Client Relations / Public Relations	☑ Clear Communication

PROFESSIONAL WORK HISTORY

GUEST SERVICE ASSOCIATE | 2009–2016 | **Olympia Country Club,** Olympia, WA

Delivered exceptional customer service as "first point of contact" to a premier and semi-private full-service country club. Controlled inventory; monitored equipment and supplies.

- As the "face of organization," worked with clients directly to accommodate and schedule their requested sports, activities, or services. Quickly responded to and resolved client issues.
- Managed men's and women's tennis leagues.
  - ✓ **Increased court use 5% and reduced complaints 60%** by implementing a new, highly efficient appointment system that optimized staff's efforts with each client.
- Increased public relations and drove brand awareness. Answered questions and provided education and information about services, events, and activities.

DIRECTOR | 2006–2009 | **Fabricon Labs,** Portland, OR

Managed departmental operations for company developing and producing Nutraceutical products.

- Inherited inefficient, poorly managed department. Rapidly identified process deficiencies and developed procedures to improve workflow, timeliness, and productivity.
  - ✓ **Tripled business in 5 months** by improving service and implementing new pricing structure.
  - ✓ **Saved company $30,000 per year** through process and efficiency improvements.
- Initiated and fostered professional relationships with physicians and medical field professionals.

DEVELOPMENT OFFICER | 2004–2006 | **Cystic Fibrosis Foundation,** Portland, OR

Steered fundraising efforts for national nonprofit organization.

- Led key events that included nationwide walks and silent auctions in collaboration with local businesses.
  - ✓ **Exceeded fundraising goals by 10%** in 2004, **16%** in 2005.

EDUCATION

Bachelor of Science Degree in Biology | 2003 | University of Portland, Portland, OR

COMMUNITY INVOLVEMENT

- Spearheaded successful fundraising activities at J.C. Green Elementary and Lakewood Middle School.
- Served as Girl Scout Leader and initiated community outreach to local food pantry and homeless shelter.

Kara Varner, MAOM, CARW, CPRW, CRS-MTC, CEIC • A Platinum Resume and Career Services, LLC • www.aplatinumresume.com
Note: Dates are minimized on this return-to-work resume, while relevant experience and impressive achievements are emphasized. Community Involvement briefly lists activities while she was a stay-at-home mom.

ANTHONY R. LINGSTRUM
EXECUTIVE CHEF

Create and deliver high-quality menu items to exceed expectations and build loyal customer base.

New York, NY 10020 ‖ 212.555.5555. ‖ anthonyrlingstrum@cmail.com

Well-respected professional with exceptional culinary, food preparation/delivery, menu design, and leadership skills. Recognized for prioritizing projects, managing personnel, and containing costs to increase market share and profitability.

Culinary Arts / Health & Safety Management / Food Preparation & Presentation / Plating / Innovative Cooking Techniques / Kitchen Operations / Banquet & Catering / Marketing / Creative Menu Development / Food & Labor Cost Control / Guest Satisfaction / Budget Projection & Management

Bachelor of Culinary Arts Degree
Certified Executive Chef (CEC) — Certified Food and Beverage Executive (CFBE)
Serve Safe Certified — New York Food Manager Certified

CAREER EXPERIENCE

STEAKS AND MORE RESTAURANT, New York, NY *(Publicly held company with 5 locations in Tristate area)* 2012–Present
Executive Chef (2015–present)
Catering Operations • Menu Development • Pricing • Inventory • Vendor Management • Food/Labor Costs • Customer Service
Direct all catering and daily kitchen operations for 2 upscale locations, with indoor/outdoor seating for 450 patrons, generating $20M+ annual revenues. Manage and control $8M+ annual purchasing and inventory budgets. Conduct food reviews, generate/submit sales and profit analysis reports to management, and ensure health and safety regulatory compliance. Recruit, train, schedule, and oversee staff of 110. Accountable for meeting sales/profit expectations.
Highlights:
- Reduced costs 16% by effectively negotiating vendor contracts and leveraging multi-site volume discounts.
- Increased profits 24% and cut food costs 32% (below industry average) through creative, organizational, and leadership skills.
- Maintain 100% rating on corporate and county health and safety inspections.
- Plan, design, and manage 150+ catered events annually with up to 250 patrons per event.
- Significantly upgraded quality of food, operations, profitability, and standards of service through innovative menu planning.
- Demonstrated exceptional talent for recruiting, hiring, and developing key support staff.

Assistant Dining Chef (2012–2015)
Line Cook • Back-of-House Prep • Staff Trainer • Second-in-Command to Dining Chef
Recognized for superior performance in mission-critical, fast-paced environments. Quickly promoted from entry-level Fryer to Chef. Assisted Executive Chef on menu and program preparation.
Highlights:
- Noted for superior culinary skills, recipe/menu development, full-service catering, and cost containment.
- Ensured compliance with all safety, cleanliness, quality, and food service standards.
- Provided hands-on instruction to staff, setting high standards for plating, service, and table presentations.

Caterer / Server / Bartender • HIGH QUALITY INN, New York, NY   2011–2013
Caterer / Server / Bartender • PLATTERS RESTAURANT, New York, NY   2009–2011

EDUCATION AND PROFESSIONAL DEVELOPMENT
Bachelor of Culinary Arts [2008] • CITY COLLEGE OF NEW YORK, New York, NY
Diversity Training [2009, 2010] — Quality Assurance [2008, 2009] — Excel [2011]

PROFESSIONAL AFFILIATIONS
National Restaurant Association • American Public Health Association • American Culinary Federation

Carol Heider, CPRW • Resumes by Professionals • www.resumesbyprofessionals.com

Note: A relevant graphic creates visual appeal, while strong accomplishments provide evidence of this chef's ability to manage both culinary and organizational aspects of a large-scale food service operation.

CHERIE RASMUSSEN

Relocating to Portland, Oregon
406.829.0999 ▪ CRasmussen@gmail.com

ELEMENTARY TEACHER: GRADES K-3

National Science Teachers' Council ▪ Teachers of Mathematics Society ▪ Montana Educators' Association

Caring, energetic teacher who creates stimulating learning environments, promotes scholastic and social development, and helps children enhance their unique potential for academic and personal success. Patient educator able to blend cooperative learning, classroom management and innovative teaching to create a foundation for lifelong learning. New graduate excited to begin a full-time teaching career in Portland as a …

- ✐ **Student Motivator:** Creating learning environments respectful of cultural diversity, physical limitations, gender differences, and religious affiliation to meet all students' needs.
- ✐ **Classroom Manager:** Initiating early academic intervention to promote positive reinforcement, mutual respect, and individual responsibility.

EDUCATION & CREDENTIALS

UNIVERSITY OF MONTANA High Honors Graduate, May 2023
Bachelor of Arts in Elementary Education – Reading, Mathematics, and Science Endorsements
K-8 Montana Elementary Teaching Certificate – SEID #12345

Trained in . . .
Dynamic Indicators of Basic Early Literacy Skills (DIBELS)
Adult, Child, and Infant First Aid and CPR, American Heart Association
Reading Well, National Center on Student Progress Monitoring (NCSPM)

TEACHING EXPERIENCE

✂ **2nd Grade Apprentice Teacher**
Seeley Lake Elementary, Seeley Lake, Montana, Spring 2023

- Created a warm, exciting atmosphere where children learned and played to strengthen reading mechanics, math readiness, and technology familiarization while developing friendships and social skills.
- Developed a stimulating classroom for 23 students, including 5 receiving Title I services, with a focus on surpassing assessment standards, improving classroom behavior, and building academic confidence.
- Orchestrated IEP in collaboration with mental health counselor, in-class para-educator, and special education teacher for student with obsessive-compulsive disorder and oppositional defiant disorder.
- Verified count of Economically Disadvantaged Students to report yearly progress per No Child Left Behind Act by assessing student records to determine those eligible for or receiving free/reduced-price lunch.

Cheryl Minnick, M.Ed., Ed.D., NCRW, CCMC • University of Montana-Missoula • www.umt.edu

Note: The Blackboard font, not commonly used for business documents, works extremely well for this elementary school teacher. The school bus graphic further expresses her expertise and her brand. Note the "relocating" mention at the top.

CHERIE RASMUSSEN

✂ K-5 After-School Program Instructor
Franklin Elementary School and Hawthorne Elementary School, Missoula, Montana, 2021 – 2022

- Developed unique after-school outdoor and fun in-class educational activities to support students' social and academic achievements by building peer relationships through play and learning.
- Awarded *Volunteer of the Year 2022* for outstanding contribution and instructional excellence.
- Taught small-group educational games and outside play for a community program targeting at-risk youth.
- Worked in harmony with parents, staff, teachers, and administrators to deliver an outstanding program.
- Invited Humane Society staff to host a "Show 'n Tell" focused on puppy and kitten care.

✂ Private Preschool Tutor and Full-Charge Nanny
Missoula and Seeley Lake, Montana, Summers 2018 – 2020

- Trusted by a high-profile celebrity couple to care for their preschool children, manage an established budget, and shuttle children to/from lessons in the family vehicle.
- Collaborated with live-in housekeeper and cook for meal planning, supply purchases, laundry services, birthday and holiday celebrations, and play-date preparation.
- Cared for children during parents' extended business travel, providing tutoring, medical treatment, and transportation services. Traveled internationally with the family.
- Encouraged children to learn through hands-on educational activities and outdoor games, teaching phonetics, math, and reading readiness in a positive, nurturing environment.

COMMUNITY VOLUNTEERISM

K-4 Soccer Coach
Missoula Public School District, Missoula, Montana, Falls 2017 – 2019
- Introduced children to soccer basics, creating a foundation for enjoyment of physical activity and competition. Taught teamwork, sportsmanship, safety, and rules of the game.

K-3 Adventure Instructor
The Adventure Club, Seeley Lake, Montana, Summer 2017
- Expanded school boundaries beyond four walls to augment classroom learning by immersing students in outdoor adventures with focus on touch, see, smell, hear, and taste. Led students on hikes, rafting adventures, and bird watching trips. Taught "Bear Basics" focused on safety in bear country.

Foster Mom
Western Montana Humane Society, Missoula, Montana, 2015 – 2017
- Provided loving, in-home medical care and socialization to underage, elderly, disabled, sick, and recovering kittens and puppies to prepare them for adoption.

Volunteer Receptionist
AniMeals, Missoula, Montana, 2015 – 2016
- Offered reception service to respond to adoption and donation inquiries at a no-kill shelter and animal food bank. Promoted the shelter at fundraising events and helped gather 9000 lbs. of donated pet food.

JOHANNA ROLLEMAN, BSN, RN

johannarolleman@gmail.com | 555.555.5555 | LinkedIn.com/in/johannarolleman

NURSE EDUCATOR

CURRICULUM DESIGN | CLINICAL EXPERTISE | CARE MANAGEMENT | PHYSICIAN & PROVIDER RELATIONS

Teach skills to foster independence and confidence in those providing in-home family care.

Registered professional nurse with deep expertise in direct patient care, family intervention, and results-focused educational leadership. Collaborator with peers, executives, and care providers across diverse touchpoints of healthcare continuum. Trusted patient support and clinical operations partner recognized for ability to develop patient-centric care models that lead to improved outcomes.

Clarify complex issues, define essence of problem or solution, and predict broad impact of important decisions, setting others up for performance success. Thrive in fast-paced environments; respond to quickly changing priorities and manage emergency situations in calm, confident manner.

Lead healthcare teams to operational excellence with collaborative coaching style while managing risk, employing cultural sensitivity and respect, and adhering to all established policies, regulations, and professional standards.

Registered Nurse – License #CA 55555-1
Basic Life Support (BLS) – American Heart Association, San Diego CPR and Education

Patient Advocacy | HIPAA Compliance | Care Planning | Resource Utilization | Staff Leadership | EMR
Curriculum Development & Delivery | Evidence-Based Research | Discharge Planning | Documentation
Data Collection, Evaluation & Reporting | Adult and Neonatal Disease States | COVID-19 Protocols
Health Assessments | Complex Care Management Principles | Integrated Team Care Rounds | Cultural Competence

PROFESSIONAL EXPERIENCE

SCRIPPS HEALTH SYSTEM – San Diego, CA   2003 – 2023

SCRIPPS GREEN HOSPITAL, La Jolla, CA | 2016 – 2023

Staff Nurse Educator | 2016 – 2023

Provided education, support, and positive reinforcement to nursing staff to achieve highest levels of care in family-centered environment. Customized learning approach to meet individualized learning needs. Promoted critical thinking skills and facilitated team communication to optimize patient outcomes. Consistently identified opportunities for education and intervention to enhance staff development and improve standards of care. Oversaw new staff orientation.

- **Delivered bimonthly training classes,** utilizing simulation and debriefing to instruct multidisciplinary staff across system, per AAP guidelines and standards. Maintained 100% staff compliance.
- **Decreased length of stay** from 14 days to 7 days for neonatal population impacted by neonatal abstinence syndrome by collaborating with cross-functional team to collect data and develop standard care policy.
- **Collaborated with neonatal and obstetric team members** to review and update obstetric and maternal child policies and procedures, making them consistent with evidence-based research.
- **Facilitated NiCU Practice Council meetings** to promote staff-based, family-centered care initiatives.

Cathy Lanzalaco, MBA, CPRW, CPCC, NCOPE, SPHR, SHRM-SCP, RN • Inspire Careers LLC • www.inspirecareers.com
Note: Capturing attention in a flash with a distinctive heading design, this resume conveys expertise and credibility throughout. DISC and Clifton Strengths details on page 2 provide insight into character and behavioral strengths.

SCRIPPS MEMORIAL HOSPITAL ENCINITAS, Encinitas, CA | 2003 – 2016

Nurse Manager | 2012 – 2016

Managed 45-member healthcare team and $650K budget for high-risk neonatal intensive care unit.

- **Supervised hiring,** onboarding, and training of all new staff members.
- **Defined roadmap to ensure 100% pass rate** for all Joint Commission audits from 2012 – 2016.
- **Introduced** *Preceptor of the Year* **award** to recognize training and leadership excellence.

Staff RN / Preceptor | 2003 – 2012

Provided comprehensive and developmentally appropriate care to all pre-term and critically ill newborns in safe and culturally sensitive manner. Collaborated with multidisciplinary care team to ensure optimal patient outcomes.

- **Recognized for leadership skills** as clinical preceptor and new RN mentor.
- **Empowered families for safe discharge** by providing advocacy, education, resources, and support.
- **Maintained best practices** through evidence-based research as member of Policy and Procedure Committee.

DISCSTYLES™ COMMUNICATION & BEHAVIORAL STRENGTHS REPORT

Sets high personal standards for self and persuade others by demonstrating competence. Sets example by demonstrating work that needs to be done. Coaches others into being more effective at reaching goals. Multifaceted operational style allows for success in variety of situations. Excellent role model for others on team. Optimistic and encouraging, which comes from natural positive spirit, high degree of sincerity, and ability to be flexible. (Aug 2022)

TOP 5 CLIFTONSTRENGTHS®

Restorative (strong problem solver)
Harmony (seeks consensus)
Individualization (values uniqueness of each person)
Input (inquisitive, likes to collect information or things)
Learner (enjoys process of continual learning)

PROFESSIONAL AFFILIATIONS

American Nurses Association – California
Professional Nurses Association of Southern California
Sigma Theta Tau International Nursing Honor Society
Member – National Association of Neonatal Nurses

EDUCATION & ADDITIONAL CERTIFICATIONS

BSN – San Diego State University, San Diego, CA

Neonatal Resuscitation Instructor – American Academy of Pediatrics, Certification #555-5555
Child Passenger Safety Technician – National Traffic Safety Administration, Certification #555555
S.T.A.B.L.E. – Stabilizing a Sick Newborn for Transport
Fundamentals of Critical Care – OB

Eric Lacroix MDEM ≫ BNSc ≫ RN

ericlacroix@myisp.com ➤ 905.456.7890 ➤ www.linkedin.com/in/eric-lacroix-mdem ➤ Mississauga, ON

DISASTER AND EMERGENCY MANAGEMENT SPECIALIST

Master's in Disaster and Emergency Management (4.0 GPA) ➤ Interned in Emergency Management at Region of Peel

Emergency Preparedness ➤ Emergency Planning ➤ Risk Assessment
Anticipate need and take a grounded, pragmatic approach to emergency management

Intuitive, forward-thinking, and **adaptable problem solver in emergency sector**. Empathetic and altruistic leader with high visual-spatial IQ. Self-directed continuous learner with **ongoing emergency management training** from Emergency Management Ontario (EMO), Office of the Fire Marshal and Emergency Management (OFMEM), and US Federal Emergency Management Agency (FEMA). **Served in Canadian Armed Forces**. Fluent in English and French.

EMERGENCY MANAGEMENT EXPERIENCE AND QUALIFICATIONS

> ➤ Rated as setting the bar high for future **Emergency Planning Specialist** interns with Region of Peel.
>
> ➤ Immersed in front-line **emergency response** as critical care RN and ex-military paramedic.
>
> ➤ Hold roles that require **rapid assessment**, **upstream thinking**, and **decisive action** to save lives.
>
> ➤ Registered member of **emergency & disaster management** and **business continuity** organizations.

Emergency Planning ➤ Emergency Preparedness ➤ Emergency Management ➤ Emergency Response ➤ Emergency Operations
Disaster Response ➤ Incident Management System ➤ Hazard Identification and Risk Assessment ➤ Contingency Planning
Risk Mitigation ➤ Training ➤ Project Management ➤ Team Leadership ➤ Relationship Management ➤ Problem Solving

PROFESSIONAL EXPERIENCE

Mississauga Central General Hospital (Mississauga, ON)   2019–Present
STAFF RN – Critical Care Float Pool

Work on small rotating niche team skilled in rapid assessment and intervention in ER, ICU, and step-down units. Assignments include ER triage, remote patient monitoring, and team lead or charge nurse in ICU.

> ➤ Collaborating on redraft of **Code Orange contingency plan** to enhance disaster readiness hospital wide.
> ➤ Adapted to new guidelines as nursing standards and care protocols evolved to treat COVID-positive patients.

Region of Peel, Department of Emergency Management (Mississauga, ON)   Fall 2021–Spring 2022
EMERGENCY PLANNING SPECIALIST – Internship

Joined as the region's first emergency management Master's intern; reported to emergency management coordinator.

> ➤ Completed 2019 **Hazards Index and Risk Assessment (HIRA)**, including current list of regional hazards and risks.
> ➤ **Wrote surge plan content for potential disastrous events** that would challenge regional capacity to respond.
> ➤ **Analyzed potential risk of cyber attacks** within regional scope and compiled executive summary.
> ➤ Updated **Critical Infrastructure (CI) database** and Geographic Information System (GIS).
> ➤ Participated in tabletop exercises for **impact assessment of terrorist attacks** on critical infrastructure.

(continued on page 2)

Brenda Collard-Mills, MRW, CRS, NCOPE • Robust Resumes and Resources • www.robustresumesandresources.com
Note: Shifting focus from nursing to emergency management, Eric brings to the forefront all of the relevant qualifications for his new career while briefly including his additional, and valuable, experience in traditional healthcare environments.

Eric Lacroix

St. Anne's Memorial Hospital (Oakville, ON)   2017–2019
REGISTERED NURSE – Emergency Department

Conducted patient assessment in all ER units (triage, trauma, acute, and minor). Oriented new hires inexperienced in an emergency environment. Served on Code Orange Committee and Professional Development Committee.

University Network Hospital (Toronto, ON)   2012–2017
REGISTERED NURSE – Critical Care Float Pool

Delivered urgent and non-urgent patient care in the emergency, ICU, and extended care departments. Earned certifications in advanced cardiovascular life support and trauma nursing.

Canadian Armed Forces (Multiple relocations in Canada)   2004–2014
PRIMARY CARE MILITARY PARAMEDIC

Provided clinical and front-line emergency and nursing care in full-time and reservist roles. Contributed to creation of training programs for junior medical staff. Certified to work in French-speaking government facilities.

VOLUNTEER EXPERIENCE

Camp Access of Southern Ontario (Burlington, ON)   2014–2020
MEDICAL DIRECTOR + STAFF RN

Hired, trained, and led medical team hosting Canada's second largest children's cancer camp. Organized schedules, updated medical equipment, and procured supplies. Reported to the non-profit's national board of directors.

➢ Performed research and upgraded contingency planning to include previously unencountered hazards.
➢ Drastically reduced infection incidents to near zero and sustained at low incident rate for balance of tenure.

INDUSTRY AFFILIATIONS

OAEM	Ontario Association of Emergency Management	2022–present
DRIE	Disaster Recovery Information Exchange	2022–present
UNDRR	United Nations Disaster and Risk Reduction	2021–present
BCI	Business Continuity Institute	2020–present
FEMA	Federal Emergency Management Agency College	2018–present
OFMEM	Office of the Fire Marshal and Emergency Management	2018–present

TRAINING AND EDUCATION

EMO and OFMEM	**Incident Management Systems 100 (IMS)**	2022
EMO and OFMEM	**Basic Emergency Management Qualification (BEM)**	2021
FEMA College	**Introduction to the Incident Command System**	2021
FEMA College	**Public Information Officer Awareness**	2021
FEMA College	**Leadership and Influence**	2020
FEMA College	**Managerial Safety & Health**	2020
FEMA College	**Incident Command Systems for Health Care Facilities**	2020

MASTER OF DISASTER AND EMERGENCY MANAGEMENT (MDEM) 4.0 GPA | York University | 2022
Member – Disaster and Emergency Management Students Association (2018–present)
Teaching Assistant and Guest Lecturer – Introduction to Emergency Management and Risk Analysis (2020–2021)

BACHELOR OF NURSING SCIENCE (BNSc) | Top Third of Class | Queen's University | 2012

LISA SMITH-JONES

PhD || DVM || BA || Dipl. ACVP

lisa.smithjones@myisp.com || 201.555.5555 || Newark, NJ 07017 || www.linkedin.com/in/lisa-smith-jones

DECISIVE SENIOR DIRECTOR ➡ TOXICOLOGY AND DRUG SAFETY

Deliver succinct regulatory submissions resulting in fewer questions and faster filings

Toxicology Strategy || Drug Development || Drug Safety || Regulatory Filings

Tenacious toxicologist, pathologist, and scientific expert in pharmaceutical drug safety and regulatory requirements. Key member and safety lead on drug discovery and development projects and leadership teams.

REGULATORY SUBMISSIONS ➡ Prepare regulatory submissions for global regulatory bodies (FDA, PMDA, EMA, and others) to support IND, CTA, and CTN filings, plus NDA, BLA, and MAA applications.

THERAPEUTIC AREAS ➡ Oncology – immunology – inflammation – neuroscience – metabolic disorders – bone.

MODALITIES ➡ Large molecule (cell therapies, biologics, T-cell engagers, monoclonal antibodies, bi-specific antibodies, antibody drug conjugates, and oncolytic viruses) and small molecule from discovery to late-stage development.

MEMBERSHIPS ➡ Society of Toxicology (2009–Present) ➡ Society of Toxicologic Pathology (2006–Present) ➡ American College of Veterinary Pathologists (2005–Present)

PUBLICATIONS ➡ Co-authored 23 publications related to toxicology, pathology, and veterinary medicine.

STRENGTHS: Toxicology || Drug Discovery || Drug Development || Drug Safety || Safety Assessment || Safety Studies || Pre-Clinical and Clinical Development || Regulatory Submissions || Contract Research Organization (CRO Management) || Good Laboratory Practice (GLP) || Regulatory Compliance || In Vitro – In Vivo Models || Problem Solving || Agility || Critical Thinking

PROFESSIONAL EXPERIENCE

ACME PHARMACEUTICAL COMPANY
Newark, NJ | 2018–Present

SENIOR DIRECTOR – Drug Safety Research & Evaluation, Therapeutic Area Lead – Oncology   2020–Present
Member – Oncology Development Leadership Team; DSRE Leadership Team; Preclinical and Translational Sciences Extended Leadership Team; Oncology Drug Discovery Unit Extended Leadership Team

➡ R&D Project Team Award || Global Project Team Award ⬅

Spearhead global oncology drug safety research across 70 programs. Oversee safety assessments; interpret and relay nonclinical toxicology data internally and to global regulatory bodies; identify potential clinical liabilities to inform trial design; contribute to strategic, financially impactful decisions on program advancement.

Held concurrent role as interim DSRE head of marketed products (400+ compounds) providing support to ensure accurate CCDS/CCSI/RSI data, labeling, and regulatory reporting; point person for health authorities.

- **Coordinated and expedited high-profile SARS-CoV-2 activities,** including clinical protocol amendments and rapid turnaround of toxicology data, and advised on data generated via in vitro and in vivo models.

- Boosted DSRE profile and strived to harmonize approaches to cell therapy programs in US and China by adding new strategic lead role; benefits led leadership team to create similar role for second therapeutic area.

- Drove creation of cross-functional, global in vivo safety study responsibility matrix to improve cell therapy regulatory submissions.

Brenda Collard-Mills, MRW, CRS, NCOPE • Robust Resumes and Resources • www.robustresumesandresources.com

Note: The theme of this resume is award-winning impact in every appointment. It is a distillation of a 12-page traditional scientific CV, focusing on relevant qualifications and contributions at the director level.

185

LISA SMITH-JONES
lisa.smithjones@myisp.com || Page 2

ACME PHARMACEUTICAL (continued)

DIRECTOR – Drug Safety Research & Evaluation, Therapeutic Area Lead – Oncology
2018–2020
Member – Oncology Development Leadership Team; DSRE Leadership Team

Led global DSRE oncology profile of programs—small molecule to biologics of various modalities—from pre-project start to post-marketing. Oversaw safety assessments from first-in-human and throughout clinical life cycle. Worked with senior members of cross-functional groups, drug discovery, and therapeutic area units on candidate drug development.

- **Won prestigious Global Project Team Award** for identifying and rectifying toxicity issues in partner safety assessments prior to presenting asset for IND filing.

DIRECTOR – Toxicology
2017–2018
Member – DSRE Leadership Team

Provided career development and mentoring to team of 9 development toxicologists. Reviewed and approved development toxicology protocols and reports for in-house and outsourced drug safety studies, toxicology lab investigations, and nonclinical packages for regulatory filings and applications. Supported immunotoxicology safety assessments and testing strategies for multiple modalities from small molecules to biologics and new modalities.

- **Initiated effort to standardize approaches to nonclinical safety assessments;** released 12 scientific and 7 operational guides for cross-therapeutic area and modality projects with 5 more guides in pipeline.

NEXTGEN PHARMA
San Franciso, CA

PATHOLOGIST DIRECTOR – Comparative Biology and Safety Sciences (CBSS)
2012–2017
Chair – Tissue Cross Reactivity Committee; Member – Regulatory Opinion Expert Working Group

➡ Acclaim Awards (6) || Applause Awards (5) ⬅

Served as project pathologist for 12 programs; nonclinical lead for inflammation product (monoclonal antibody) and coordinator for all nonclinical sections of BLA filing; CBSS lead for metabolic disorders compound and 3 related neuroscience compounds (large and small molecule) in early-stage development.

- **Identified error in peer-reviewed pathology data of late-stage compound** and activated pathology working group, resulting in removal of toxicity liability and compound having more favorable profile than competitors.

- Tightened regulatory report writing for studies done internally and by contract research organizations.

- Performed program-level survey advocating for in vitro and ex vivo studies and animal welfare conscious study selection and design aimed at reducing, refining, and replacing animal use in drug development.

ABC THERAPEUTICS
San Diego, CA

PRINCIPAL VETERINARY PATHOLOGIST – Research and Development
2006–2012

➡ R&D Star Award (2009) ⬅

FORMAL EDUCATION AND ACCREDITATION

DACVP – BOARD CERTIFIED IN VETERINARY ANATOMIC PATHOLOGY
American College of Veterinary Pathologists

PHD – EXPERIMENTAL PATHOLOGY || DVM – Cum Laude
Stanford University

BA – ZOOLOGY – Cum Laude
University of California, San Diego

LILLIE BROWN

Mobile, AL ▪ 555-352-2345 ▪ lilliebrown@gmail.com ▪ www.LinkedIn/in/LillieBrown

AWARD-WINNING FUNDRAISING EXECUTIVE
Connecting the community with mission-based causes and positioning underperforming markets for sustainable growth.
Nonprofit Leadership | Community Engagement | Sponsorship Cultivation

Nonprofit executive with high-performance background in building and growing effective fundraising programs that generate year-over-year revenue growth for large-scale community-based organizations. Transparent leader who accepts shared accountability with staff for surpassing goals and transforming declining relationships into income-generating opportunities that expand organizational territory presence. Gregarious mentor and trainer known for combining excitement and clearly defined strategies with collaboration to support the organizational mission.

Fundraising Strategies ▪ Constituent Relations ▪ Corporate Partnerships ▪ Stewardship ▪ Executive Board Leadership
Policy Development ▪ Major Gifts ▪ Annual Giving ▪ Budgeting ▪ Performance Management ▪ Training

PROFESSIONAL EXPERIENCE

Alabama Public Health Association – Mobile, AL　　　　　　　　　　　　　　　　　**2022–2023**
SENIOR DIRECTOR OF EVENTS

Relocated to provide strategic oversight and accountability of $6.1M income target for event-related and advocacy activities. Supervised, coached, mentored, and trained 9 full-time employees.

- **Secured $2.1M in 9 months,** executing 21 community fundraising events while mobilizing 600+ volunteers.
- **Accelerated awareness for mission-related events** to improve outcomes for undeserved patients, including indoor air, oral chemo, and insurance coverage for colonoscopies under 50.

Birmingham League of Stars – Birmingham, AL　　　　　　　　　　　　　　　　　**2019–2022**
DIRECTOR OF COMMUNITY ENGAGEMENT

Led implementation and planning of policies and programs, including major gifts, planned giving, and high-profile event activities, to achieve mission and income targets. Grew fundraising support through relationship management and engagement of local corporations, volunteer leadership groups, and community-based assets.

> *"...... is willing to accept challenges and motivates others to follow her leadership."*
> —National Board Member

- **Boosted payroll deduction income to $250K+,** recovering contributions from former event campaign to support annual giving program.
- **Raised $100K+ in new income,** incorporating district-wide fundraising initiatives in 50 AL high schools.
- **Generated additional $100K** by soliciting athletic directors to participate in special events program.

Community Health Coalition – Birmingham, AL　　　　　　　　　　　　　　　　　**2016–2019**
STATE VICE PRESIDENT, ALABAMA

Devised statewide strategies and plans for fundraising, advocacy, patients served, and leadership engagement to reach year-over-year income increases. Partnered with government officials and C-Suite executives at major retailers to rebuild Board of Directors. Served on executive board for Nonprofit Coalition and National Healthcare Center. Acted as staff liaison to division board members.

> *"Her talent is only exceeded by her extraordinary commitment to service. She has continued to produce excellent results with her teams."*
> —Division Board Member

- **Gained 9% income spike,** empowering staff to exceed performance outcomes and fundraising goals.
- **Received first $1M gift** for Mid-South Division, prospecting donor leads and establishing trust through meticulous needs assessment and connection to cause.
- **Organized conference planning committees for events with up to 5K attendees.** Developed agenda, trained facilitators, negotiated vendor contracts, and scheduled opening/closing ceremonies.
- **Recognized as only State VP to earn largest growth** in advocacy memberships across Mid-South Division.

Ashley Watkins, NCRW, NCOPE • Write Step Resumes • writesteresumes.com

Note: Bullets start with strong, bolded achievements, many of them quantified. The boxed endorsements add even more impact, interest, and credibility.

LILLIE BROWN

Mobile, AL ◼ 555-352-2345 ◼ lilliebrown@gmail.com ◼ www.LinkedIn/in/LillieBrown ◼ Page 2 of 2

Ending Hunger – Birmingham, AL   2015–2016
EXECUTIVE DIRECTOR

Positioned market to experience increases in income and patients served for first time in 6 years. Planned and executed income growth strategies for gala, Board of Directors, major gifts campaign, and health initiatives objectives. Supervised 5 event staff.

- **Reached $150K goal,** landing prestigious venue for sold-out, high-profile event and leveraging social elite committee to host Birmingham Gala.
- **Garnered 100% funding** for nonprofit program over 5 years by cultivating relationships and securing major gifts from top executives at BigTime Corporation.

Giving Foundation, Inc. – Birmingham, AL   2013–2015
AREA DIRECTOR, CENTRAL ALABAMA

Embraced aggressive sales culture to secure $1.9M and preserve territory goals and objectives. Supervised, coached, and trained 7 full-time employees.

- **Led state in staff and volunteer retention** for 2 consecutive years.
- **Secured $50K grant,** forging partnership with foundation director.

Building Brighter Futures – Birmingham, AL   2008–2013
COMMUNITY REPRESENTATIVE, CENTRAL ALABAMA

Hired to drive forward momentum for community events, galas, and golf tournaments. Salvaged declining relationships with disgruntled volunteers in 5 counties. Secured corporate payroll deduction accounts to meet income goals. Recruited, trained, and supervised 700 volunteers.

- **Netted $300K+,** launching "Major Gifts Kick-off Breakfast" and business luncheon fundraiser.
- **Won National Summit Award 5 consecutive years** for surpassing income and program goals.

Emerging Leaders, Inc. – Birmingham, AL   2004–2008
PRESIDENT

Orchestrated business operations functions, including budgeting, hiring, performance management, training, and community relations. Cultivated relationships with Executive Board of Directors and Fortune 1000 CEOs to garner corporate-level support. Planned and executed special events, fundraisers, promotions, and major gifts initiatives. Strategized individual giving and marketing campaigns, bowl-a-thons, golf tournaments, and galas. Supervised 9 staff.

- **Increased revenue 50% in 9 months** and recruited 178 volunteers in first 12 months, reaching $1.1M goal.

EDUCATION

Bachelor of Arts in Event Management
University of Alabama – Tuscaloosa, AL

TRAINING

Consultative Sales | Crucial Conversations | Constructive Feedback Delivery | Performance Evaluations | Focus Meetings
Stand-Ups and Corrective Action | Public Speaking | Presentations

LAWRENCE MCMASTER

Montreal, PQ H3C 1V2 Canada

lmcmaster@hotmail.com • 514.222.1111

SERVANT LEADER | PRESIDENT & CEO | BUSINESS TURNAROUND EXPERT

Award-Winning Association Executive driving organizational change and fiscal accountability in highly competitive environments. Change driver for socially responsive organizations requiring **sustainable business transformation.**

Critical Competencies

- Strategic Planning
- Fund Development
- Change Management
- Program Development & Delivery

- Media & Government Relations
- National Health Policy Development
- Volunteer Recognition & Rewards
- Donor Relationship Strategies

- Capital Development & Project Planning
- Zero-Based Budgeting & Cash Flow
- Community Relations & Advertising
- Corporate Governance | Risk Control

Professional Experience

PRESIDENT AND CEO　　　　　Lung Association of Canada　　　　　2014 – Present

Non-profit dedicated to preventing and managing lung disease through research, advocacy, patient services, and education.

Reorganized underperforming association to a sustainable, results-oriented charity business.

CEO with full planning, operating, marketing, financial, legislative, regulatory, and administrative responsibility for programs, services, and business affairs. Reporting to Board of Directors, lead staff of 10 and $1.2M operating budget.

Organizational & Industry Leadership

- **Reversed 7-year decline in net revenue** by redesigning direct-mail program and annual Christmas Seals campaign.

- Co-Chaired Canadian National Health Strategy Committee and **secured $300K** disbursement to guide the delivery of lung health services across Canada.

- Negotiated purchase and renovation of 11,000 sq. ft. commercial property to serve as association headquarters and provide lucrative tenant revenue stream—resulting in **zero rent expense** for the association.

- **Generated $200K** from Public Health Agency of Canada to create "Asthma Aware," an evidence-based program to educate community leaders with children in their care.

Fundraising & Community Programs

- Exceeded $800K goal for planned-giving program with a **$1M planned gift.**

- Increased participation in Credit Union "Lung Run" from **280 to 850** and revenues from **$17K to $116K** in 5 years.

- Grew "Airway Run" revenues from **$32K to $65K,** partnering with Montreal International Airport Authority.

- Orchestrated and created "**Learn to Run for Smokers**" program—now delivered in 3 provinces.

BUILDING SOCIALLY RESPONSIVE ORGANIZATIONS THROUGH INNOVATION, OPERATIONAL EXCELLENCE, AND LEADERSHIP.

Maureen Farmer, CHRP, CCMC, CRS, CCS • Word Right Career • wordrightcareer.com

Note: Bold graphics highlight key achievements that are further detailed in bullet points. Although rich in content, the resume has ample white space and is very readable. A branding statement serves as a footer on both pages.

PRESIDENT AND CEO	Special Olympics of Canada	2001 – 2014

**Created the most successful athlete recruitment program in Canadian Special Olympics history …
invited to present program to Special Olympics International Congress in Washington, DC.**

Initially hired as the Provincial Program Director; led the creation of the athlete/coach development programs and the current competitive structure. Named nationwide General Manager in 2000 and the first President and CEO in 2003.

Organizational & Industry Leadership

- In partnership with core leadership team, recruited, motivated, and engaged a high-profile Board of Directors featuring numerous corporate and community leaders.

- Implemented sustainable system of volunteer and staff professional development and established a leadership structure within each of the **15 Special Olympic regions,** building future sustainable growth.

- Attended as Chef de Mission at 5 National Games and **directed 23 provincial multisport games** featuring 4–7 sports and approximately 1000 coaches and athletes.

- Served on the initial Special Olympics Canada Site Visit Team along with Dr. Frank Hayden—**world founder** of Special Olympics—evaluating programs and structure of Special Olympics British Columbia.

- **Elected by colleagues** to National Sport Program Committee, Special Olympics Canada, and Sport Manager Team Canada at World Special Olympics Summer Games in New Haven, CT.

Fundraising & Community Programs

- Grew revenues from **$250K to $450K and** diversified the fundraising program.
- Increased sustainable public funding from **$6K to $42K** annually as a result of a successful provincial government assessment. Result: Special Olympics of Canada ranked 7th of 60 national sport organizations.

- In partnership with National Tire, created the "National Tire Asthma Awareness School Program," presented to **12,000+ school children** and 350 teachers in inaugural year.

Fueled $200K in private + $36K public funding

Education and Professional Development

Bachelor of Arts in Economics and Marketing | University of New Brunswick, Fredericton, NB | 1999
Successfully Leading and Selling Change | Dalhousie University | Halifax | 2015
Strategic Planning to Lower Fundraising Costs and Boost Revenues | Ottawa University | Ottawa | 2015
Certificate in Leading Innovation | Saint Mary's University | Halifax | 2014
Governor General's Canadian Leadership Conference | 2014 and 2021

Awards and Accolades

- Awarded **Queen Elizabeth II Diamond Jubilee Medal** by Special Olympics of Canada in 2018 in recognition of exemplary past contributions.
- Earned Stamp of Excellence for transforming Special Olympics of Canada from an unrecognized sport organization to ***NATIONAL SPORT ORGANIZATION OF THE YEAR in 2011*** — awarded by Sport Canada.

BUILDING SOCIALLY RESPONSIVE ORGANIZATIONS THROUGH INNOVATION, OPERATIONAL EXCELLENCE, AND LEADERSHIP.

ANDREA SHACKELFORD

San Dimas, CA | 714-555-4835 | andreashack@gmail.com

TARGET: MARKETING ASSISTANT

High-performing business graduate prepared to assume entry-level marketing position within sports industry. Motivated professional with tireless work ethic, competitive drive, and determination to excel.

Quick to step up and take on tough challenges and leadership roles. Strong willingness to learn paired with ability to adapt to new environments. Highly effective at solving complex problems and remaining calm under pressure. Unique blend of creative and analytical skills.

Proficient in Adobe Creative Cloud, Canva, Final Cut Pro, and Microsoft Office Suite (Excel, PowerPoint, Word).

EDUCATION

Bachelor of Business Administration – Sports Management ◆ University of California, Irvine, CA (expected May 2023)

Honors Program | Minor: Communications | GPA: 3.8

- Varsity volleyball player, 3 years. Recognized by Orange County Collegiate Volleyball League for academic excellence.
- Member, Pi Kappa Alpha Fraternity. Led content development process as Board Secretary (2021–2022).

High School Diploma ◆ Torrey Pines High School, San Diego, CA (2019)

GPA: 4.2 | Magna cum Laude | Baseball, football, volleyball, and basketball player

EXPERIENCE

MARKETING & BUSINESS DEVELOPMENT INTERN, Gold's Gym, Fullerton, CA (2022)

> *Gained hands-on marketing experience, training, and education during 4-month internship at personal training gym.*

- Developed and executed social media content strategy that more than doubled Instagram engagement in 2 months.
- Utilized Canva to create new marketing brochure with more engaging and professional design and layout.
- Built and presented comprehensive business plan for second store location. Created market and competitive analysis, marketing and sales strategy, operating plan, and financial projections.

ASSISTANT STORE MANAGER, Dick's Sporting Goods, Fullerton, CA (2021–2022)

> *Promoted from sales associate to assistant store manager after 4 months. Developed critical skills in diverse areas of retail management, including marketing, sales, finance, operations, communications, customer service, and conflict resolution.*

- Played key role in designing and executing product assortment strategy, resulting in second-highest sales in region.
- Exceeded expectations for customer rewards program, achieving 91%+ enrollment (10% above quota).
- Recognized for successfully deescalating and handling stressful situations and conflicts in workplace.

SUMMER CAMP SUPPORT INTERN & COUNSELOR, Mount Palomar Summer Camp, Palomar, CA (2019–2020)

> *Provided ongoing support to summer camp leaders, ensuring camp programs ran smoothly and effectively.*
> *Developed and managed social media presence. Designed and implemented innovative and engaging camp programs.*

- Successfully leveraged Facebook to enhance community outreach and increase summer camp enrollment.
- Built trust with parents and boosted camper retention by promptly and efficiently addressing questions and concerns.

Kelly Gadzinski, ACRW • KG Career Services • kgcareerservices.com

Note: To help Andrea stand out in a large pool of entry-level candidates, her resume is focused on results rather than responsibilities. The headline makes her target crystal-clear.

JANE BROWN

215.555.7654 – JBROWN@GMAIL.COM – PHILADELPHIA, PA

SOCIAL MEDIA MANAGER

- Expert in social media platform functionality, engagement, analytics, scheduling, and search engine optimization.
- Direct, concise, compelling communicator.
- Key contributor and project leader who clearly executes creative direction, brings new ideas to the team, and thrives in highly collaborative environments.

EXPERIENCE

MMO Gaming, Inc., Allentown, PA   2021–Present
Community Manager

- Lead team of 60 social media specialists to provide online customer assistance to **4.3M subscribers globally**.
- Eliminated phone wait times to customer lines through introduction of weekly Twitter chat (#MMONews) to brief customer base on changes from latest expansions or patches, **saving company $1.2M** annually in staffing hours and operating costs.
- Collaborate with IT, UX, and executives as tester on development team to ensure mobile, PC, and tablet accessibility.

E-Gaming Accessories, Philadelphia, PA   2017–2021
Social Media Manager

- Increased follower base **85% within 4 months** by optimizing website for searchability and reporting out on activity analytics.
- Initiated online promotions to improve in-store traffic, resulting in **35% quarterly sales increase**.
- Managed and coordinated monthly blog to share news and product updates from owners.

Datacom Industries, Trenton, NJ   2015–2017
Social Media Specialist

- Drafted posts for corporate blog and social accounts.
- Researched industry trends and presented topics at monthly meetings.
- Corresponded with public across accounts using various management tools and analytics.

SKILLS

Core Competencies: Strategic Planning, Engagement, Community Management, Search Engine Optimization (SEO), HTML

Software & Platforms: Proficient on both Mac & PC. Skilled in design for promotional content using Photoshop, Prezi, Illustrator, Dreamweaver, InDesign, Canva.

Social Media: Twitter, Facebook, LinkedIn, Vimeo, Instagram, Snapchat, Pinterest, WordPress, Vine, Blogger, Google+, YouTube

Management Tools: Tweepi, Hootsuite, Tweetdeck, Google Analytics, Klout

Microsoft: Word, Excel, Project, Outlook, PowerPoint

FOLLOW ME ONLINE

WWW.JBROWN.COM   /JBROWN

/IN/JANEBROWN   /JBPINNING

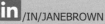

EDUCATION

University of Pennsylvania – **Bachelor of Arts Degree in Communication** – 2015
Concentration in Journalism and Marketing

Erica Tew, CPRW • CT Department of Labor • ct.gov/dol

Note: Erica's resume rewards readers with valuable information in every glance. Her target is clear and supported by relevant job titles. Her achievements are prominent, her skills are showcased, and her online presence (key for her target role of Social Media Manager) is visibly displayed.

ELVIRA PETERSEN

London, UK   📞 + 44 (020) 3444 7895 | ✉ elvira.petersen@hotmail.com | 🔗 linkedin.com/in/elvira-petersen

CREATIVE DIRECTOR

Strategic Brand Design | B2C2V | Contract Negotiations | International Sales Management | Customer Journey | Media Content

- Appointed national Managing Director at age 27. Built major player on European market in 3 years. Trilingual (Italian, English, Swedish).
- Reputation for building relationships at all levels and composing and training high-performing sales teams.
- Negotiated €800.000 to €2.6M framework agreements.
- Outperformed 4 other organisations' turnover and profitability within 2 years of launch.

CAREER & ACHIEVEMENTS

Global Media Awards (GMA)   2013–Present

Leading content marketing agency producing 300+ specialised cross-media campaigns/year across Europe. 150+ staff.

MANAGING DIRECTOR, GMA UK, London, Apr 2016–Present

Full P&L (6-8 M€) and staff (35 FTE, 8 direct reports: sales director, business developers, corporate recruiter, content studio, financial administrator). Report to 3 owners. Member of 4-person UK management team.

- Asked by owners to head up new office in UK; found and negotiated office facility, recruited 10 employees, negotiated contracts with distributions channels, trained sales staff, and set budget.
- Captained pioneering launch of independent lifestyle magazine (BXC) distributed monthly with London's leading daily newspapers.
- Streamlined onboarding process and initiated job ads with best dividend yields utilizing LinkedIn, IG, and FB.

Achievements (select):

- Delivered 100% increased YoY revenue over 4 years. GMA now major player on European market.
  - Built most commercially successful GMA operation out of 5, with sales director.
  - Initiated and launched new roles, bonuses, and salary model.
  - Launched annual awards for best project management, sales, and employees.
- Negotiated exclusive contracts with 3 largest distribution channels in UK.
  - Saved 21% (€950,000→€750,000) by analysing communication (email and dialogue).
- Secured exclusive deals with 4 leading daily newspapers by outcompeting majority of competition.
- Saved €10,000–€15,000/month and improved deliveries by building 360° content studio from scratch.

> **AWARDED**
> within 2 years
> for highest
> turnover,
> profitability, and
> growth in group.

HEAD OF PRODUCTION, Malmö, Sweden, May 2013–Apr 2016

- Recruited to 4-month old startup and team of 5 to be Art Director and run everything from brand profile/graphic design, to layout of magazines, to creating ads and coordinating with 3 printing houses.
  - Handled bookings, relationships with printing companies, editorial staff, and project manager.
  - Created ads for Mercedes Benz, PEAB, Vattenfall, and others.
- Directed editions in Sweden, Germany, and Denmark and 100 releases/country/year.
- Co-developed with CEO and founder internal business school to grow talent.

ABCD Weekend   2012–2013

Founded in 2005, 190,000 circulation, distributed 10 times/year to households in Southern Sweden.

EDITOR-IN-CHIEF, Oct 2012–May 2013
GRAPHIC DESIGNER, Jan 2012–Oct 2012

- Recruited to direct 13 different 30–40-page editions from concept to printed product.
- Developed magazine's format together with AD and designed all 16 editions.
- Created content (feature stories and editorials), oversaw layout, produced ads, coordinated with advertisers, and sent magazine to print.
- Co-directed deadline schedules and maintained relationships with customers and printing company.

EDUCATION & ADDITIONAL

BA in Design and Visual Communication, Copenhagen Business School, Denmark   2011
Lecturer (yearly), Copenhagen Business School (students in design program)   2013–Present
Languages: Swedish (native), Italian (bilingual), Dutch (95% understanding), English (fluent), Danish (conversational)

Birgitta Moller, ACRW, MRW • Cvhjälpen • cvhjalpen.nu

Note: A 1-page format highlights Elvira's rapid rise, numerous accomplishments, and impressive awards. The content is tightly written and energetic.

JANE HOWARD

(213) 875-5555 | jhoward@gmail.com | www.linkedin.com/in/jhoward | Los Angeles, CA

SENIOR SALES PROFESSIONAL
B2B SALES ▪ B2C SALES ▪ TEAM LEADERSHIP ▪ STRATEGIC MARKETING

- Personally closed deals with 4700+ clients, generating $4.7M and regularly ranking in the top 5% companywide.
- Led team to a 125% increase in new corporate memberships in first 2 years as Sales Manager.

"I would bet on you for any problem-solving, strategy, or sales management competitions." –GM, All Star Athletic Clubs

▪ SALES EXPERIENCE ▪

All Star Athletic Clubs   Pacific Palisades, CA | 2012 – Present
An upscale health club with 11 locations and 40,000 members
Sales Manager | 2019– Present • **Senior Sales Representative** | 2016 – 2019 • **Sales Representative** | 2012– 2016

Market and manage B2B and B2C membership sales, renewals, and personal training. Heighten company brand awareness through innovative corporate initiatives such as outreach programs and promotional events.

Cultivate and maintain an extensive network of contacts/clients through prospect lead generation, cold-calling, lead tracking, marketing campaigns, and print advertising. Recruit, train, and lead sales representatives.

B2B SALES

- Led Santa Monica sales team that increased total corporate revenue 59% and new corporate memberships **125%** over past 2 years by mining, targeted cold-calling, cultivating and developing C-level relationships, and offering exclusive programming for businesses.
- Closed **8** new corporate accounts; maintained and grew 12 existing accounts.

B2C SALES

- Regularly ranked in top **5%** among **60–80** sales reps.
- Achieved a consistent average of **114%** of quota.
- Averaged **60%** success rate in cross-selling personal training packages, exceeding corporate average of **41%**.
- Generated **48%** of sales from referrals.

TEAM LEADERSHIP

- Led sales team to generate **$2.8M** in sales and close deals with 2700 clients. Met or exceeded median club performance **19** out of **22** months, despite increasing local competition.
- Personally produced **$1.2M** with **1400+** clients while leading sales team during past 2 years.
- Surpassed goals for new membership units, with a team average of **111%** over quota in first year as Sales Manager.
- Achieved highest team renewal rate companywide, with **6%** increase from prior year.

TECHNOLOGY ACCOMPLISHMENTS

- Created a robust Excel customer tracking system to supplement outdated CRM.
- Selected as company beta-tester for Salesforce.com and Motionsoft.

▪ EDUCATION ▪

PEPPERDINE UNIVERSITY | Bachelor of Arts in Psychology, With Highest Honors | Malibu, CA | 2009

Lucie Yeomans, NCOPE, CEIC, CGRA, OPNS • Your Career Ally • yourcareerally.com
Note: The first thing that catches your attention on this resume is the graph that illustrates revenue growth. That strong first impression is reinforced when you read Jane's many accomplishments, organized for quick scanning and filled with bold numbers and results.

Fred Johnson

LinkedIn Profile | 857-554-4444 | fred.johnson@gmail.com

Sales Manager – Specialty Foods
Commodity Food Items — Major Food Categories — Imported & Domestic
Fluent in English & Italian

- Transformed stagnant revenue stream into a thriving $14M+ business.
- Closed 6-figure deals while maximizing profitability.
- Drove rapid company growth through consultative, relationship-based sales.

Endorsements

Fred is dedicated and excellent at his sales job. He has in-depth knowledge of all his customers' buying patterns and has great perception on price in the marketplace.
*- Sarah Seaborn, **Field Sales Manager at MB Food Distributors***

His passion for food and knowledge is quite extensive. He has been a great help in providing and sourcing items. Fred is a "get the job done" kind of guy.
*- Richard Garcia, **Foodie's Urban Market***

He is delightful to work with. Customer oriented, responsive, detailed and thorough. Perfect!
*- Keisha Jones, **Downtown Food Emporium***

Areas of Expertise

Solution Selling	Relationship Building	Account Management
Revenue Generation	Rapid Growth & Expansion	Contract Negotiations
Profit Optimization	Customer Service	Promotion Planning

Professional Experience

MB Food Distributors, East Boston, MA
Wholesale distributor, selling more than 24,000 ingredients to the bakery and supermarket industries.

Sales Director *(2018 – Present)*

Report directly to owner while managing all aspects of sourcing, pricing, and selling both commodity and specialized food items. Sell to a portfolio of 250+ accounts comprising restaurants, wholesalers, distributors, and hotels. Process daily orders ranging from $200 to more than $100K, perform pricing analysis, develop revenue forecasts, and anticipate market trends to create new sales opportunities.

- Boosted overall revenue stream from $3M to $14.5M, accounting for 23% of $60M annual income.
- Consistently generated the highest gross margins among entire sales force of 30 since second year of tenure.
- Single-handedly expanded product line from 12 commodity items to 200+ specialty food items including non-GMO, gourmet pastries, and organic foods.
- Cultivated lucrative partnership with a major account by eliminating contracts, simplifying pricing structure, developing buying incentives, and offering seasonal promotions.
- Earned *Supplier of the Year Award* for Foodie's Urban Market, becoming their preferred vendor in 2020.

Continued...

Melanie Denny, CPRW, CIPCC • melaniedenny.com
Note: Ample white space and attention-getting Endorsements create strong visual appeal, while quantified achievements and ample industry-specific experience will attract future employers.

Fred Johnson

LinkedIn Profile | 857-554-4444 | fred.johnson@gmail.com | Page 2 of 2

Chelsea Foods, Inc., Chelsea, MA
$50M specialty foodservice distributor, specializing in high-end hotels and restaurants

Customer Service Sales Representative *(2011 – 2018)*

Serviced customer accounts, ensuring product offerings aligned with customer needs to build trust and loyalty. Enhanced product line by introducing imported specialty items, ultimately improving profit margins.

- Launched and directed specialty cheese division, achieving up to 40% margin versus 20% among colleagues.
- Expanded market reach and generated $8M in revenue by leveraging relationships with industry suppliers.

Boston Wholesalers, Boston, MA
One of the largest importers and distributors of fresh produce and specialty foods in Northeast and Mid-Atlantic.

Sales Representative *(2008 – 2011)*

Recruited to expand regional produce sales. Recognized opportunity to tap into dairy space and lobbied new dairy sector to company president.

- Gained approval to start and run entire dairy division from the ground up.
- Expanded facility to store inventory within 2 months.
- Leveraged industry contacts to pre-sell $20K–$30K in cream cheese on day 1 of department opening.

Prior

Served as Quality Control Manager at International Food Corporation, ensuring the accuracy and quality of incoming and outgoing orders of specialty imported foods, particularly limited production international cheeses.

Education

University of Massachusetts, Boston, MA
Bachelor of Science in Business Administration – Concentration in Food Science

ROGER LITTMAN

941-663-3663 | rlittman@gmail.com | LinkedIn

SALES MANAGEMENT EXECUTIVE—COMMUNICATIONS & TECHNOLOGY SECTOR
B2B SOLUTION SALES | PIPELINE DEVELOPMENT | SALES TEAM BUILDING & LEADERSHIP

Leading exceptional sales team performance and aggressive revenue growth amid rapid change.

→ **Results above target in every role, and virtually always through significant organizational transition,** including post-merger integration, business startup, turnaround, and business model transformation. Double-digit growth in each of the last 3 years; significant share in all markets.

→ **Deep sector expertise and insights** through experience with BigCom, ComSouth, CorporateCom, and ABCCom. Find and cultivate revenue opportunities. Develop and adapt product/service positioning and compelling value propositions to executive-level prospects and customers at leading companies.

→ **High-impact team building and leadership,** driving clarity of purpose, engagement, and the highest levels of consistent performance. Invaluable ability to assess team capabilities and gaps and steer strategic realignment.

> **ADDITIONAL KEY COMPETENCIES**
>
> CLIENT RELATIONSHIP MANAGEMENT
>
> GO-TO-MARKET STRATEGY
>
> M&A INTEGRATION
>
> SALES OPERATIONS
>
> COMMUNICATION & PRESENTATIONS
>
> TEAM ASSESSMENT & TRANSFORMATION

PROFESSIONAL EXPERIENCE

BIGCOM (FORMERLY MIDCOM)   **2018 – Present**
VICE PRESIDENT OF SALES

Joined MidCom to steer turnaround of the wholesale and enterprise sales team. Following the acquisition of MidCom by BigCom (2016), **tapped to drive post-merger team integration and sales momentum across 16 markets,** accelerating growth and evolution from traditional cable provider to leading-edge tech company.

- Led the post-acquisition transformation of the legacy BigCom team, integration of both companies' sales teams, and double-digit revenue growth over each of the last 3 years.

- Spearheaded new business development with the 4 largest wireless carriers in the US, attaining strong market share where the company operates, including 80% share in legacy MidCom markets.

- Developed and turned around first MidCom team, executing 15 new multi-year customer contracts and expanding revenues from $1 million to $20+ million in 2 years, and later to $72 million.

- Completely revamped the customer proposition, connecting more effectively with key targets.

- Assessed team capabilities and streamlined team from 15 to 8, focusing on core strengths and realizing immediate performance improvement.

- Facilitated introduction and business partnership that resulted in acquisition of XYZ Communications.

> → **Double-digit YOY growth post-merger**
> → **Leading market share**
> → **Team turnaround: 20X growth in 2 years**

Cathy Alfandre, MBA, MILR, MRW, CCMC, NCOPE • Catherine A. Alfandre, LLC • cathyalfandre.com
Note: Designed to make Roger's results and value jump off the page, this resume combines detailed bullets with high-impact shaded boxes—one for each of his positions—that feature the most notable results in shortened form.

COMSOUTH   2009 – 2018
SENIOR DIRECTOR OF SALES (2014 – 2018)

Promoted to lead not only continued growth of enterprise and wholesale markets, but also to transform the under-producing international access division. Led sales and sales support organization of 30 people.

- Drove cross-business YOY growth to $200+ million.

- Achieved profitability of global division in first year and accelerated sales in Europe and South America markets from $5 million to $50 million within 2 years.

- Identified and implemented cost-saving opportunities, including integration of teams, resource sharing, and closing of 2 offices.

- Conceived and spearheaded product repositioning to attract and secure business from global Fortune 500 companies.

> → **Multi-unit growth to $200+M**
> → **Turned around global division and achieved 10X growth**

DIRECTOR OF SALES (2009 – 2014)

Led startup sales group to serve enterprise and wholesale market segments, with a focus on repositioning the brand from a stodgy, regulated experience to an agile and innovative service.

- Drove growth to >$20 million in the first year of operation and consistently exceeded all targets with one of the highest performing sales teams across the company.

- Hired, developed, managed, and mentored sales and marketing team that grew to 70 employees.

- Forged and sustained key client relationships, including with leading companies in multiple sectors.

- Selected for ComSouth's Gateway for Leadership Program.

> → **Startup to $20+M in 1 year**
> → **Developed vital new enterprise client relationships**

Prior sales leadership experience with:

CORPORATECOM

ABCCOM

> → **Built division from startup to $120M**
> → **Top performing team**

EDUCATION

WASHINGTON UNIVERSITY, St. Louis, Missouri
BA—MAJOR: ECONOMICS, MINOR: MARKETING

SALLY JOHNSON

https://www.linkedin.com/in/sallyjpr

Open to Relocation ♦ 737.995.6463 ♦ sallyjohnson@mac.com

PUBLIC RELATIONS / COMMUNICATIONS

Dedicated and creative new professional with an eye for detail poised to excel in the communications field. Proven track record as a social media innovator, gaining loyal followers and building brands to boost company profits.

- ♦ Strategic communicator who successfully pitched stories and ideas to bloggers and journalists.
- ♦ Confident public speaker spurring others to action. Impeccable organizer for high-profile events.
- ♦ Publisher of articles circulated to 40K+ students within campus community through social media tools.

Proficiencies & Technical Skills

Social Media Management │ Event Planning & Management │ Blogging │ Research │ Email Marketing │ Publicity │ Editing │ Press Releases │ Media Alerts │ Photoshop & InDesign │ AP Style │ MS Office │ Google Analytics

PUBLIC RELATIONS EXPERIENCE & INTERNSHIPS

Fashion Public Relations Intern, 2022–2023 ♦ BEVERLY SHAW IMAGE CONSULTING AGENCY, Orlando, FL

Selected out of 3 interns to deliver styling advice as part of high-profile event for 450 socialites.

Sought out new business opportunities and partnerships for fashion consultancy re-engaging with audience after a 1-year hiatus. Researched, targeted, and identified 12+ local events and drafted and disseminated proposal letters to introduce services. Developed promotional campaigns, pitch sheets, and press kits using InDesign.

Public Relations Chair, 2022–2023 ♦ DELTA SORORITY, Orlando, FL

Planned a community-service mentoring event for 6 junior high schools in Orlando.

Established local chapter presence of national service-based organization with 50K+ members. Managed social media presence (Facebook, Twitter) and increased website analytics 60% from prior year. Carried out publicity, organized 10 donation events, and coordinated charity clothing drive collecting 300 apparel items in just 3 days.

Public Relations Intern, 2022 ♦ KEY BRIGHT COMMUNICATIONS, Washington, D.C.

Pitched branded Look Book, an idea that increased sales within 30 days of implementation.

Drafted press releases, wrote media pitches, developed communication strategies, and authored web content for 8 clients as part of virtual internship. Built trust with CEO and audience, increasing social media presence by 365 followers within 5 months. Diagramed and sketched website wireframes during business rebranding process.

Director of Publicity, 2021–2022 ♦ ON-CAMPUS COUNCIL, Orlando, FL

Introduced new cinemagraph technique, Flixel, for promoting campus events.

Brought on to turn around low social media following. Collaborated with 10 event directors and organized brainstorming sessions with executive directors. Coordinated celebrity comedy events and concerts.

Social Media Intern, 2020–2021 ♦ SOCIAL SAVVY, Cocoa Beach, FL

Pitched paper products line, an idea that was successfully implemented in Fall 2013.

Created social media presence for event management firm. Grew Facebook page to 852 fans. Researched speaking engagements and managed photo shoots for annual social media conference.

EDUCATION

BA in Communication, Public Relations Concentration, 2023 ♦ SUNSHINE COLLEGE, Orlando, FL

Dean's List ♦ Member of Public Relations Society of America

Sophia Marshall, MHR, ACRW, BCC • MeSheet • mesheet.com

Note: Sally's resume is rich with keywords—appearing everywhere from her Summary, to Experience, to Education. A highlight of each position is pulled out into a highly visible 1-liner below each job title.

JASON OKORO

jason.okoro@gmail.com | LinkedIn.com/in/jason-okoro | 555-456-7890

HUMAN RESOURCES BUSINESS PARTNER
Change Management | Data Analytics | Performance Management

Human Resources professional with dual Master's in Human Resources/Industrial Relations and Business Administration. Passionate about enabling organizations to effectively achieve their business objectives and create a best-in-class employee experience. Experienced in labor relations and performance management, providing short- and long-term solutions for complex problems. Worked in a multinational, fast-paced, high-performance culture.

CAREER HIGHLIGHTS

- ☑ **Achieved 75% employee retention rate** by facilitating employee resource groups, counseling, and coaching.
- ☑ Revamped corrective action policy, ensuring consistency with corporate policy and **improving efficiency by 20%.**
- ☑ **Implemented change management strategy,** achieving fast adoption of ERP software, resulting in **40% increase in productivity.**

Employee Relations | Compliance | Recruiting | Human Resource Management | HRIS | Onboarding | Succession Planning | Human Resource Policies | Talent Development | Employment Law | Problem Solving | HR Generalist Functions

WORK EXPERIENCE

ABC Company, Pittsburgh, PA
HR Business Advisor & Labor Relations Representative (Jan. 2022 – Present)

Collaborate with Corporate Labor Relations team, updating them on Union Representative contracts and annual audits. Lead grievance investigations, gathering information on complaints and providing solutions for 800+ employees. Complete trainings on cyber security, learning how to safeguard the workplace against cyber threats.

- ☑ **Recruited 165 hourly workers** and coordinated the onboarding process.
- ☑ **Credited as key contributor to 75% retention rate** of both exempt and non-exempt employees—compared to 56% in prior year. Supported workers through employee resource groups, counseling, and coaching.
- ☑ **Increased employee morale 30%,** coaching and advising workers on human resource issues, performance management, and conflict resolution.
- ☑ Elected program manager for the ABC African-American Network, **developing programs to increase membership engagement, community service, and professional development.**

National Distributors, Inc., Chicago, IL
Human Resources Intern (Supply Chain) (May 2021 – Oct. 2021)

Served as human resource business partner for traffic center with 100+ drivers, building engagement and maintaining open communication. Advocated for frontline workers, leading investigations, recommending strategies to improve workplace culture, and building rapport with workers.

- ☑ **Coordinated diversity, engagement, and training** events for 30 interns.
- ☑ **Improved efficiency 20%** by revamping the corrective action policy to streamline implementation and ensure consistency with the corporate national policy.

Human Resource Intern (Sales) (May 2020 – Aug. 2020)

Provided support to 28 sales interns in Midwest, guiding and coaching them on optimizing their professional development. Investigated grievances involving frontline field workers, advocated on their behalf, and recommended solutions.

- ☑ **Boosted employee satisfaction 15%,** collaborating with national project teams on strategizes to optimize the hiring and onboarding process.

EDUCATION

University of Illinois at Urbana Champaign, IL	Champaign, IL
Master's In Business Administration	Graduation: December 2021
Master's In Human Resources & Industrial Relations	
University of Lagos	Lagos, NG
Bachelor Of Science In Economics	Graduation: December 2016

Kareem Rogers, NCOPE • HR Depot, LLC • hrdepotllc.com

Note: Offering rich, relevant experience through employment and internships, this young professional is poised to advance in the field of Human Resources. His resume shows career progression and substantial contributions in each role.

JACQUELINE J. JONES

Miami, FL | 205-352-4212 | jacqui-jones@gmail.com | www.linkedin.com/in/jjjones

SENIOR HUMAN RESOURCES BUSINESS PARTNER / TALENT MANAGEMENT ADVISOR

Organization Effectiveness | Professional & Career Development | Project Management

Accelerating peak performance through employee-centric recruiting, orientation, and onboarding strategies.

$600K Revenue Growth ★ 6X Outstanding Recruitment Achievement Nominee ★ 2X "Top 50 Recruiter" Nominee

4X-Certified HR Pro drawing from global recruiting and talent management expertise to amplify organizational achievements for cross-functional business units. Inspire peak performance and culture of excellence through mutually beneficial partnerships, consistent follow-up, and accountability. Coach and mentor business leaders, internal clients, and key employees, delivering company-wide training workshops and centralizing processes to influence positive change.

CAREER HIGHLIGHTS

 Formulated global recruitment strategy across multiple business lines in the U.S., Canada, and South America.

 Generated $600K in revenue for talent firm in 2–3 years by placing associate- to executive-level candidates.

 Yielded 6% employee attrition rate and raised productivity 35% while improving workplace communication.

Workforce Planning | Performance Improvement | Associate Management | Leadership Development | Budgeting
Organizational Development | Policies | Employee Assessments | Compensation | Benefits | Labor Relations
Metrics & Analytics | Mentoring & Coaching | Federal & State Labor Laws | Safety & Health

Software Knowledge: Human Resources Information Systems (HRIS) Tools and Web-based Applicant Tracking Systems, including Taleo, Peopleclick, SAP SuccessFactors, PageUp, and LinkedIn Recruiter.

PROFESSIONAL EXPERIENCE

Chemical X Firm – Dhahran, Saudi Arabia   **March 2017–Present**

REMOTE TALENT MANAGEMENT ADVISOR *(April 2021–Present)*

Promoted to lead 9-member team in design, implementation, and delivery of programs for 4K+ employees based in US and Saudi Arabia. Serve as critical point of contact for complex HR projects, including $3.5M onboarding overhaul, metrics reporting, assessment center, new employee orientation program, and monthly expatriate visa processing (up to 200 hires). Recruit key talent and control employee experience from background check facilitation to off-boarding. Advise employees through career pathing process to drive professional development and fortify succession planning.

★ Lowered turnover to 7% during early tenure in role.
★ Shortened new hire training period 4 weeks, capturing buy-in from team to revamp onboarding process and integrating technology that centralized procedures from sourcing through first 90 days.

SENIOR TALENT ACQUISITION ADVISOR – Staffing and Workforce Analysis *(March 2018–April 2021)*

Entrusted to fill management and business-critical roles, partnering with internal stakeholders on recruiting and succession planning activities to accelerate peak performance. Designed workflow processes for recruitment and new hire onboarding. Sourced and identified top talent through workshops and social media campaigns on LinkedIn and Bayt to boost retention for Saudi employees.

★ Slashed external agency usage 45% and improved quality of hires 67% after refining recruiting procedures and redesigning new employee orientation.

Ashley Watkins, NCRW, NCOPE • Write Step Resumes • writestepresumes.com

Note: The Summary is a powerful snapshot of expertise and achievements, most notably in an eye-catching Career Highlights box. Jacqueline's value is further supported by details in Professional Experience, and the sharp layout and ample white space make this resume inviting to read.

JACQUELINE J. JONES

Miami, FL | 205-352-4212 | jjjones@gmail.com | Page 2

ONBOARDING AND ORIENTATION SUPERVISOR *(March 2017–March 2018)*

Hired to guide full life cycle onboarding and mobilization process for Saudi National and expatriate employee groups. Managed analytics, visa processing, background checks, travel management, and program development. Designed and facilitated employee/expatriate Welcome Tour, New Hire Orientation, Apprentice Graduation, and YaHala Welcome Center to enhance the employee experience. Supervised 9 onboarding specialists.

Worldwide Petroleum Corp – Houston, TX   June 2011–March 2017

SOURCING SUPERVISOR

Led 5 recruiters in steering corporate recruitment and organizational branding strategy to fulfill high-volume hiring needs for technical and non-technical roles in upstream petroleum division. Designated as 3rd party agency liaison, coordinating fee negotiations, executive search engagements, and service level agreements (SLAs). Served as 1 of 3 recruitment leads for industry job fairs, corporate-wide Employee Referral Program (ERP), and H1-B visa recruitment program.

★ Rolled out Topgrading interview method, delivering monthly workshops with 65 hiring managers and interview panelists.
★ Tracked agency partner performance, implementing program with metrics assessments and annual evaluations.
   o Cut 3rd party agency fees 25% and boosted employee engagement and retention after introducing ERP.

EARLY CAREER

Lyndon Corp – Miami, FL   1 year

CONTRACT TALENT ACQUISITION AND RECRUITMENT SPECIALIST

USA Corp – Ft. Lauderdale, FL   7 years

SR. RECRUITER / TRAINING SPECIALIST

Professional Search Firm – St. Petersburg, FL   3 years

LEAD RECRUITER

Bob, Jack & Jill – Jacksonville, FL   3 years

EXECUTIVE RECRUITER

EDUCATION

Ruckers College – Miami, FL
Bachelor of Science in Organizational Human Resources Development

Nova University – Orlando, FL
Bachelor of Arts in Business Management (magna cum laude)
Graduate Certificate in Conflict Mediation and Negotiation

Certifications: Human Resources Business Professional (**HRBP**), Global Human Resources Professional (**GPHR**) Senior Professional in Human Resources (**SPHR**), and Certified Personnel Consultant (**CPC**)

AWARDS

Top 50 Recruiters in FL Nomination | Florida Association of Recruiting Consultants   2 consecutive years
Outstanding Recruitment Achievement Nomination | Miami Association of Recruiting Consultants   6 consecutive years

Maya Musa

504.222.6324 | mayamusa@email.com | Marrero, LA, 70072 | linkedin.com/in/mayamusa

VICE PRESIDENT - DIVERSITY, EQUITY, INCLUSION
Mission-Driven, Growth Focused Change Agent: Nonprofit & Public Sector

TEDx Speaker | Board Member | Award-Winning Community Builder | Social Change Advocate

DIVERSITY EXECUTIVE advancing racial and disability equity by leveraging social and financial capital in higher education, nonprofit, and government agencies. A natural leader with fresh insights drawing diverse stakeholders to philanthropy and assessment tools to build community and system advocacy.

Signature career achievements:

- Educate national audiences as an **eight-time plenary speaker and workplace trainer on issues of race, equity, and disability** on prominent stages such as the United Nations and Ivy League institutions.
- Increased sense of belongingness by **75%** in the Black student population at Ivy University in a two-year period.
- Recovered **$80M+** with three new revenue streams and achieved solvency in first nine months as Vice President.

Leadership Expertise: Community Engagement, Organizational Development, Program Development, Coalition Management, Diversity Training, Leadership Development, Fundraising, Program Evaluation, Staff Development

Relevant Experience

Hearing Connections – New Orleans, LA   2022 – Current

VICE PRESIDENT – Community Engagement
Overview: Took historically bleeding department to solvent in nine months, doubling revenue sources in one year.
- Oversee close to **$1M** budget with **72%** of FY22 revenue goal met **11** months before end of fiscal year.
- Nurture **20**-person staff's professional growth with five direct reports receiving promotions in the last year.
- Invented certification programs that secured nine higher education partners.
- Grew income streams from two to five with from-scratch fundraising efforts that cultivated corporate sponsorships.
- Launched first donor management system (CRM) and Social Assessment division for the large global nonprofit.

Ivy University – Portland, ME   2019 – 2022

DIRECTOR | ASSISTANT DEAN OF STUDENTS – The Office of Diversity, Equity & Inclusion
Overview: Addressed Black student disconnect by more than doubling campus-wide belonging via social capital.
Community Building
- Won 2021 Student Affairs Award for increasing belongingness **75%** in underrepresented students.
- Increased Black student engagement by acting on institutional and student assessment outcomes:
  - Initiated Black student graduation ceremony and the annual Black Legacy Month, traditions still alive today; named unofficial member of the Black Class of 2021.
  - Almost tripled Greek system presence from two to five houses within two years.

Fundraising & Administration
- Raised over half of the **$90K** budget each academic year (**57%** in FY19/20 and **68%** in FY20/21).
- **Promoted to Director after four months.** Supervised cross-functional team of **13**.

Meg Applegate
Note: Tight writing (most bullet points are 1 line), lots of white space, clear division between items and sections, and a crisp font (Tahoma) make this resume easy to read. What you notice most are Maya's impressive achievements, exactly as intended.

Relevant Experience cont. | Ivy University Cont...

Program Management
- Led and developed **15** campus-wide programmatic initiatives annually, addressing racial equity and system change.
- Advised on academics, leadership, and identity development with the **450**-student caseload.

USA Hearing Advisory (USAHA) – Boston, MA   2016 – 2019

DIRECTOR OF POLICY & GOVERNMENT
Overview: Expanded organization's national political impact by engaging U.S. congressional committees.
- Secured a longstanding seat on the National Communication Disability Advisory Committee.
- Collaborated with the **10**-member executive board and three staff members.

State University – Boston, MA   2014 – 2016

COUNSELOR – Employment & Disability Services
Overview: Led 250-student advising program and achieved a 95% graduation rate for students with disabilities.
- Accomplished **84%** job placement rate, securing internships and jobs for students with disabilities.
- Spearheaded holistic advising/mentoring program for **58** students. Recruited **100%** of student caseload.
- Decreased missed appointments by **76%** through automated follow-up and online scheduling/rescheduling tool.

Advisory Board & Council Membership

ADVISORY BOARD MEMBER
Ivy University, Dept. of Communications & Allied Health   2019 – 2022
Center University Black Graduate Women's Association   2017 – 2018

ADVISORY COUNCIL MEMBER
U.S. Disability Advisor Council   2018 – 2020
Commonwealth of Massachusetts Developmental Disabilities Council – Appointed by Governor   2015 – 2016

Education & Certification

M.S.Ed Higher Education – with Honors, Gem Foundation Research Scholar – Center University

M.A. Counseling – with Honors – Ivy University

B.A. Sociology – with Honors, Mable R. Senior Scholar – Florida University

Public Dialogue Facilitator | Restorative Justice Practitioner

JOANIE PETERS

123-456-7890 | Dennis, MA 02634 | email@bryant.edu | www.linkedin.com

BACHELOR OF SCIENCE IN BUSINESS ADMINISTRATION
TARGET: FINANCIAL SERVICES

Highly regarded team leader with project experience in market research, competitor analysis, and business plan development. Self-directed, focused, flexible problem solver keen to identify opportunities and provide solutions. Personable and professional communicator who forms collaborative relationships with peers, superiors, and clients.

EDUCATION
Bryant University *Smithfield, RI* | May 2023
BACHELOR OF SCIENCE IN BUSINESS ADMINISTRATION | Financial Services Major; Sociology Minor
3.5 GPA | Dean's List | Alpha Kappa Delta, International Sociology Honor Society

COURSE HIGHLIGHTS

**Individual Taxation | Investments, Financial Institutions, and Markets | Risk Management and Insurance
Law of Financial Institutions | Multinational Finance | Real Estate Finance | Management of Banking Institutions**

BUSINESS COURSE PROJECT TEAM LEADER

Foundations of Marketing Management
- Collaborated with national consulting company, ALKU. Conducted market research and competitor analysis to determine effective means of recruiting millennials. Presented recommendations.

Management Principles and Practice
- Partnered with Rhode Island Military Organization to help connect active-duty personnel, veterans, and disabled veterans with services. Redesigned website, networked with agencies, and helped establish volunteer system.

Bryant IDEA
- Utilized design thinking process to develop marketing plan for car dealerships. Recommended showroom changes and social media campaign.

Global Foundations of Business
- Developed business plan and marketing strategy for new product. Researched current market trends.

CAPSTONE PROJECT

Race & Ethnicity | Studied effects of stereotypes and perceptions of ability among races and within higher education.

WORK EXPERIENCE
BUSINESS ANALYST INTERN, Georges Resources, Ltd. *Boston, MA* | September 2022 – June 2023
- Conducted studies for capacity and representative pricing on life insurance policies as part of periodic evaluation of ultra-high net worth portfolios. Met with policyholders to assure alignment with objectives.
- Partnered with banks to quantify impact of loan rate changes on life insurance policies. Identified discrepancies and recalculated benefits.

ADMISSIONS FELLOW, Admissions Office at Bryant University *Smithfield, RI* | August 2022 – June 2023
- Chosen to represent Bryant University to prospective students and families. Interviewed applicants, conducted tours, and worked open houses. Wrote handwritten thank-you notes on behalf of Admissions Office.
- Helped new students, transfers, and athletes by answering questions and providing valuable insight. Contributed unique perspective and experiences to enrich the Fellow program.

HOST / SERVER / BARTENDER, Baxter's Grille *Truro, MA* | Summers 2019 – 2022

COMMUNITY SERVICE | Bryant Best Buddies, Executive Board Member | CALO, Committee Member

Stacie Fehrm, Med, CPRW • Stacie Writes Resumes • staciewritesresumes.com

Note: The heftiest portion of this resume is Education, where relevant class projects are described in some detail. A valuable internship and other employment are presented under Work Experience.

ASTRID NILLSEN

AMN@email.com | 555.222.1111 | linkedin.com/in/astridnillsen

 I attribute my own professional success to my partnership with Astrid – she motivates and coaches in a manner rarely seen.

PROFILE OF A FINANCE PROFESSIONAL: Catalyst for essential change

✳ **10 years' experience developing and directing award-winning finance teams; recognized for exceptional revenues, team performance, and client engagement and retention.**

- **Distinguished and charismatic leader** who mentors for top performance, achieving results that exceed expectations and raise the bar. People-oriented. Decisive. Resourceful.
- Keen ability to **create a vision that disrupts status quo**, stirs admiration, earns accolades, and paves the way for a resilient business future. Dynamic. Entrepreneurial.
- **Genuine leader and team builder** who contributes significantly, ensures ethical decisions, and steers through challenges with composure. Fact- and principle-driven.

Business Skills	High-Performance Leadership	Technical Skills
Annual Business Plan	Change Management	CRM Salesforce
Financial Management	Business Development	MS Office
Risk Analysis/Management	HR Programs and Initiatives	Naviplan
Community & Public Relations	Performance Management	Univeris
Client Relationship/Engagement	Sales Leadership and Coaching	Zoom

PROFESSIONAL EXPERIENCE: Visionary leader recognized for excellence

Liberty & Life Financial | Portland, Oregon | Industry leader in insurance, wealth solutions, and customized health programs

FINANCIAL CENTER MANAGER   2013 – 2023

Team: 3 Managers, ~30 Advisors, 4 Administrative staff | Salaried & Commissioned

Overall Achievements: Spearheaded cultural, operational, and performance transformation.

- **Transformed underperforming center into Award of Merit-recognized center, achieving ongoing top 5% standing each quarter after year two (measured alongside 90 other financial centers).**
- Mentored and motivated financial advisors to write viable business, without pause, leading team to qualify our team of >400 in 9 consecutive campaigns, an unprecedented effort and achievement.
- Achieved up to 126% of wealth targets and clean annual financial center audits, YOY, after initial operational transformation in year one.
- Invited by President to share intellectual property as panel member of *Pygmalion Group*, company's top performers.
- Introduced client experience improvements that were rolled out to all financial centers nationwide.

Methodology: 100% responsibility and 0% excuses

- **Focus:** Proactively addressed governance, recruitment and retention, sales strategies, performance and training/mentoring, and other human resource and operational issues.
- **Balance:** Appropriately bridged center's management within corporate structure, effectively blending entrepreneurial and corporate requirements for risk management and governance.
- **Annual Planning:** Created business and financial plans that incorporated and genuinely contributed to community presence – sponsoring >10 local sports teams, clubs, and other charities.
- **Performance:** Communicated high expectations, sharing best practices, conducting joint work, and creating annual full-day event that offered training and recognized achievements.

Stephanie Clark, BA, MCRS, MRW • linkedin.com/in/stephaniebclark-wordsmith/

Note: This resume opens with a powerful endorsement, then continues with a Summary that conveys character as well as expertise and achievements. Category headings, and a page turn, break up what would be an over-long list of bullet points needed to describe a 10-year span in one job.

Methodology: continued

- ○ **Data Analysis:** Leveraged internal software to conduct forecasting—risk, ratings, and quality of business. Closely monitored performance-to-goal with monthly spreadsheets and discussions.
- ○ **Human Resources:** Fulfilled accountability for all HR functions—recruitment, code of conduct, change management, benefits and compensation, succession planning (12 in last 3 years), and more.
- ○ **Client Services:** Maintained tight control on service delivery, approving each transaction and connecting with each new client. Partnered with advisors for best outcomes and high client retention.
- ○ **Operational Processes:** Managed spend, addressing inefficiency by actively seeking input. Managed recruitment and training to reduce turnover. Conducted surveys for to gain perspective and identify new opportunities.
- ○ **Compliance:** Rectified audit-compliance issues, partnering with internal investigators as Head of Compliance and actively accepting accountability for every aspect of business.

Union Securities Inc. | Seattle, Washington | A leading wealth management firm in Washington State since 1901

INVESTMENT ADVISOR   2001 – 2013

Mandate: Through networking, cold calling, COI relationship building, and client referrals, attracted and retained high-net-worth clients with minimum account size of $500K in investible assets.

- ○ Retained all but 2 clients in 12 years.

Overall Contributions:

- ○ Recognized for achievements as 3x recipient of President's Club Award.
- ○ Achieved Wealth Management Award of Excellence.

EDUCATION

Washington State University | Business Administration
United States Securities Institute | CSC, CPH, Ethics, PFP, WMT, FMA
Insurance Council of Oregon | Individual—Life, Accident & Sickness
Investment Funds Institute | Branch Manager Course

Professional Development:

- ○ In-house training (Liberty & Life) in leadership and management, human resources, communications, conflict resolution, workforce planning, talent management, succession planning, and more.
- ○ Annual conference attendee at International USA annual Leadership and Management Program (financial services industry's premier annual event draws 3000+ global leaders and executives).

BILL SMITH, CPA, MBA

Lakewood OH 44107 • 216-456-6543 • bill.smith27@gmail.com • www.linkedin.com/in/billsmithcpa/

CHIEF FINANCIAL OFFICER – CHIEF ACCOUNTING OFFICER

Award-winning Senior Accounting and Financial Executive with 20+ years of fast-track experience leading initiatives in financial reporting, SEC documentation, and M&A for Fortune 100 public organizations.

- ➲ **Transformational change agent** who turns around struggling financial and accounting functions by optimizing workforces, accelerating reporting, streamlining processes, and igniting cultural change.

- ➲ **Mergers & Acquisitions consultant** who advises on optimal tax and divestiture strategies. Integration leader who combines accounting and financial teams and policies.

- ➲ **Empowering servant leader** who develops employees to achieve goals and attain promotions. Sought-after mentor followed by many direct reports to new companies. Earned reputation for making a difference in employees' careers.

- ➲ **Collaborative director** who aligns cross-functional teams around shared goals.

> **Recipient "Crain's CFO of the Year—Atlanta"** for transforming accounting offering, exuding strong management style, and orchestrating successful partnerships with vendors.

EXECUTIVE COMPETENCIES

Leadership: Coaching & Mentoring | Succession Planning | Team Building | Employee Engagement | Performance Reviews | Employee Development

Finance & Accounting: Internal & External Reporting | Benefits Accounting | Audit | Tax | Bankruptcy | SEC Reporting | Earnings Call Preparation | Technical Accounting | Sarbanes Oxley | Treasury | Credit & Collections

Human Resources: Talent Acquisition | Benefits | Workforce Transformation | Compensation

Mergers & Acquisitions: Integration | Due Diligence | Tax Strategies | Accounting Policies Integration | Balance Sheet Valuation Diligence | Divestitures

PROFESSIONAL EXPERIENCE

XYZ Inc., Atlanta, GA   8/2016–Present

Executive Vice President, Chief Financial Officer, and Treasurer (1/2020–Present)

Lead and manage general accounting functions, including generation of financial statements for SEC reporting. Oversee financial reporting and technical accounting research. Manage finance team with treasury, credit, collections, and financial planning and analysis. Direct all tax activities for company's annual federal and state income tax returns. Manage enterprise-wide human resources functions: talent acquisition and management, benefits, performance reviews, and compensation. Prepare and facilitate Board and Audit Committee materials on quarterly and annual basis.

- ▪ **Awarded distinguished "Crain's CFO of the Year—Atlanta"** for transforming accounting organization, exuding strong management style, and collaborating with internal and external customers.

- ▪ **Served on senior management team that facilitated sale of XYZ business in 2020 for $330.8M.** Supported data requests with carve-out audit and completed on time. Provided board with accounting guidance discussion points. Evaluated tax strategies on deferring tax gain for sale of property.

- ▪ **Reduced rent expense by $43.1M** as part of team that repurchased 20 leased sites from SVC for $308M.

- ▪ **Renegotiated company's $200M credit facility syndication.**

- ▪ **Enabled accurate evaluation of capital projects** by developing processes that generated realistic scope, cost, ROI expectations, and time projections.

- ▪ **Promoted 10 direct reports within five years** by providing mentoring and coaching.

Rebecca Bosl, MBA, MLS, CERM, NCRW, CPRW, CJSS, CCMC, CPPC, CEIS, WPB5, NCOPE, Reach Personal Branding Strategist • Dream Life Team • dreamlifeteam.com

Note: Bill's resume clearly communicates that he can turn around struggling organizations, has deep M&A (mergers and acquisitions) experience, and excels as an empowering manager. A shaded box in the Summary calls attention to a prestigious award.

BILL SMITH, CPA, MBA | PAGE 2

XYZ Inc., continued

Senior Vice President and Chief Accounting Officer *(8/2016–12/2019)*

Transformed the accounting, tax, and financial reporting departments/activities following a period of material weaknesses and deficiencies within the organization. Created information for and attended audit committee meetings, board meetings, and earnings calls.

- **Reduced costs by bringing tax function in-house.** Streamlined processes and fixed material weaknesses. Received millions of dollars in tax refunds.

- **Orchestrated workforce transformation** by hiring VP of Tax, Manager of General Accounting, and Manager of Financial Reporting and by downsizing underperforming employees. Reorganized department to support normal cadence of SEC filing and to instill sense of urgency.

ABC Corporation, Cleveland, OH   11/2010–8/2014

Publicly traded global power management company with $21.6B in revenue and 99,000 global employees.

Vice President Technical Accounting and Reporting

Led a financial reporting and technical accounting team of five and provided guidance to senior management for complex transactions. Managed mergers and acquisitions (M&A) team of five in due diligence, valuation of assets and liabilities, and integration activities. Oversaw SEC reporting and Sarbanes Oxley (SOX). Participated in and provided schedules for earnings press releases. Interacted with and reported to audit committee regarding upcoming accounting standards changes in US GAAP.

- **Directed integration activities for $10B XZZ Lighting acquisition,** by converting XZZ into ABC's accounting policies and procedures and by recording acquisition on balance sheet. Led SEC reporting and purchase accounting efforts, including SEC filings, responding to SEC comment letters, and opening balance sheet valuation diligence.

- **Elevated quality of public filings** to provide more transparency and better structure.

- **Created culture of excellence** by hiring strong talent and motivating teams to perform at high levels.

EARLY CAREER

Director, **Financial Reporting, ABC Corporation,** Benton Harbor, MI   12/2009–10/2012

Senior Manager | Manager, **ABC Consulting Firm,** Boston, MA   2/2002–11/2009

EDUCATION

MBA, Boston University, Boston, MA

BBA, University of Michigan, Ann Arbor, MI, *summa cum laude*

CERTIFICATIONS & AFFILIATIONS

Certified Public Accountant, State of Georgia | Member, Financial Executives International (FEI)

Marty Basso

(860) 749-5611 – Hartford, CT - BassoM@email.com

TRADES APPRENTICE

Diligent Trade Worker offering more than 5 years' electrical and iron work experience in commercial, industrial, and residential settings. Reliable, dependable, and trustworthy.

Strong technical background; able to quickly learn new tasks and troubleshoot problems. Capable of performing in all conditions and environments including inside, outside, hot, cold, tight/narrow, and elevated worksites. Exceptional interpersonal skills; able to professionally interact with customers and work as a team.

Proficient with CAD software, security systems, automated systems, MS Word, Excel, and Adobe Illustrator.

SKILLS SUMMARY

Equipment Expertise		Areas of Strength	
➢ Voltage Meters	➢ Torches/Welders	➢ Equipment Operation	➢ Maintenance
➢ Wire Cutters	➢ Drills	➢ Diagnostics	➢ Blueprint Reading
➢ Benders	➢ Power Tools	➢ Wiring Circuits	➢ Low/High Voltage
➢ Hand Tools	➢ Measuring Devices	➢ Inventory Control	➢ Service Installs

VOCATIONAL EXPERIENCE

Electrical
- Measured, cut, bent, and installed metal and plastic conduits above ground and buried.
- Utilized voltage meters to troubleshoot short circuits and test amperages.
- Installed and wired switches (single, 3- and 4-way), outlets (interior, exterior, and GFCI), fixtures, appliances, safety devices, and equipment.
- Diagnosed and performed electrical repair on energized and non-energized circuits, including industrial high-voltage panels and residential service installations.
- Mounted panels, installed circuit breakers, ran homeruns, buried grounding rods, and labeled wires.

Iron Work
- Utilized welders, torches, grinding wheels, saws, and benders to work with iron.
- Operated lifts, jackhammers, cement mixer, pumps, and heavy vehicles (trucks).
- Designed custom fittings for residential and commercial projects.

General
- Performed work in basements, attics, rooftops, commercial, industrial, and residential settings.
- Maintained inventory by recording parts used and identifying parts needed.

EXPERIENCE

Maintenance Worker	*Garner Institution*, New London, CT	2016–2019
Electrical Apprentice	*Johnny Electric*, Groton, CT	2014–2016
Ironworker	*Roger Wrought Iron*, New London, CT	2010–2014

EDUCATION

3 Semesters of Electrical Apprenticeship, Valley Community College, Essex, CT
Diploma, New London High School, New London, CT

Christopher McCormack, CPRW • CT Department of Labor • ct.gov/dol

Note: Marty's functional resume plays up his skills and experience as they relate to his current objective: a position as a Trades Apprentice. His brief Experience listing minimizes the fact that he is returning to the building trades after a gap.

Jeffery James

 Jeffjames2918@gmail.com

 912-378-9080

 Charleston, SC

Cargo/Freight
Transportation & Distribution

Inbound | Outbound

Comprehensive experience in the realm of logistics, port operations, freight transportation & distribution, seaport embarkation and debarkation (domestic and international); specialize in the operation of transportation vehicles, port, warehouse, distribution, and heavy equipment. Excel in aspects of cargo movement, distribution, and regulatory compliance.

Professional Experience

05/2015-Present

South Carolina Ports Authority, Charleston, SC
JOCKEY TRUCK DISPATCHER

- Facilitate container movements within Port of Charleston region.
- Enforce compliance with Maritime Transportation Security Act of 2002, facility security plans (FSP), and security measures and procedures. Reduce risk and mitigate exposure to threats and/or terrorist activity.
- As **Driver Trainer,** train drivers to move containers between terminal rail facilities and ships. Move up to 100 containers per shift.

02/2002-05/2015

Trek Transport, Columbia, SC
HEAVY TRUCK DRIVER

- Drove up to 3000 miles per week, nationally and into Canada. Maintained a safe, accident-free driving record, accumulating >1M safe miles.
- Capitalized on proficiency in the French language to develop relationships with customs agents at the Canadian border.
- Bilingual assets enhanced company business relationships, leading to requests for future services; generated >$750 in new business.

02/1999-02/2002

KBR, Houston, TX
MOVEMENT CONTROL TEAM SUPERVISOR

- **Camp Kuwait Naval Base (KNB)** — Supervised a team of 20 civilians monitoring the Kuwait port area and vessels coming from U.S. ports.
- **Battle Command Sustainment Support System (BCS3)** — Managed Camp Arifjan BCS3 to augment OIF supply chain and sustainment operations.
- Supervised 10 U.S. truck drivers servicing 12 military camps in Kuwait and 18 other camps geographically dispersed throughout Iraq.

Education

2015

Bachelor of Science
Major in Business Administration
COLUMBIA COLLEGE, SC

Certifications

- Jockey Truck Operator
- Class A Commercial Driver License
- TWIC Credential
- SC Ports Authority (GPA) Credential
- Transportation of HAZMAT, KBR
- Occupational Safety and Health, KBR
- TEREX Crane Operations, KBR

Network Partners

- Homeland Security
- Department of Defense
- Port Authority Police Department
- Certified Peace Officers
- Customs & Border Patrol
- Immigration and Customs Enforcement (ICE)
- Regional Transportation CEOs
- South Carolina Ports Authority

Lisa Parker, CERM, CPRW, CEIP • Parker-CPRW • parkercprw.com

Note: Preparing to interview for a promotion at his current employer, Jeffery needed a document that would set him apart from other internal candidates. His visually distinctive resume concisely conveys the length of his experience and depth of his expertise to make him an exceptional candidate.

ENGINEER – PROJECT LEADER

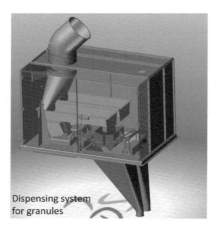

Dispensing system
for granules

EDUCATION
BS Mechanical Engineering, 2010
Concentration in Machine Construction
University of Washington, Seattle, WA

TECHNICAL SKILLS
• **Software**
Microsoft Project – SolidWorks –
Solid Edge – Dynamic Designer

• **Mathematics Programs**
Mathcad – Matlab – Mathematica

• **Programming Tools**
GX Developer – GS Works – IX Developer

• **Construction**
Ansys

LANGUAGES
English & **Norwegian** – bilingual
German – conversational

Z conveyor, maintenance free for 10 years

AMY BLACK

206-270-8857 ■ amyblack@gmail.com ■ LinkedIn ■ Seattle, WA

DESIGN ENGINEER: Innovator, troubleshooter, skilled programmer, and machine constructor with a reputation for paying great attention to detail and always exceeding expectations.

- Designed innovative conveyor that has performed flawlessly—without maintenance or repair—for 8 years.
- Developed pioneering concept turned high-profile research project at University of Washington. Received industry-wide praise. Invited to lecture at research conference in 2019.

ENGINEERING CONSULTANT / MACHINE CONSTRUCTOR
RF Technology, 2015–Present

Perform consulting assignments for a variety of clients, including the company's #1 customer, DFG Mills.

Core Skills: Production Flow Analysis – Investment Documentation – Procurement – Machine Programming – Process Programming – Project Management – Installation – Hydraulics – Pneumatics – Process Engineering – Special Tool Construction

Key Projects:

- **Dispensing system for granules** with special hygiene and flexibility request. *Concept design, procurement, monitoring, installation, programming, and deployment.*
- **Belt conveyor** for bread traveling through 2 floors, from bakery to packing. *Design, project management, programming, and installation.*
- **Packing lines** for 2 mill sites. *Design, project management.*
- **Z conveyor** (food-approved) with special requirements for cleaning access. *Design, project management, deployment.* **8 years of 100% maintenance-free operations.**

> *"Amy's ingenuity and problem-solving skills are exceptional."*
> (President, RF Technology)

MECHANIC, T. H. Workshops, 2013–2015

Created prototypes and manufactured test samples for production runs of instruments, wooden toys, and furniture for customers that included renowned Thomas Mosier Cabinetmakers. Customized products for clients and designed tools to streamline production.

Key Projects:

- **Mechanical control system** for external profile milling. *Installation of circuit diagrams and deployment.*
- **New PLC control system** for 5 machines filling and closing bags of pellets. *Installation of circuit diagrams and deployment.*
- **Development of new, fully automated packing machine.** *Design, manufacturing, and deployment.*

> *"Amy is smart, resourceful, and a natural problem solver."*
> (Production Supervisor, T. H. Workshops)

Birgitta Moller, ACRW, MRW • Cvhjälpen • cvhjalpen.nu

Note: The 2-column format is an effective strategy for showcasing examples of Amy's own work, plus her technical skills, without detracting from the core text—her relevant experience, skills, projects, and accomplishments.

MARVIN FELDSTEIN

Open to Relocation | 809-956-4322 | marv@feldcom.com

MANUFACTURING ENGINEERING ♦ PROJECT MANAGEMENT ♦ CROSS-FUNCTIONAL TEAM LEADERSHIP

Top-performing engineering professional with demonstrated success increasing operational efficiency, improving product quality, and reducing cost for world-leading automotive manufacturer. **Driven project manager** energized by projects on cutting edge of technology, juggling demands and expanding knowledge to meet dynamic business requirements. **Collaborative and engaging leader** who excels at building and leading high-performing teams and communicating with stakeholders at all levels.

PROFESSIONAL EXPERIENCE

CARPATHIAN MOTOR WORKS (NYSE: CMW), Taos, NM   2014–Present

SENIOR PROJECT ENGINEER –TOOL & DIE (2021–Present)

Promoted to drive Industry 4.0 (smart manufacturing) initiatives for 325K+ sq. ft. facility that engineers and constructs tools and dies for fabrication and assembly of sheet metal body parts. Challenged with developing and executing engineering strategies that improve tool design, reduce product defects, and maximize productivity. Assume end-to-end ownership of product lifecycle and provide direction on highly technical projects to global team of technical group leaders. Manage $8M budget.

- Selected to lead global team in developing first smart production stamping tool with real-time production monitoring capability. Developed fabrication strategies, performed failure modes and effects analysis (FMEA), and determined machining tools and process.

- Exceeded leadership expectations, met budgeting goals, and identified $170K+ cost savings while taking on increased level of responsibility following organizational restructuring.

- Led cross-functional team through root cause analysis of dimensional and surface issues for line of tools required for upcoming high-profile vehicle launch. Thrived in high-pressure situation, beating strict turnaround deadline by 5 days.

- Created tool design strategy that reduced build time and improved surface quality on outer metal parts. Realized cost savings of $55K per year.

OPERATIONS MANAGER – TAOS TOOL & DIE (2019–2020)

Promoted to lead team of 32 unionized employees through end-to-end product development process for automotive stamping tools. Challenged with delivering tools requiring high surface quality and dimension accuracy on-time to stamping plant. Consistently recognized by management as top performer and positive contributor while attending graduate school part-time.

- Applied engineering theories acquired through graduate work to reduce downtime at Taos assembly plant. Built highly complex models and simulations that identified major bottleneck, leading to 17-vehicle increase ($19K) in daily production.

- Improved draw tool engineering strategy, resulting in 4-day reduction in build time and $35K annual cost savings.

- Avoided delays in production due to reduced workforce during COVID-19 pandemic by implementing plant safety protocols, ensuring all employees were equipped with appropriate PPE, and quickly responding to and resolving issues.

- Effectively handled major increase in job responsibilities after group leader was reassigned. Created systems and processes that improved communication and set clear expectations and priorities, increasing overall team efficiency and productivity.

MANUFACTURING ENGINEER (2014–2019) ♦ MANUFACTURING ENGINEER INTERN (2014)

Completed 2-year engineering rotational development program for new graduates, acquiring supervisory experience in machining, assembly, verification, planning, and design of auto body dies. Provided technical direction and oversight to diverse workforce in high-pressure, high-volume manufacturing environments while driving continuous improvement initiatives.

- Improved tool development time by creating work order system, utilizing new metrics to better manage team workload.

- Reduced part transfer station downtime 15% by leveraging visual management system to generate real-time issue alerts.

PRIOR ENGINEERING EXPERIENCE: Manufacturing Engineering Co-op at Caterpillar (NYSE: CAT) in Deerfield, IL (2012–2013)

EDUCATION & PROFESSIONAL AFFILIATIONS

Master of Engineering in Global Automotive and Manufacturing Engineering – University of Texas (2019)
Bachelor of Science in Mechanical Engineering – California Institute of Technology (2013)

Member, Electrical Subteam – Caltech Hybrid Electric Vehicle Team (2012–2013)

Kelly Gadzinski, ACRW • KG Career Services • kgcareerservices.com
Note: A 1-page presentation packs a lot of information into an easily skimmable format that clearly shows Marvin's record of achievements and rapid progression to roles of increasing responsibility.

TRENDALL MILLER, P.Eng., MBA

TARGET: CHIEF OPERATING OFFICER | ENGINEERING

Toronto, Ontario P1P 0P0 • 416.111.2222 • trendall.miller@gmail.com

DRIVING GLOBAL CORPORATE TRANSFORMATION THROUGH INNOVATION AND VERSATILITY

15+ years of diverse experience in dual technical & financial capacity

Poised to be effective—and offer best-in-class global influencing skills—by possessing the versatility of a Swiss Army Knife, deep knowledge of business and finance, and unstoppable determination.

When you have a distinct problem in need of a detailed solution, I am your guy! I am respected for carving out something new to create solutions on the fly. I am a *versatilist* with a depth of talent in the vital areas of technical engineering, operations, and finance; and a breadth of talent that covers all the necessary skills required to lead corporate operations to peak performance.

> *"Combining his extensive engineering expertise with his strong analytical capability, Trendall adds significant value to the company's long-term planning, forecasting, and financing initiatives".*
>
> - Senior VP Finance, ABC Resources

VERSATILITY IN ACTION

➢ **Reshaped** key operating contracts to **slash material costs by 20%** across business during oil price decline and COVID 19-enforced standby conditions on operations.

➢ **Chiseled out alternative financing and investment options** to fund ~$240M of capital requirements in Iran for an internationally focused exploration and production company.

➢ **Forged strategic business partnership** to secure 2-year contract valued at $15.3M/year to improve operational efficiency and performance capability.

CORE COMPETENCIES

BUSINESS EXPANSION	FINANCIAL DIRECTION	STRATEGY & EXECUTION	LEADERSHIP
Business Intelligence	Business Assessment	Process Improvement	Shareholder Relations
Asset & Revenue Growth	Risk Mitigation	Strategic Roadmap Design	Influencing & Negotiating
M&A Strategy	Financial Investments	Business-Tech Alignment	Partnership Building

CAREER HIGHLIGHTS

ABC RESOURCES, *Canada, Iran & UAE*   **2013 – Current**

> *Internationally focused, independent exploration and production company engaged in acquiring, exploring, developing, and producing crude oil and natural gas in the Iranian Region.*

SENIOR LEADER, JOINT VENTURE OPERATIONS *(2019 – Current)*
Annual Work Program & Budget: $100M+ | Annual Revenue: $150M+

Promoted to company representative embedded in Iranian Partner's Dubai Head Office.

➢ **Implemented** AFE controls system to manage JV spending and provide robust project controls over capital authorization for development spending.

➢ **Launched** redesigned field workover program to increase long-term well productivity by 10%.

➢ **Transformed** cost management initiatives with a 12% reduction in Operating Budget and reduction in Production Operating Cost from $4.60/bbl to $3.68/bbl in 6 months.

➢ **Delivered** total annual Work Program & Budget (WP&B) expenditures within 5% and 9% in 2021 and 2022 with a budget of $110M and $75M, respectively.

➢ **Negotiated** settlement in an international environment by building interfirm collaboration and trust to forge consensus on common strategy and transformed company into leading regional player.

➢ **Honoured** with 5-year service award: special recognition for boosting JV collaboration and alignment.

Skye Berry, CGRA, CMRW, CCTC, CRS, CIS, CES • Skye Is The Limit Resume & Career Solutions • skyeisthelimit.ca

Note: Starting with the Summary, this resume exudes personality as well as professional expertise. It is enhanced throughout with effective graphics that call attention to impressive results.

Trendall Miller ▪ Page 2 ▪ 416.111.2222

ABC Resources, continued

LEAD, ECONOMICS, PLANNING & EVALUATIONS *(2017 –2019)*
Estimated Capital: $240M | Annual Revenue: $75M

Selected to provide senior management with financial intelligence and insights on the dynamics of energy markets across the Iranian region. Evolved to become SME for Joint Venture technical matters. Led scenario modelling, economic evaluations, and investment analytics for take-private transaction during corporate downsizing initiative.

> **Directed** monthly and quarterly cash flow analysis with objective to maintain >20% IRR and attractive project NPV's for primary investor in Iranian projects.
> **Collaborated** with investment team in sourcing and economic analysis of new project investments, including asset sales and M&A activities.
> **Secured** alternative investment with major shareholder for cash consideration of $0.28 share, representing a 70% premium to Common Share closing price and an implied value of $225M CAD.
> **Slashed** 18% in co-venturer partner expenditures through strict evaluation and management of $75M annual capital budget.
> **Attained** a 60% increase in Proved plus Probable ("2P") Reserves and a 250% increase in net present value to $114M USD of company's primary asset.

Unlocked Asset Value: 60% increase in 2P reserves & 250% increase in net present value.

Reduced Near-Term Financing Costs: 18% reduction in co-venturer partner expenditures.

SENIOR DRILLING & COMPLETIONS ENGINEER *(2015 – 2016)*
Supervised: 30+ | Procurement Contracts: $9.5M | Optimization Budget: $3M+ | Annual Revenue: $15M

Guided the development of core asset areas within Iran and prepared annual development capital forecasts and AFE with yearly realized expenditures within 8% of approved budget.

> **Expanded** daily well production rate by 16% with 51% production efficiency uptime improvement.
> **Created** enhanced reservoir treatment program that generated 33% reduction in well OPEX, with 6% reduction in capitalized development expenditures.
> **Facilitated** a 16% increase in reserves estimates that delivered a projected 180% well productivity growth on future developments.

ADDITIONAL ENGINEERING EXPERIENCE   2008 – 2015

SENIOR DRILLING & COMPLETIONS ENGINEER | Xell Exploration Inc., Canada/West Indies (2015)

SENIOR DRILLING ENGINEER | DBE Energy Ltd., Iran (2014 – 2015)

SENIOR COMPLETIONS ENGINEER | Delta Exploration Ltd., Toronto, Canada (2012 – 2014)

DRILLING & COMPLETIONS WELLSITE ENGINEER | GD Group Ltd., Canada/Norway/Australia (2008 – 2012)

EDUCATION & PROFESSIONAL DEVELOPMENT

EXECUTIVE MASTER OF BUSINESS ADMINISTRATION (eMBA), Finance Specialization, Dean's List | **2018**
Alex School of Business – University of Ontario

BACHELOR OF SCIENCE: MECHANICAL ENGINEERING (Cooperative Program) with Honors | **2006**
University of Ontario

Negotiation Skills for the Oil & Gas Industry | 2019

World Fiscal Systems for Oil & Gas: Ontario Petro Academy | 2017

Quality Management Systems Lead Auditor Training Certification | 2008

PROFESSIONAL MEMBERSHIPS

Association of Professional Engineers and Geoscientists of Ontario (APEGO)—Professional Engineer (P.Eng.)

Society of Petroleum Engineers (SPE)—Member

215

CYNTHIA FRAZETTI

Little Rock, AR | 501-270-5000 | cfraz@outlook.com

GLOBAL DIRECTOR — PURCHASING & SUPPLY CHAIN

✓ **HIGH-IMPACT PURCHASING & SUPPLY CHAIN LEADER** with track record of success building global, top-performing teams; optimizing business cash flow; and delivering millions of dollars in cost savings across diverse industries.

✓ **FORWARD-THINKING BUSINESS PARTNER** highly skilled at collaborating cross-functionally to develop and execute best-in-class sourcing and supply chain strategies. Trusted resource, advisor, and executive collaborator.

✓ **EXPERT RELATIONSHIP BUILDER & COMMUNICATOR** recognized for fostering critical business partnerships with key suppliers and stakeholders that deliver measurable ongoing value. Talented negotiator and decision maker.

LEADERSHIP EXPERTISE

Strategic Planning & Execution ♦ Supplier Relationship Management ♦ Global Cross-Functional Team Leadership
Supplier Sourcing & Negotiations ♦ Cost Savings ♦ Change Management ♦ Process Standardization & Improvement

PROFESSIONAL EXPERIENCE

MECHANICO — Parent Company: GGH Holdings — Little Rock, AR   2021 to Present
Industry-leading contractor for fabrication, construction, and maintenance in power, chemical, oil and gas, water/wastewater, and heavy industrial markets.

DIRECTOR OF SUPPLY CHAIN

Lead team of 3 direct reports managing $65M annual spend on tools and consumables, rental equipment, subcontractors, and construction materials. Challenged with building and implementing supply chain, centralized purchasing, and cost reduction strategies from ground up. Drive efficiency by setting and monitoring KPIs and creating best-in-class processes. Nominated by CFO to serve as head of internal Women in Leadership Committee. Report directly to COO.

➢ **Delivered $1M+ cost reductions** through supplier pricing negotiations, rebate programs, and tariff exemptions.

➢ **Improved cash flow $5.4M in 16 months** by negotiating extended payment terms with key suppliers.

➢ **Nominated by president of GBH Holdings** to lead supply chain committee. Conducted supplier spend analysis to optimize decision-making process and leverage cost improvement opportunities across all 5 companies.

➢ **Proactively conducted supply chain risk assessment** and prioritized critical focus areas during global pandemic.

➢ **Managed efficient transition of purchasing activities to align with SAP conversion** at newly acquired location.

WATER STORM– Parent Company: Banff Labs (NYSE: BANL) – Denver, CO   2012 to 2021
World's largest independent manufacturer of chemical injecting, proportioning, dispensing, and medicating equipment.

GLOBAL DIRECTOR OF PURCHASING & SUPPLY CHAIN (2019–2021)

Promoted to manage and develop high-performing team of 14 direct reports located across US, UK, and China responsible for $48M annual spend on custom plastics, electronics, and metals used for chemical dispensing systems. Delivered strong results through continuous improvement in inventory management and reduction, working capital, supply forecasting, and regulatory compliance.

➢ **Improved inventory turnover 15%** through increased supplier collaboration, talent development, just-in-time inventory management, and new inventory stocking programs and planning systems.

➢ **Increased cash flow $2.7M in 4 months** by negotiating improved payment terms with key suppliers.

➢ Designed and executed global expedited freight process that **delivered 40% reduction ($250K) in annual expenses.**

➢ **Grew talent pipeline and built organizational capabilities** via student engagement project with University of Illinois.

Kelly Gadzinski, ACRW • KG Career Services • kgcareerservices.com

Note: Tight writing and a clean, modern format make for an attractive, readable resume that puts the spotlight on Cynthia's many quantified achievements as well as her strong career progression. A concurrent (and relevant) consulting job is briefly mentioned in a separate section on page 2.

WATER STORM, continued

GLOBAL DIRECTOR OF PURCHASING (2018)

Led global purchasing team in identifying cost-saving opportunities, sourcing for new products, and strengthening supplier relations. Established and achieved aggressive cost-reduction goals.

➢ **Orchestrated and led global sourcing summit** that generated winning cost reduction ideas and strategies.

➢ **Achieved $1.75M cost savings** through value engineering, price negotiation, and strategic sourcing initiatives.

NORTH AMERICA SOURCING MANAGER (2016–2018)

Promoted to plan and execute new supplier sourcing strategy for North America. Managed sourcing specialist and $36M annual spend. Forged enduring supplier relationships through business reviews, site visits, and contract negotiations.

➢ **Realized $1.5M annual savings** across multiple product categories through value-added business initiatives, supplier consolidation, and complex price negotiations.

BUYER/PLANNER (2012–2016)

Managed $14M annual spend on electronics and plastics from China and Taiwan. Challenged with optimizing inventory of products with long lead times. Collaborated with buying team to uncover cost-saving opportunities.

➢ Overhauled and streamlined purchase order process, **reducing purchase order transactions 35%,** which freed up buying team to tackle more strategic, value-added initiatives.

➢ **Lowered key supplier inventory 36% ($650K)** by detecting and correcting process inefficiencies.

ENVIRO SYSTEMS, Louisville, KY
2010 to 2012

Manufacturer of rugged and transportable mobile enclosures, environmental control units, and power generators.

PURCHASING SPECIALIST II

Oversaw end-to-end purchasing process for wide variety of environmental control systems for military, involving highly complex purchase orders. Ensured strict adherence to government policies and regulations.

➢ Led contract renegotiation with major German supplier that **yielded $600K+ savings** for company.

➢ **Secured $1.5M+ savings** through negotiations on material pricing and payment terms and alternate sourcing tactics.

FRAWLEY ENTERPRISES (NYSE: FRAW), Cincinnati, OH
2005 to 2010

Nation's largest wholesale distributor of residential and commercial plumbing supplies such as pipes, values, and fittings.

PROJECT MANAGER – STRATEGIC SOURCING (2008–2010) ♦ BUYER (2005–2008)

Promoted to develop and implement nationwide sourcing strategies for multiple product categories. Identified preferred suppliers and negotiated volume incentive rebate programs. Communicated and managed sourcing improvements.

➢ **Realized $750K+ cost savings** by building deep supplier partnerships and monitoring usage across all US locations.

CONSULTING EXPERIENCE

PACIFIC FOODS CORPORATION, Cincinnati, OH
2022 to Present
CONSULTANT – *Provide supply chain management consulting and mentoring at multifaceted food distribution company.*

EDUCATION, CERTIFICATIONS & PROFESSIONAL DEVELOPMENT

BS, Purchasing Management and Decision Sciences—St. Louis University

Certified Purchasing Manager (CPM)—Institute for Supply Chain Optimization

Nominated for and completed multiple leadership development and training programs during tenure at Water Storm.

CALVIN BROWN

NATURAL RESOURCE MANAGEMENT
Stream Permitting | Cultural Restoration | Water Quality

123.456.7890 • calbrown@gmail.com • Spokane, WA • www.linkedin.com/in/calbrown/

CONSERVING, DEVELOPING, PROTECTING & MANAGING NATURAL RESOURCES
in partnership with local government, state agencies, conservation districts, and private landowners

Resource Conservationist dedicated to protecting land, watershed, wildlife, and cultural resources. **Environmental Scientist** skilled in extracting field data, generating scientific reports, and monitoring landowner, state, and federal projects to assist senior scientists with research and archaeological fieldwork.

MANAGERIAL SUPPORT	• Groundwater Monitoring & River Sampling • Flow System Calibration & Water Discharge • Project Management & Fieldwork Logistics • Data Preparation, Assessment & Reports	• Technical Research, Writing & Editing • Fieldwork Logistics, Planning & Collection • Wetlands Restoration & Mitigation • Artifact Inventory, Illustration & Storage
PERMIT KNOWLEDGE	• Federal Rivers & Harbors Act, Section 10 Permit • EPA & State Water Quality Standards (WQS) • Law, Rules, Technical Forms & Applications • Natural Streambed & Land Preservation, 310 Permit	• Stormwater Discharge, General Permit • Water of the State Investigations • Federal Clean Water Act, 404 Permit • Stream Protection Act (SPA)

PROFESSIONAL EXPERIENCE

CLEAN WATER ACT & TURBIDITY PERMIT COODINATOR (GRADUATE INTERN)
State of Washington Department of Environmental Quality (DEQ), Spokane, WA, August 2022–June 2023

- Reviewed Clean Water Act (CWA) 404 permit compliance for state hydroelectric and water quality-related projects, offering the public and state agencies technical assistance and cultural resource protection education.
- Delivered timely water quality permits, permit renewals, and permit modifications aligned with SOPs and internal and external regulatory changes to federal CWA and state Water Quality Standards (WQS).
- Managed data in Excel and Access, aided process improvements, and reviewed reissuance of five-year U.S. Army Corps of Engineers Nationwide Permits (NWP) to ensure accurate administration within required timeframes.
- Enforced water permit requirements and administrative rules via review of WAC 173 Authorizations for temporary turbidity exceedances associated with construction projects in state waters.

FIELD ARCHAEOLOGIST (SEASONAL FIELD TECHNICIAN)
Archeological Services & Environmental Consulting, Dillon, MT, May–August 2020 & May–August 2021

- Provided Project Archeologist topographic maps, town/county histories, digital photographs, soil maps, and literature reviews to prepare for state-funded archaeological and cultural resource protection projects.
- Planned fieldwork logistics for archaeological investigations, cultural resource surveys, and historic preservation projects. Trained volunteers to identify, evaluate, and protect cultural resources and to write technical reports.
- Conducted ArcMap GIS analyses and archaeological material lab analysis. Submitted recommendations to Project Manager to prepare highly complex National Register of Historic Places (NRHP) eligibility reports.

TECHNICAL SKILLS

Trimble XT GPS Navigation Systems; Garmin eTrex GPS & Garmin MapSource; Rhino GPS Navigation System; Terrain Navigator Pro; ESRI ArcGIS 10.2.2 & ArcGIS 10; Web Soil Survey Maps; Silva & Brunton Mapping Techniques; Windows Distance 6.0; Topographic Map Reading & Orienteering; Microsoft Excel, Access, Word, PowerPoint, Outlook.

EDUCATION

Master of Science (MS) in Resource Conservation, *University of Montana, May 2023*
Bachelor of Arts (BA) in Anthropology, Minor in Cultural Archaeology, *Washington State University, December 2020*

Cheryl Minnick, M.Ed., Ed.D., NCRW, CCMC • University of Montana-Missoula • www.umt.edu

Note: Professional Experience shows highly relevant internship and seasonal positions that support this new graduate's goal of natural resource management. Skills are neatly presented in table format with clear headings as part of an information-packed Summary.

George Stam

Detroit, MI | 555-345-2345 |georgestam@email.com

CHEMIST | TECHNICAL EXPERT | SOLUTIONS PROVIDER
Develop new products as innovative formulator. Increase sales by speaking customer's language.

Tenacious, intellectually curious problem solver who exercises sound judgment. Bridge builder who fosters an environment of open communication with all levels of stakeholders. Trusted client technical liaison. Safety champion with deep experience in product formulation and testing.

Strengths – Formulation | Research | Quality| R&D Production | Operations | Safety | Communication
Technical Skills – Chromatography (GC, IC, HPLC) Infrared Spectroscopy Elemental Analysis (ICP-AES, RDE, XFR) | Wet Chemistry (KF, TAN, TBN, TA)

FLUIDS & OILS EXPERTISE INCLUDES METAL WORKING, HYDRAULIC, STAMPING & VANISHING

PROFESSIONAL EXPERIENCE

DIRECTOR OF TECHNICAL SERVICES | Midwest Fluids Corp |*$50M Lubrication Distributor, Detroit, MI* | 2017–Present
Recruited by customer to focus on product development. Pivoted after acquisition as SME and revenue facilitator developing new product lines through reverse engineering. Currently dual Chemist formulating and testing products and Technical Expert and Sales Support helping close more business by bridging the knowledge gap for clients. Report to CEO.

TECHNICAL EXPERT / SALES SUPPORT PARTNER. In-house sales advisor, go-to client technical advisor and product SME. Partner with reps to identify and solve client business challenges across products, processes, and proper components.
- Instrumental in strengthening or salvaging key manufacturing client accounts: Chrysler, Cummins, Rolls Royce.
- Respond to all email queries regarding products and product recommendations as member of Technical Services Group.
- Expedite SAP conversion by classifying/exporting data and maintaining transparency with conversion team.
- Lead metalworking course covering Basic Lubrication for Sales Team.
- Maintain ISO certification by owning problem resolution of quality issues from investigation to corrective actions.

CHEMIST/FORMULATOR. Generate income by engineering competition-displacing products that performed equal to or better than competition, 90% of time at lower cost – which serves as catalyst to capture full range of client products.
- Saved $380K in R&D costs by reverse-engineering 15 blends in-house, paving the way for new product lines.
- Lowered customers' VOC emissions by developing several low-VOC rust preventatives.
- Assisted Purchasing by sourcing, negotiating, and approving vendors; create SDS and PDS for Sales and Marketing.

RESEARCH CHEMIST | UP Lab, | *$21M Full Service Fluid Analysis, Traverse City, MI* | 2014–2017
Recruited by R&D Manager to own Fuel Dilution and SimDis testing in support of company's most significant client.
- Saved client thousands of dollars and improved fleet health by eliminating lubricant problems from the fuel dilution process.
- Improved quality, accuracy of test results, and reporting with consistent, nationwide validation and testing methods.
- Significantly reduced safety concern (explosion risks) by rewriting procedures and retraining staff on GCs.

CHEMIST | Major Oil | *$200M Employee-Owned Supplier Industrial Solvents, Houston, TX* | 2012–2014
Began in quality and quickly morphed into product development in conjunction with R&D with a major focus on supporting sales.
- Slashed GC run times from 40 to 10 minutes. Decreased downtime between runs by becoming inhouse GC expert.
- Saved top-tier client significant product replacement costs by developing innovative new cleaner.
- Helped General Motors meet government-required VOC regulations as team member of new low-VOC cleaner.
- Developed green-heat transfer fluid for geothermal systems that could be used to heat homes/buildings.
- Helped develop a fluid to go into machines to make fake snow—used during Taylor Swift's CMA performance.
- Trained and certified in ISO 9001:2000. Worked individually or in partnership with ISO coordinator in investigations.

EDUCATION | ASSOCIATIONS

Bachelor of Science (BS) Biology | 2012 | Associate of Science (AS) Chemistry | 2011 – Indiana University
Member, Society of Tribologists and Lubrication Engineers (STLE) | American Society for Testing and Materials (ASTM)

Note: George's current position, which spans 2 distinct areas of performance, is presented with separate sections that make each role—and its many accomplishments—clear. A branding statement below the headline is supported with numerous examples throughout the resume.

Lorraine Jones, M.S.

Floral Park, NY 11001 • (516) 555-7255 • lorraine.jones@email.com

Director of Data Science – Causal Inference (Healthcare Analytics)

Combine great storytelling with machine learning, algorithm design, and AI modeling to develop and implement novel, cloud-based analytics solutions that shape data-driven healthcare strategies

Process-oriented Data Analytics Executive with 7+ years of experience, **3+ years in a director capacity,** initiating and managing large-scale analytics projects for fast-paced healthcare startups and integrated hospital systems. Develop and mentor data science teams in building high-quality tools from initial concept and prototype design to QA testing and product deployment. Blend expertise in data structures, population health, and medical claims data with operational and financial knowledge to deliver best-in-class clinical healthcare products with **Fortune 25/50** and **Global 500** stakeholders.

Analytics Tools: SQL Server, SSRS, SSIS, T-SQL, PostgresSQL, Python, PowerBI, Tableau, JIRA, Alteryx, and AWS

Areas of Expertise

Causal Inference Methodologies	Technical Leadership (25–30 staff)	Project Management Methodology
Product Development/Deployment	Executive Presentation & Interface	Automated Quality Assessment
Applied Statistical Modeling	Senior Stakeholder Engagement	Code & Documentation Practices
Data Science Strategy Development	Verbal & Written Communication	Population Health Problems
Quality Metrics: HEDIS, NCQA, NQF	Technical Training & Mentoring	Enterprise Data Warehouse

Professional Experience

NOVASYTE HEALTH   Floral Park, NY
Manager, Implementation Analytics   Jan 2022 – Present

Recruited to work with the VP, Implementation Analytics, and drive quality analytics and payment performance solutions based on HEDIS, NCQA, and NQF frameworks for episode-based care delivery models. Designated HEDIS subject-matter expert for all Novasyte stakeholders: provider partners, health plans, and government programs. Lead in-depth metric analysis and validation in substance use disorders, pharmacy management, medication adherence, provider quality, patient-reported outcomes, breast cancer episode development, and internal marketing and business development.

➤ Presently **building a first-rate infrastructure team** focused on designing and evaluating alternative payment and episode-based models to improve high-quality care coordination and delivery while reducing costs.

➤ Tapped to analyze a pilot program focused on creating a closed loop between identifying and tying social needs, program enrollment, and service coordination to quality, satisfaction, and health and financial outcomes.

➤ Using SQL and Python, defined, validated, and implemented substance use disorder metrics into the provider chronic quality scorecard and client reports for contracted Medicaid health plans based on vague claims data. This was a key milestone for the analytics quality initiative due to its **potential to save Medicaid billions.**

➤ Leveraged data analytics to deliver a major executive presentation focused on pharmacy Rx levers and the root cause of medication nonadherence issues involving asthma, antidepressant, and statin treatments.

➤ Strengthened problem-solving skills by providing ongoing technical mentoring and training to junior analytics staff on writing, programming, and troubleshooting algorithms for ETL processes.

OLYMPUS GENERAL HOSPITAL   Cleveland, OH
Data Scientist   Jun 2020 – Jan 2022

Promoted as the **first Data Scientist** in a new department to **work in a director capacity** with administrative and clinical leaders and execute projects requiring full data science pipelines. Led the integration of disparate and centralized information into data marts, data mining, statistical models, dashboard design, and custom and ad-hoc care analytics reporting solutions in SQL environments that drove measurable outcomes for population health systems. Served in a data scientist capacity on the CliniSync Health Information Exchange committee focused on enabling interoperability.

Kate Williamson, MS, CPRW, NCOPE, CRS+ES, CRS+IT, CRS+HM, CRS+AF • Scientech Resumes LLC • scientechresumes.com
Note: Positioning Lorraine for the next step up in her fast-moving career, this resume highlights both technical and leadership strengths and accomplishments. Judicious use of bold type highlights several "firsts" and other notable details.

➢ Boosted HEDIS ratings **from 2 to 4 stars**, resulting in bonus payouts and **millions in YOY insurance payments** by auditing SQL codes and SSIS packages to identify and close capture rates gaps.

➢ Partnered with Optum to identify new outreach strategies, close HEDIS care gaps, and draft a data closure plan for securely extracting, loading, and transferring large file batches to and from external systems.

➢ Expedited gap closure by leading Humana and Cigna IT partners to design and **deploy the first prototype algorithm** and integrated SSIS package workflow to transfer terabytes of patient data from FTP servers.

➢ Reduced readmission and achieved cost avoidance by developing and presenting an automated RCA tool—**still in use**—to HR management that analyzed serious adverse events and identified the top 10 readmission factors.

➢ Improved patient care response by establishing data-driven processes, including algorithms, to streamline risk assessment and referral to specialty clinics for conditions such as sleep apnea, hearing loss, and obesity.

➢ Played an integral role in **centralizing disparate data sources** from EHR/EMR, insurance claims, and health information exchange databases across the UH Population Health system using SQL Server data mining.

IT Report Developer   Apr 2019 – May 2020

Drove modernization by designing and implementing clinical analytics and Power BI reporting tools, including user-friendly dashboards, to monitor healthcare KPIs and automate reporting for different enterprise functions. Collaborated with managers, customers, database administrators, developers, and data architects across the project management lifecycle, including requirements gathering, prototype design, user acceptance testing, documentation, and production release.

➢ Recognized with a **WOW award** for deploying a process mining dashboard in operating rooms that leveraged real-time analytics, including case volume metrics and utilization rates, and delivered drill-down visualizations that identified the top 10 surgery delays, improved OR decision-making, and **earned CIO support**.

➢ Earned a **Bright Idea award** for designing algorithms, developing SQL procedures, and creating intuitive dashboards that integrated an independent surgical application with Allscripts EMR/EHR platform.

➢ Utilized time and workflow management talents to spearhead the timely resolution of Tier 1 issues for on-call and UH initiatives; developed report feature guides and maintenance procedures before production deployment.

IT Operations Specialist   Jul 2017 – Apr 2019

Brought on to manage and maintain various business reporting systems, including the IT Manager Center Intranet and the Office of the CIO SharePoint sites. Assisted the Executive VP in preparing the annual IT OPEX and CAPEX budget. Interfaced with finance managers to analyze and report key financial data and application metrics for IT Tower leadership and represented IT in legal meetings to ensure prompt contract negotiation, review, and approval.

➢ **Boosted population health management** initiatives by partnering with IT leadership to deploy a comprehensive Allscripts clinical manager platform that centralized data from disparate clinical systems.

➢ Streamlined new hire training and reduced liability risks by creating and circulating an IT operations manual with documented change management, troubleshooting, and training procedures.

Education

NATIONAL UNIVERSITY   San Diego, CA
Master of Science (**M.S.**), E-Commerce
Bachelor of Business Administration (**B.B.A**)

EMPIRE COLLEGE   Santa Rosa, CA
Bachelor of Science (**B.S.**), General Sciences

Professional Development

Microsoft Certified BI Developer – SQL Server Reporting Service (SSRS)

Professional Affiliations

Member, AMERICAN COLLEGE OF HEALTH EXECUTIVES (**ACHE**) | Currently working toward achieving ACHE Fellowship

LUCY SIMPSON

lucysimpson@nu.edu | **617.555.2345** | linkedin.com/in/lucysimpson
https://www.lucysimpson.com/portfolio

COMPUTER ENGINEER

High-achieving Northeastern University graduate seeking computer engineering opportunity in the Greater Boston area.

Results-driven, self-motivated, and appreciative of team environments where members share ideas, promote industry best practices, and learn from each other.

"I'm ready to get to work!"

Software Development | Team Leadership | Collaborative Work Style | Multi-Project Management

EDUCATION

NORTHEASTERN UNIVERSITY, Boston, MA — *Bachelor of Science, Computer Engineering | 2023*
Minor in Math, Computer Science, and Software Engineering | GPA 3.85

COMPUTER LANGUAGE AND PROGRAM PROFICIENCY

Java	C/C++	MatLab
Progress	VHDL	Python
CUDA	Assembly	mySQL

MS Office Suite	Rhinoceros 3.0	Flamingo
Penguin	NetBeans	MS Visual Studio
Alice 3.0	Vivado	PlanAhead
Eclipse Neon	Logger Pro	Quartus 13.0+
Anaconda	Dependency Walker	Code Warrior

PROJECT HIGHLIGHTS

Semi-Autonomous Car
- Constructed semi-autonomous cars based on the NXP Cup (embedded programming).
- Documented entire design process from requirements specification to test plan.
- Developed two separate cars on individual microprocessors with different ARM processors.
- Interfaced CMU5 PixyCam and an array of photodiodes for vision purposes.

Digital Drawing Tool
- Created tool with Xilinx's Nexys4 board in VHDL.
- Responsible for output via VGA from RAM to the monitor.
- Utilized potentiometers to control the X-Y coordinates via an ADC chip using I2C protocol.

Educational Android App
- Designed simple Android app to teach children how to discern differences between numbers

PROFESSIONAL EXPERIENCE

VMWARE, New York, NY   5/2022 – 8/2022
Research Assistant, Internship
- Self-taught Python programming language; applied Python and CUDA to complete graph analysis project.
- Researched suitable algorithms and tested run times with multiple Python packages, applying different graph data structures for memory management.
- Implemented CUDA code into Python for both handwritten kernels and third-party functions to further client research.

RIVERSIDE TECHNOLOGIES, INC., Boston, MA   5/2021 – 7/2021
Software Developer
- Self-taught Progress programming language to develop Point of Service systems.
- Worked independently and remotely; provided documentation of daily progress reports to office-based manager.

Cathy Lanzalaco, MBA, CPRW, CPCC, NCOPE, SPHR, SHRM-SCP, RN • Inspire Careers LLC • www.inspirecareers.com

Notable: A colorful gear graphic is the focal point of this new-grad resume, along with a neat chart showcasing technical proficiencies. Highlights of college projects are featured in their own section.

ELLA WADELL

Washington, DC 20001 | ellawadell@gmail.com | (202) 212-7210 | linkedin.com/in/ellawadell

SOFTWARE DEVELOPER

Determined and creative professional, decisively applying out-of-the-box thinking to conceptualize fresh ideas, learn and apply innovative technologies, and design new concepts. Initiate and accept challenges and successfully work on team and solo projects, with or without supervision. Consistently use exceptional communication, analytical, and collaboration skills to solve complex business process issues by using advanced technical capabilities.

Areas of Knowledge

Bizagi	Business Process Modeling (BPM)	C++	Aspen Process Simulation Software
UiPath	Technical Support	HTML	VHDL Simulation Modeling Language
Robotics Software Engineering	Data Process Modeling	CSS	Python, Java, JavaScript
RPA – Robotic Process Automation	Common Data	SQL	MS 365
Software Development	Structures & Algorithms	MATLAB	Windows 10 OS

EXPERIENCE

JR. SOFTWARE DEVELOPER | BPM AUTOMATION – WASHINGTON, DC   **2022–PRESENT**

Create business process models (BPM) to demonstrate processes and turn models into executable processes. Participate in business meetings with clients and demonstrated RPA capabilities for automating and improving business operations, products, and services. Refine processes and perform software testing and troubleshooting.

- **Projects**: Federal Aviation Administration (FAA)
  - **Business Process Modeling:** Mapped out the entire grievance process into a BPM application, automated the grievance filing process, and demonstrated how the application optimizes grievance procedures.
  - **Recruitment Automation:** Developed an automated form to facilitate targeted recruiting via LinkedIn. Presented a demonstration to FAA's Human Resources Division.
- **Accomplishment**: Tested for and passed the UiPath RPA Developer exam in 4 months (ahead of 6-month employer-mandated deadline), advancing my technical knowledge and capabilities for projects.

PROCESS ENGINEERING INTERN | BLUE NILE NATIONAL LABORATORY – WALDORF, MD   **05/2021–07/2021**

Designed diagrams and models to simulate chemical processing to gather research data. Conducted research and attended weekly meetings to discuss project status and onsite safety.

- **Project:**
  - **Modeling & Simulation:** Simulated the Plutonium (IV) Oxalate Precipitation process by using the Aspen Simulation Software for modeling.

EDUCATION

Bachelor of Science in Computer Engineering | 3.4 GPA | Virginia Tech University | 05/2022
- **Courses:** Software Engineering, Networks & Systems, Digital Systems Design, Circuit Analysis, Digital Logic, Computer Program Design, Telecommunication Networks
- **Projects:**
  - **UAV / UGV Design:** Teamed to build, program, and combine UGV and UAV designs using Python and C++.
  - **Digital Systems Design:** Simulated the washing machine process by programming FPGA boards using Xilinx software.
  - **Software Engineering:** Worked through the planning phase for creating a grocery delivery service app.
  - **Algorithms:** Executed algorithmic techniques to implement process management, storage management, processor management, file systems, security, distributed systems, performance evaluation, and real-time systems.
  - **Cisco Networking Academy:** Setup productivity workstations comprised of computer hardware components.
  - **Digital Imaging:** Administered MATLAB for digital imaging processing and editing.
  - **Coding:** Used VHDL Simulation Modeling Language to code FPGA boards.

PROFESSIONAL MEMBERSHIPS

Society of Women Engineers (SWE) | National Society of Black Engineers (NSBE)

Tammeca Riley, MS, CPRW, CRS+MCT, ACRW-Federal, NCOPE • Infinite Potential Resumes • infinitepotentialresumes.com

Note: This resume makes the most of Ella's somewhat limited experience by highlighting her current position, a prior internship, and extensive college projects. Technical competencies are prominently featured in a table as part of the Summary.

ANDREW GARCIA

(555) 577-3172 ◆ garcia@abcmail.com
linkedin.com/in/andrewgarcia ◆ Los Angeles, CA 25251

HELP DESK SUPPORT TECHNICIAN

Resourceful, solution-driven IT professional adept at mastering technology tools, resolving the root cause of technical issues, and cultivating relationships to sustain business continuity, IT security, and client satisfaction.

Skills, Competencies & Relevant Coursework

Hardware & Software Desktop Support ● Diagnosis & Troubleshooting ● Physical & Virtual Operating Systems
Malware Security ● Network Protocols ● Scrum Methodology ● Active Listening ● De-escalation ● Windows & Linux
Active Directory ● Google Suite ● Zoom & MS Teams ● MS Excel ● Adobe Creative Cloud ● Web Ex ● Spanish Fluency

PROFESSIONAL EXPERIENCE

LINKEDIN CORPORATION (A SUBSIDIARY OF MICROSOFT CORP) – *New York, NY*

Help Desk Support Technician Intern   **Jan 2023–Present**

Ensured end-user productivity and system security by providing first-level IT support for 10,000+ employees throughout the U.S. for the world's largest professional social network of 740M members across 200 countries.

- Chosen to troubleshoot Slack, Google, and Adobe apps, fielding 15+ client phone calls and 25+ email inquiries daily.
- Reduced ticket resolution time 10% through efficient Service Now request classification, assignment, and tracking.
- Maintained 100% accuracy utilizing Active Directory to process shared permissions for distribution and security.
- Reduced malware impacts by promptly running Symantec End Point Protection and ADW cleaner scans.

GAP, INC. – *New York, NY*

Customer Service Associate   **Jan 2022–Jun 2022**

Promoted in 5 months to work in flagship store of apparel retailer based on technical and communication skills.

- Ensured customer satisfaction by processing 100+ returns per day and assisting customers with exchanges.
- Reduced inventory loss 5% by reporting previously undetected shoplifting attempts in fitting rooms.

Retail Sales Cashier   **Aug 2021–Dec 2021**

Processed 200+ daily transactions on point-of-sale system and tracked stock replenishment with mobile inventory app.

- Ranked #1 of 12 cashiers for selling the most credit card applications for 3 consecutive months.
- Trained 2 new cashiers in point-of-sale system and stock room inventory control and tracking processes.

SHAKE SHACK – *New York, NY*

Host Cashier   **May 2019–Mar 2020**

Served hundreds of customers per day, 40 hours per week, including greeting patrons, processing orders, collecting payment, and serving meals in a fast-paced environment for one of the most rapidly growing food chains in the U.S.

- Provided service to 500+ guests per day, ensuring order accuracy, food safety, and timeliness.
- Selected to cross-train on each station due to demonstrated ability to pitch in, quickly learn, and cover all roles.

EDUCATION AND RECOGNITION

YEARUP College-Level Business Education Program—Information Technology Concentration—2022–2023
Selected for competitive national program of 6 months of intensive business training and 6-month internship.
Relevant Coursework: Computer Applications, Project Management, MS Excel, Communications, Customer Service
Awards: Earned **YearUp Student of the Month Award** for Training Colleagues in New Technology Tools

Julie Wyckoff, M.Ed., CPRW, CCTC • Custom Career Solutions • customcareersolutions.com

Note: Andrew's relevant experience comes from his current internship with LinkedIn, earned through his selection for the highly competitive YearUp program (described under Education). His prior experience adds value by clearly demonstrating his work ethic and technical aptitude.

GWEN MORGAN

gwen.morgan@gmail.com ▪ 860.675.5555

INFORMATION TECHNOLOGY SPECIALIST

CCNA Training	Operations Analysis	Troubleshooting
Data Control Functions	Diagnostic Procedures	Customer Service
Computer Programming	Installation / Maintenance	System Evaluation

Results-driven and Cisco-certified technical professional offering deep knowledge of information technology systems. Highly effective communicator with strong presentation, project management, and networking skills. Natural problem solver and efficient troubleshooter; detail oriented and skilled in testing programs. Outgoing representative with expertise in customer service.

Project Management	InsightIQ, Operations Manager, Analytics, Oracle Enterprise Manager, MS Visio, MS Project
Network/Infrastructure	VLans, Trunking, LAN/WAN links, NAT, PAT, TCP/IP, ACL, Routing
Languages/Frameworks	PostgreSQL 8, HTML, JAVA, Visual Basic, C++, Ruby
Software Proficiencies	Oracle ZFS, Hitachi HCP/HDI, Dreamweaver, Flash, Microsoft Office Suite: Word, Excel, PowerPoint, Publisher, Outlook

PROFESSIONAL EXPERIENCE

FREEDOM CLAIMS AND LIFE INSURANCE, Springfield, MA
Network System Analyst   2021 – Present

Reduced ticket issues 35% by training users and developing "Troubleshooting FAQ Guide," a user-friendly, self-directed, online resource manual.

- Monitor network to ensure network availability to 75 system users and perform maintenance.
- Provide technical support on-site or remotely through analysis, testing, and troubleshooting.
- Diagnose and resolve hardware, software, and other network and system problems while informing users of necessary changes, issues, and timelines.
- Perform network maintenance to ensure optimal network operation.
- Install, configure, and support local area networks.

CERTIFICATION & EDUCATION

Cisco Certified Network Associate – 2018

Bachelor of Science – Information Technology Systems – 2021   New York University, New York, NY

Coursework included…
Workflow Diagrams, Database Management, Information System Ethics, Project Management, System Analysis & Design, Desktop Build & Installations

VOLUNTEER SERVICE

HARTFORD HIGH SCHOOL, West Hartford, CT
Head Track Coach   2021 – Present

Erica Tew, CPRW • CT Department of Labor • ct.gov/dol

Note: Gwen's resume is jam-packed with relevant keywords, from the Summary through Experience and Education. A strong, measurable achievement in her current job is set off in bold type in a shaded box.

BRIAN PATTERSON

Seattle, WA 98101 | ☎ 253-444-6289 | ✉ Brianpatterson1@live.com
www.linkedin.com/in/brian-patterson | 🖥 Top Secret Security Clearance / SCI

VIDEO GAME PRODUCER

Program & Project Manager – Video Engineer – Communications & Operations Professional – Instructor
B.S. degree—Graphic Arts & Coding

Creative professional with a strong passion for playing and developing diverse and emergent video games. Possess expert knowledge and extensive experience with online gaming architecture, game systems and mechanics, and game development methods. Utilize technical expertise as part of a dynamic team chosen to participate in research and development processes for critical military programs within the United States Air Force. Control multimillion-dollar assets/facilities with 100% accountability.

CORE SKILLS

Project Management Oversight	Comic-Con Convention Logistics	Advanced Technology Integration
Staff Management & Training	Written and Oral Communications	Simulator Development / Utilization
Collaborative Work Style	Technical Writing / Storytelling	Research & Development
Excellent Scheduling / Deliverables	Multi-genre Experience	Complex Design / Troubleshooting
Detail Orientation / Quality Control	Emotional Intelligence	Multimillion-Dollar Asset Management
Business Law / Critical Thinking	Cultural Diversity & Inclusion	Product Testing / Viability

Simulator Experience

✓ Instructor on PAVE PAWS and UEWR simulator software *[Created realistic scenarios to train military flight crews on potential missile launches and satellite operation.]*
✓ Worked with contractors to develop new Rendezvous and Proximity Operations software to stimulate highly precise maneuvers in a variety of space orbits by providing real-world experiences.

Select Comic Con Workshops & Training

✓ Gears, Green Screens, & Gaming	✓ World-building & Storytelling
✓ Writing for the Computer Gaming Industry	✓ Creating Diverse Worlds & Cultures
✓ How-to Show Your Story, Don't Tell It	✓ Building Worlds Across Entertainment Mediums
✓ What to Think About Before You Start Writing	✓ New Realities—VR, AR, & Gaming
✓ How-to Plot Structure—Creating the Foundation	✓ Stories Across Screens with Emil Pagilarulo
✓ Film School 101&102: Preproduction/Screenwriting	✓ How-to: Dynamic Story Creation in Plain English
✓ Film School 103: Directing & Crew Management	✓ Creating Immersive Game Story
✓ Film School 104: Editing & Producing	✓ Three Rules for Protagonists

Volunteered at San Diego Comic Con 2022—Gained hands-on knowledge and experience in the inner workings and behind-the-scenes processes for producing and conducting a successful convention.

CAREER NARRATIVE

UNITED STATES AIR FORCE

VISUAL PRODUCTION SPECIALIST   Mar 2020 to Present
2d Audiovisual Squadron, Hill Air Force Base, UT

Project Leader: Supervise crew and plan, coordinate, and execute video production and documentation of DoD and Air Force contingency/humanitarian operations. Create videos that educate, inform, and inspire Air Force core values. Manage $500K in equipment and the Air Force's only Mobile Production Satellite Truck valued at $1.8M.

Expert Trainer: Trained new Public Affairs personnel on cameras, audio, lighting, technology, and editing techniques.

➡ **Key Projects & Accomplishments:**
- Contributed to 52 video productions and 12 live streams, 23 of which were personally directed.
- Chosen as Producer/Director for production of "Mission Out" video, which aired live to 187,000 people and won a 1st place award for video production.

Kara Varner, MAOM, CARW, CPRW, CRS-MTC, CEIC • A Platinum Resume and Career Services, LLC • www.aplatinumresume.com

Note: As he transitions from the military, Brian wants use the professional skills he gained in video production, along with his avid interest and many volunteer experiences in video gaming, to land a job in the video gaming and convention business. His resume clearly conveys his extensive qualifications.

BRIAN PATTERSON | Resume Page – 2

VISUAL PRODUCTION SPECIALIST, continued

- Selected as Public Affairs Liaison during regional response training exercise; coordinated presence at 8 events and media training for 20,000 state personnel. Promoted preparedness for Disaster Preparedness Campaign.
- Provided media coverage intended to increase public awareness for prevention campaigns and programs in support of National Domestic Violence Awareness Month, National Child Abuse Prevention, Month of the Military Child and Month of the Military Family, Military Spouse Appreciation, Suicide Awareness Month, and other community-oriented events and activities.
- Trained and directed junior airmen to be lighting technicians, camera operators, and audio technicians and how to conduct live streaming setup. Presented video to the 388th Commander.
- Steered transition to digital media archive; cataloged and delivered 400 tapes for conversion. Modernized and preserved media history.

COMBAT BROADCASTER   Oct 2017 to Mar 2020
Various domestic/international operating locations, Hill Air Force Base, UT

Planned, coordinated, and executed video production and documentation of Department of Defense and Air Force contingency and humanitarian operations in overseas contentious locations.

 Key Projects and Accomplishments:
- Documented and produced a video detailing a fellow Airman's recovery from injury. Provided video copy to the base Resiliency Program as a resource for over 10,000 military personnel.
- Selected as Lead Audio Technician for Space Command business trip. Shot key satellite using time lapse feature.
- Documented F-35A rollout ceremony/live broadcast. Produced stream for web that reached 300,000 people.
- Received Intercontinental Ballistic Missile briefs before completing 8+ hours of shooting and editing. Received Letter of Achievement from Combatant Commander Air Force for "commitment to nuclear readiness."
- Head of Production for creation of "going away" videos. Three military members recognized for storytelling abilities. Won 2nd place Air Force Visual Information Awards Program award.

SATELLITE OPERATIONS MANAGER | FLIGHT CHIEF   2014 to 2017
1st Space Operations Squadron | Schriever AFB, CO

Directed operations and staff executing Air Force Space Command's $530M Multi-mission Satellite Operations Center. Leader of three-section flight providing operations training, personnel scheduling, and weapons and tactics support. Managed weapon system acquisition launch and early-orbit anomaly resolution and disposal for unique Intelligence Surveillance and Reconnaissance assets.

 Key Projects and Accomplishments:
- Safeguarded $2.9B in assets while streamlining security procedures supporting 49 visitor requests, 15 distinguished visitor tours, and clearance of 90 personnel.
- Established launch and early orbit procedures for $150M space vehicle, coordinated early operational acceptance with headquarters, and provided critical Intelligence Surveillance and Reconnaissance products to USCENTCOM.

EDUCATION | PROFESSIONAL DEVELOPMENT

Bachelor of Science — Graphic Arts & Coding — May 2019
Washington State University, Seattle, WA

Associate's Degree in Public Affairs | Community College of the Air Force | Gunter AFB, AL — May of 2014

Broadcast Journalist | Intermediate Videography Course | Defense Information School (DINFOS)

Undergraduate Space Training / PAVE PAWS Training Course | Vandenberg AFB, CA
Advanced Orbital Mechanics | Space 200 | National Security Space Institute — Peterson AFB, CO

TECHNICAL ACUMEN
Microsoft Office Suite, radar control interfaces, 2D/3D software, Adobe Flash, Adobe Photoshop and Dreamweaver

AMELIA HIGGINS

www.linkedin.com/in/ameliahiggins | ameliahiggins@outlook.com |Okemos, MI | 517.954.8058

SOFTWARE ARCHITECT
SOFTWARE DEVELOPMENT — PROCESS IMPROVEMENT — TECHNICAL LEADERSHIP

Team Leadership **Agile/Scrum Leadership** **Dev Ops Architecture** **Systems Architecture** **QA Process Development** **Requirements Gathering** **Performance Analysis** **Server Configuration** **Acceptance Testing**	Analytical, highly adaptable professional with progressive experience leading teams and development projects spanning systems, software, and services. Proactive project leader able to anticipate future needs and design products, processes, and systems to meet them. Software design and development expert with demonstrated success taking end-user needs from concept to implementation for clients across industries. Excellent communicator known for identifying talent and managing agile teams that deliver results, exceeding company goals and objectives.

CAREER HIGHLIGHTS

- *Primary Solution Architect for complex, multi-year project development of suite of custom-built software applications with a $22M budget.*

- *Technical Lead & Recruiter for team of 20+ software **developers**; maintained **80% end-of-project retention rate.***

- *Champion of more agile scrum-based software development in a largely waterfall-based organization.*

- *Driver of faster delivery time, establishing development ops process for IT software development organization using API server and custom-built software tools.*

PROFESSIONAL EXPERIENCE

F500 ACCOUNTING · Okemos, MI   2020–Present
ASSOCIATE DIRECTOR, INTELLIGENT AUTOMATION DEVELOPMENT
Provide technical and product leadership on intelligent automation to empower f500's tax, audit, and advisory verticals.

- Managed implementation of custom process automation designed to drastically reduce time and personnel required to analyze complex data files by using on-shore and off-shore teams.
- Collaborated with senior leadership to identify product roadmap for chatbot-based automations for internal use, with eventual goal of availability to external clients.
- Identified technical and business needs associated with proposed firm-wide RPA platform; collaborated with Managers and Architects from all 3 business verticals and forwarded recommendations to Directors.
- Designed programs to foster innovation throughout firm using combination of targeted and crowd-sourced ideation, hackathons, and limited engagement development initiatives.

Technologies: *Automation Anywhere, Javascript, Java*

NATIONAL CHARTER HERITAGE · Grand Ledge, MI   2014–2020
SOFTWARE ARCHITECT
NCH is an education management organization that oversees 80 charter institutions nationwide.
Infrastructure Strategy

- Implemented on-premise Team Foundation Server environment as part of DevOps evolution to support source code control and packaging, automated builds, releases and search.
- Created and led development of comprehensive software ecosystem with the goal of maximizing software reuse through componentization and service orientation.
- Built and launched comprehensive series of software development, quality assurance, and production server environments to support application design, development and delivery

Monica Marcelis Fochtman, PhD, CPRW · Sheldrake Consulting, LLC · sheldrakeconsulting.com

Note: This resume emphasizes both leadership and hands-on technical activities to support Amelia's goal of transitioning from a Big 4 consulting company to a smaller company as an individual contributor.

AMELIA HIGGINS

ameliahiggins@outlook.com | 517.954.8058

Technical Leadership
- Designed, built, and implemented custom software development framework that became foundation for $10M suite of proprietary software applications. Involved at macro and micro levels to manage its growth and progression.
  - Re-usable components designed to standardize and streamline web services within the API layer and to align more thoroughly to RESTful best practices.
  - Data retrieval and manipulation framework leveraged both Repository and Unit of Work patterns to streamline data access and abstract the underlying technology toolset.
  - Framework for system security designed to provide authorization in a claims-based environment, allowing web services to respond to requests by interrogating a set of ADFS against known set of approved roles.
  - Distributed caching model designed to provide output caching to our web services layer as well as in-process caching for system configuration values via a standalone Redis server.
  - Series of common utilities designed to provide advanced, structured, logging via Serilog to all services, repositories and business logic throughout the entire ecosystem.
  - Series of common utilities designed to provide access to a distributed job queuing system for basic task scheduling.

Technologies: .NET 4.5, C#, HTML/XML, Angular JS, JQuery, Web API, MVC, Signal R, Redis, SQL Server 2014/2016, SQL Reporting Services, Team Foundation Server 2012/2017, Release Management, Hangfire, Ninject, NewRelic, ProGet, Serilog, Seq, Entity Framework

PRIVATE DESIGN · Grand Rapids, MI   2012–2014
PRINCIPAL CONSULTANT & OWNER
Technology consulting agency focused on custom software development and collaboration solutions.

- Designed and built custom software that provided cutting-edge analysis of toxicology data for IonTox, an international biotechnology company that provides in vitro toxicology expertise to global clients across industries.
- Collaborated with an existing development team to develop suite of SharePoint 2010 applications to support business and financial advisory operations of Accounting Firm.
- Provided technical assistance, platform extensions, and data migration services as part of team deploying *SumTotal* LMS to independent business affiliates throughout Asia.

Technologies: .NET 4.0, C#, SharePoint 2010, SumTotal, SQL Server Integration Services, Microsoft CRM 4.0/2011, Subversion

CMF TECHNOLOGIES, INC · Okemos, MI   2007–2012
SENIOR CONSULTANT
CMF provides engineering, business, and IT solutions for aerospace, manufacturing, and public sector clients.

- Served as Senior Developer on teams that provided custom .NET web applications within the SharePoint platform for companies such as Dow Corning, Houghton Mifflin, and ThinkWise.
- Led team responsible for development of web application to proactively engage writers, publishers, and editors in the publication process.
- Developed series of proof-of-concept applications to provide call center functionality and location triangulation information for on-campus public safety at Waterford University.

Technologies: .NET 1.1 – 4.0, C#, Visual C++, Visual Basic, SQL Server, SQL Server Integration Services, Entity Framework

PRIOR CAREER PROGRESSION
Senior Software Engineer, Analysts International · Grand Rapids, MI
Consultant, Petoskey Stone Consulting · Grand Rapids, MI
Software Development Consultant, Dynamic Computer Services · Grand Rapids, MI
Programmer/Analyst, Brainy Group · Grand Rapids, MI

EDUCATION AND CERTIFICATIONS

WESTERN STATE UNIVERSITY   **SCRUM ALLIANCE CERTIFICATIONS**
BACHELOR OF SCIENCE: COMPUTER SCIENCE   SCRUM MASTER (CSM), SCRUM PRODUCT OWNER (CSPO)

ENRIQUE MARTINEZ

555-679-9876 | enrique.martinez@gmail.com

TARGET OPPORTUNITY: QUANTITATIVE ANALYST

Financial Markets | Securities | Hedge Funds | Risk Management | Corporate Finance
Applying Mathematical & Statistical Methods to Guide Companies in Making Sound Financial & Business Decisions

PROFESSIONAL QUALIFICATIONS

➔ Hands-on experience in data collection and analysis, research planning and design, research methodology, results reporting, trend analysis, computer modeling, and project management.
➔ Strong mathematical, computational, and analytical skills. Creative problem-solving and capable decision-making.
➔ Work well independently, with teams, and as team coordinator. Intuitive, articulate, and enthusiastic.

TECHNOLOGY PORTFOLIO: MS Office Suite, MatLab, Wolfram Mathematica.
Basic programming experience with Java.

EDUCATION

BS – Mathematics (Pure Math Specialization), Harvard University, 2023
Magna Cum Laude, GPA 3.87/4.0, Dean's List (all semesters)

Honors & Awards
Pi Beta Kappa Honorary Society • Presidential Scholarship Award
Mathematics & Statistics Departmental Honors & Faculty Award (2022)
Oscar Zariski Academic Award (2021) • Sophomore Achievement Academic Award (2021)

Research Projects
➔ **Probability & Statistics Project** (2022–Present). Collaborate with research team to investigate the repetition of mathematical procedures for problem solving and the relation of probability and statistics to modern economic theory. Coordinate team assignments that leverage each individual's talents. Pending publication in *Journal of Probability & Statistics,* Summer 2023.
- Honored with "Outstanding Poster Presentation" displaying research methodologies, calculations, and findings at 2023 Joint Mathematical Meeting of American Mathematical Society and National Association of Mathematicians.
- Expanded scope of research to include application for financial markets research and market volatility.
- Recognized by industry experts for development of unique formulas for analyzing economic theory.

➔ **String Theory Project** (2021). Year-long independent research of string theory, a branch of pure mathematics with relevancy to financial markets, economics, medicine, chemistry, and other sciences. Applied mathematical tools and concepts to investigate uncommon topics for mathematical study.
- Awarded departmental honors for quality of work.
- Presented findings at Undergraduate Achievement Conference.

EMPLOYMENT EXPERIENCE

Manager / Waiter – Harvard Square Bistro, Cambridge, MA, 2020–Present
- Coordinate scheduling, inventory, deliverables, sales reporting, cash management, and customer service.
- Train and manage 6-person kitchen and wait staff.
- Demonstrate strong customer service, communications, and interpersonal relationship skills.

Wendy Enelow, MRW, CPRW, JCTC, CCM • Enelow Enterprises • wendyenelow.com
Note: A key element of this new-grad resume is a detailed presentation of award-winning mathematical projects. The Headline and Professional Qualifications succinctly capture the expertise and value he offers to a prospective employer. Ashley Watkins, NCRW, NCOPE • Write Step Resumes • writestepresumes.com

SHARON THOMAS

ORLANDO, FL • 205-352-4212 • SHARONTHOMAS@EMAIL.COM • WWW.LINKEDIN.COM/IN/CYBERSHARON

SENIOR CYBERSECURITY LEADER

Strengthening security governance and risk management processes for leading technology organizations.

- *Goal-driven cybersecurity professional* with performance history of consulting with cross-functional IT, security, and systems engineering teams to drive audit readiness and deliver compliance solutions for large-scale projects.

- *Analytical thinker* who researches cost-effective methods for automating and streamlining business processes to guarantee successful compliance and technology audits while clarifying ambiguous situations.

- *Compliance-centric consultant* known for building strong stakeholder relationships and proactively implementing control systems that offer swift resolution of challenging problems in a remote work environment.

Audit Readiness | Compliance Testing | Continuous Improvement | People Management | Risk Mitigation
Software Development | Design, Release & Maintenance | Operations | Leading Technical and Non-Technical Teams

ISC² CISSP • ISACA CISM • ISACA CRISC • NIST Cyber Security Framework • NIST 800-53 • COBIT • ISO27001 • PCI DSS
FedRAMP ATO • SSAE 16/SOC 2 • SANS CIS • Microsoft Office Suite • Word • PowerPoint • Excel • Visio • Project

PROFESSIONAL EXPERIENCE

Top Tier Security, Inc. – Orlando, FL   June 2020–Present
SENIOR SECURITY CONSULTANT
Consult on network cybersecurity programs to drive audit readiness and minimize compliance gaps for global leaders in technology services and digital transformation. Lead internal security audits, remediation, information security assessments, data storage activities, and security application vulnerabilities. Oversee application infrastructure and advise on audit requirements, GRC tools, compliance testing, reporting, and Florida Consumer Privacy Act (FCPA) readiness.
- Achieved 100% pass rate on cybersecurity exam by monitoring workflow and coaching 5-member team on establishing relationships and defining curriculum specifics for study materials and practice groups.
- Collaborated with pre-sales team to identify RFPs, contractual requirements, and project-specifics, including deliverables, timelines, pricing, standard regulatory terms, and governance conditions.
- Educated clients and internal stakeholders on GRC processes, policy and risk management, and FCPA compliance.

NextLevel Cyber – Orlando, FL   September 2015–June 2020
CYBERSECURITY ENGINEER
Chosen as first point of contact to advise clients on change management and security issue resolution. Monitored compliance with contracts and SLAs and contributed to improvement and implementation of cybersecurity. Acted as subject matter expert in McAfee security technologies and developed surveillance tools to detect threats. Maintained detailed knowledge of Ransomware, Malware, Network Intrusion Prevention, and Security Information Event Management systems. Conducted quality assurance assessments.
- Selected as lead engineer on 3 contracts and guided 5-member team in producing deliverables within budget and timeline requirements.
- Achieved 30% compliance increase for SLAs across 5 clients on scheduled changes and yielded 90% drop in irrelevant data exposed to clients' point of contact.
- Improved productivity, training 10-member team on information mapping, ticket updates, and email templates for following up with system owners on change requests pending approval.
- Defined and implemented SOPs aligned with stakeholder's requirements and professionally developed 3 engineers capable of carrying vision toward successful completion.

Continued on next page...

Ashley Watkins, NCRW, NCOPE • Write Step Resumes • writestepresumes.com

Note: Although highly detailed and filled with technical terms, Sharon's resume remains highly readable because of concise writing and clean formatting. A branding statement under the Headline helps focus the resume in Sharon's preferred niche of cybersecurity.

SHARON THOMAS   203-352-4212 • SHARONTHOMAS@EMAIL.COM • PAGE 2

CYBER SECURITY ENGINEER | NextLevel Cyber – Orlando, FL (Continued...)

- Uncovered client's breach of Service Level Agreement and minimized risk and financial loss by leveraging keen eye for detail to address issue before project completion.
- Significantly reduced errors and ensured quicker response times to stakeholders by boosting efficiency during monthly vulnerability scanning tasks.
- Developed mitigating solutions that curtailed risks and threats by researching anti-virus protection, host intrusion prevention, data loss protection, email/web gateway, attack vectors, and best practices.

ABC Administrators Technical Solutions, Inc. – Orlando, FL   **November 2011–April 2015**
INFRASTRUCTURE SPECIALIST
Evaluated and recommended necessary changes in performance tuning, infrastructure design/monitoring, endpoint security, perimeter security, and vulnerability management. Spearheaded initiative to install, configure, and maintain applications within IT infrastructure. Conducted complex technical evaluation and suggested proposed physical architectures and detailed designs. Executed long-range strategic plans for IT, including operational aspects of application execution within infrastructure.

- Automated manual tasks and software systems by analyzing problems, evaluating technical issues, and generating infrastructure-related scripts to streamline operational activities.
- Named key point of contact entrusted to maintain company's compliance with regulatory requirements for HIPAA and HITECH.
- Consulted with company on business continuity and disaster recovery planning, testing, and training.

CompassTech – Vinje, Norway   **November 2005–September 2010**
PROJECT MANAGER
Managed testing phases for Big Data and Prediction Modeling projects. Partnered with engineering and executive staff to coordinate team scheduling, develop metrics/KPIs, conduct performance evaluations, and identify process improvements to assess program performance.

EDUCATION & PROFESSIONAL DEVELOPMENT

National College – Orlando, FL
Master of Science in Cyber Security & Information Assurance, 2017

Florida State University – Tallahassee, FL
Master of Science in Business Management, 2012

Information Mapping® Professional™ (IMP) Certification Training (2016)
RSA University (2018): -RSA Archer Suite Training; - RSA NetWitness® Platform Training
Splunk (2018): Splunk Fundamentals, Advanced Searching and Reporting, Advanced Dashboards and Visualizations
McAfee (2015/2017): McAfee ePolicy Orchestrator, Endpoint Security, Data Loss Prevention, Host Intrusion Detection

CERTIFICATIONS

CRISC – ISACA	June 2021
CISM – ISACA	February 2021
CISSM – ISC²	September 2019
CNSSI-4012 National Information Assurance Training Standard for Senior Systems Managers	May 2018
NSTISSI-4011 National Training Standard for Information Systems Security (INFOSEC) Professionals	May 2018
CompTIA Security+ Certification – CompTIA	November 2017

MARK JACOBS III

San Francisco, CA 00093 | LinkedIn Profile

902-106-9444 | mark@gmail.com

SENIOR MANAGER INFORMATION TECHNOLOGY

Known for outstanding analytical abilities in resolving complex issues

Certified Support Center Analyst providing high-quality and timely technical support in multi-faceted service-based organizations. Award-winning technology engineer, consistently presented with progressively challenging roles; earned 5+ promotions for taking initiative in adopting industry best practices that improved metrics, maximized efficiency, and expedited technical resolution.

TEAM LEADERSHIP — Leading teams of 12+ technical employees; respected among peers for hands-on leadership style and applauded by management for boosting team productivity.

PROCESS IMPROVEMENT — Identifying opportunities for improving existing processes, then devising and executing plans to enhance workflows.

TECHNICAL SUPPORT — Delivering concierge support to internal and external customers while handling high-volume technical support desk with up to 300+ daily trouble tickets.

TECHNICAL EXPERTISE

Technology Operations	Technical Support
Network Infrastructure	Project Management
Enterprise Network Operations	Troubleshooting
System Upgrades	Technology Deployments
End-User Support	Preventative Maintenance
System Configurations	Desktop Support

> *"Mark was such a great addition to our team. His analytical mind was just what we needed to raise our SLAs, speed up time to resolution, and streamline our internal processes."*
> – Fred Jackson, VP IT Services, Pipe Piper, Inc.

CAREER PROGRESSION

Pipe Piper, Inc.; San Francisco, CA — 2018 – Present

Senior Support Specialist Level II

Provide 24/7 on-call technical support for 60 commercial accounts via phone and email. Clients include Wells Fargo, BB&T, Morgan Stanley, Aegon, American Equity, Allianz, AIG, Allstate, Mass Mutual, Jackson National, Merrill Lynch, Nationwide, New York Life, TD Ameritrade, and Metlife.

- ▶ **Shortened average resolution time 71% from 7 days to 2–3 days** after initiating tiered support model that standardized support protocols and enabled prioritization of high-profile tickets.
- ▶ **Single-handedly address and close an average of 40 cases per month within 3 days or less.**
- ▶ **Eliminated instances of overlooked inquiries** by filtering requests through Salesforce.com software versus receiving requests through unregulated shared inbox accessible to all team members.
- ▶ **Devised and established trouble ticket distribution system** to evenly assign 150+ weekly cases among team of 7.
  - ○ Took initiative to conduct team meeting to overcome resistance, foster collaboration and gain buy-in for new rotational ticket distribution process.
- ▶ **Earned promotion to Senior Support role** in June 2022 to serve as team leader and point of contact for procedural questions.

> Won Stickman Award Q4 2022 for demonstrating extraordinary leadership, collaboration, and contributions to the global organization.

Continued…

Melanie Denny, CPRW, CIPCC • melaniedenny.com

Note: Design elements include bold category headings, a boxed endorsement, and an impressive award—all of which convey the expertise and value of this IT Senior Manager.

MARK JACOBS III

902-106-9444 | mark@gmail.com | Page 2 of 2

Seventy-Five, Corp.; Monaco, CA   2011 – 2018

Desktop Technical Support Analyst *(2016 – 2018)*
Assessed and resolved average of 17 daily new client incidents onsite and via remote desktop interfaces. Handled all HP certified hardware repairs; replaced laptop screens, hard drives, CPUs and motherboards.

▶ **Resolved all site-wide issues** related to user software, user telecom issues, and switch upgrades within allotted SLAs.

▶ **Streamlined methods for reimaging computer systems** for work-from-home employees; cut process times in half.

Supervisor – Technical Support Helpdesk *(2014 – 2016)*
Promoted to supervise team of 9 tech support agents and manage daily average of 85 new incidents while monitoring agent metrics. Performed all managerial duties to include conducting interviews, creating shift schedules, authorizing vacation time, approving time sheets, and addressing employee issues.

▶ **Appointed acting manager** of technical support helpdesk and facilitated transition to overseas vendor.

▶ **Oversaw the execution of 300+ daily trouble tickets,** generating reports to analyze daily workflow and call volume.

▶ **Revamped department SOPs,** including Level 1 escalation procedures and attendance policy.

Technical Support Helpdesk Representative *(2011 – 2014)*
Supported 16,000+ in-house and work-from-home employees on various technical issues via online chat as well as inbound and outbound phone calls. Solved customer issues related to internal systems, third party software, network trouble, and printers.

▶ **Resolved up to 230 incidents per week** while consistently maintaining a 97% customer satisfaction rating.

▶ **Frequently ranked as #1 producer** with 35% more resolutions than team average.

Technology Solutions, Inc.; Oakland Park, FL   2008 – 2010

Store Manager *(2009 – 2010)*
Led team of 15 in daily operation of computer repair store. Interviewed candidates, trained new hires, groomed existing personnel, and delegated workload across team. Handled store opening and closing procedures.

▶ **Boosted overall revenue 15%** by training staff in customer resolution strategies.

▶ **Established standard procedures** and measurable processes.

Repair Manager *(February 2009 – August 2009)*
Supervised team of 12 technicians while monitoring all repair projects. Served as escalation point for unresolved problems and customer complaints.

▶ **Implemented preventive maintenance procedures,** including data backup solutions and software updates.

Hardware Technician *(2008 – 2009)*
Analyzed and resolved hardware and software computer errors for remote and on-site customers.

EDUCATION & TRAINING

UCLA; Los Angeles, CA | **Bachelor of Science in Business Administration, Major: Technology Operations** *(2009)*
Skill Path Management Certificate *(2020)* | **HDI Support Center Analyst Certification** *(2015)* | **ITIL** *(2014)*

TECHNICAL SKILLS

SOFTWARE	VMware, MS Office Suites, Microsoft Windows Server 2008, 2012, 2016, Splunk Enterprise Monitor, JIRA, XMLSpy, LANDesk Management Suite, SMS, BMC Magic, Salesforce, ImOnCall, Webex, MOVEIt, Adobe Products, Active Directory, Gmail Enterprise Email
HARDWARE	CPU, hard drives, RAM, network cards, laptops, printers, scanners, servers, custom computers
SERVER APPLICATION	Microsoft SQL Server Management Studio, Exchange, SharePoint, Oracle, Domino
NETWORK	LAN, WAN, TCP/IP, Juniper, VPN

Susan G. Evans

Memphis, TN • (555) 222-4444 • sge@gmail.com

Disruptive MedTech Executive & Chief Solutions Architect
Holistic Strategy — Design Thinking — Theoretical Modeling — Innovation for Ethical & Societal Impact

Entrepreneurial Product Innovation & Engineering Leader with multiple patents to go with track record of success **designing and developing revolutionary new products** and **leading discovery in medical science.** Inspirational communicator and team leader adept at optimizing performance by matching team member strengths to available tasks.

UVA MBA Candidate (Quantitative Finance) with deep passion for driving disruptive MedTech solutions using theoretical and mathematical modeling.

Computational Fluid Dynamics, Systems Engineering, Mechanical Engineering, Lasers, Electronics (Oscilloscopes, Signal Generators, Piezoelectrics, Magnetic/Micro Circuits), Fabrication (Lathe, Mill, Weld, Water-Jet, Etching, Extrusion, Casting, Machining, 3D Printing, CAD Modeling), Software (Ansys, Agilent ADS, Chemkin, Matlab, Mathematica, LaTeX, DesignSpark Mechanical, SolidWorks, COMSOL Multiphysics, MS Suite), Programming (C++, Fortran, Python, HTML5, CSS3, Javascript)

ENTREPRENEURIAL & PRODUCT INNOVATION EXPERIENCE

PARADOX ENGINEERING LLC, Ideator & Product Innovation Leader | Founder   August 2022 – Present
Launched holding company and assembled and led technical and product teams to enable invention and product discovery in healthcare, medical devices, engineering, and defense sectors. Direct solution ideation, MVP product/prototype development, use case design, white paper creation, and patent/IP functions.

- Designed and built working prototype for OQR-Type Rotational Gravity Gradiometer with sensitivity to perform General Relativity experiments to define curvature of space-time.
  - ✓ Engineered product for simple, low-cost manufacturing.
  - ✓ Built commercial use cases for mapping earth density with no digging, chemical testing, or jamming.
  - ✓ Developing software for results analysis using complex mathematical models and algorithms.
- Directing patent effort for energy-beamed missile disruption device.

PERCIPIENCE LLC, Chief Innovator & Product Developer | Founder   August 2021 – Present
Founded new business entity and built team focused on medical device product invention. Lead all aspects of product strategy, product design and engineering, and MVP product development.

- Invented device to remove medical implants with reduced incision size and patient pain levels using continuum mechanics theory for implant extraction.
  - ✓ Designed device to be purely topical, achieving Class 1 Medical Device status for reduced legal liability and accelerated FDA approval timeline.
  - ✓ Engineered single-part solution with fully compliant features to optimize quality, reduce manufacturing and parts costs, and eliminate assembly.
  - ✓ Driving commercial viability with product completion and FDA submission in August 2023.
- Led market research and analysis, identifying opportunity for 2.3M medical implants removed each year in the US, including devices for birth control and to treat depression, macular degeneration, and more.

EDUCATION & CREDENTIALS

Master of Business Administration (MBA)
University of Virginia Darden School, August 2023
Quantitative Finance, Economics & Accounting

Pre-Medical Studies
University of Tennessee, 2018

Master of Science (MS) in Aerospace Engineering
Johns Hopkins University, 2013
Full Scholarship with the Applied Research Lab

Bachelor of Science (BS) in Mathematics & Physics
University of Missouri (Dual Honors), 2010
Jones Mathematics Award & Scholarship Recipient

Post-Graduate Certificate in Artificial Intelligence & Machine Learning (AI/ML), University of Texas at Austin, 2021
President & Science Officer, Johns Hopkins University Student Launch Initiative
STEM Coach & Mentor, OneGoal

LinkedIn Profile: www.linkedin.com/in/sg-evans

Stephen Van Vreede, CPRW, ACRW, MCS, OPNS, Phello Certified Career Networking Expert • ITtechExec • ittechexec.com
Note: Experience is broken into 2 distinct groups—on page 1, medtech product development experiences, and on page 2, medical and scientific research posts—to position this inventor to transition from entrepreneurial ventures to a medical device company.

Susan G. Evans

Page Two • (555) 222-4444 • sge@gmail.com

SCIENTIFIC RESEARCH & MEDICAL EXPERIENCE

JOHNS HOPKINS APPLIED RESEARCH LAB, Research Assistant – High-Energy Transmission & Storage Division
Performed research on ultra-short pulse high-energy lasers, laser and matter interaction, plasmas, microwaves, RF circuits, and electromagnetic phenomena in collaboration with the DoD/US Navy. Engaged with Research Principals to fabricate devices, prioritize projects, fulfill grant requirements, comply with agency regulations, and prepare reports.

- Conducted theoretical modeling for optimization and diagnostics of weapons-grade lasers and high-energy transmission and storage solutions.
- Created new methods for device calibration and error detection.
- Applied Collision Theory, Electronic Theory of Solids, and Solid-State Physics concepts to solve an anomalous melt depth problem related to ultra-short pulse laser drilling of metals.
- Wrote Master's Thesis on laser–matter simulations and design of differential equation methods.

JOHNS HOPKINS AEROSPACE ENGINEERING, Research Assistant – Advanced In-Space Propulsion Program
Supported novel space propulsion design projects, from feasibility and proof-of-concept (POC) development to systems and solution design to laboratory testing. Applied Empirical and Theoretical Analysis for experiment POC. Calibrated and maintained lab and test devices. Ran electromagnetic–molecular interaction simulations in C++.

- Designed solution for Rydberg-induced state of water for in-space propulsion, installing vacuum plumbing, gauges, and microwave and RF circuitry.

UNIVERSITY OF MISSOURI PHYSICS DEPT., Research Assistant – Particle Astrophysics Program
Performed theoretical modeling and analysis, error and regression analysis, mechanism simulations, and working model design in support of particle astrophysics research.

- Created model to analyze unknown Terra-Electron-Volt source in Cygnus OB2 region of Milky Way.
  - ✓ Authored paper, published in peer-reviewed journal; Abstract and Article in university Archives.
  - ✓ Created and exhibited poster at Undergraduate Research Conference.
- Built best-fit model using regression analysis for insights into proposed causal mechanism of relativistic pion–pion particle and double Lorentz-boosted nucleon–gamma ray interactions.

ELITE MEDICAL SCRIBES LLC, Certified Medical Scribe
Documented physician–patient interactions and examination findings taking SOAP medical notes. Authored admissions and discharge diagnoses and care instructions. Managed documentation of patient orders, lab and radiology tests, and medications in electronic health record (EHR/EMR). Ensured HIPAA compliance.

PATENTS — PUBLICATIONS — PRESENTATION

Implant Removal Devices and Methods, *Intl. Patent App#:* PCT/US2021/018427, *Pub#:* WO/2021/265211 A1.
Rotational Gravity Gradiometer, *US Patent App#:* 14770258, *Pub#:* 20160240116; Granted 04/2017.
Rotational Gravity Gradiometer, *Intl. Patent App#:* PCT/US2013/069888, *Pub#:* WO/2015/065492.

S.G. Evans, **Solving the Classical Physics Problem of Saint-Venant's Principle of Stress Concentration by Challenging How Continuum Mechanics is Conceived.** *Phys. Rev. D.* 2022, In Submission.

L. Anchordoqui, H. Goldberg, S.G. Evans et al., **Present and Future Gamma-Ray Probes of the Cygnus OB2 Environment.** *Phys. Rev. D.* 80 (2009) 103004.

E. Mohseni Languri, S.G. Evans, et al., **An Approach to Model Resin Flow through Swelling Porous Media.** *10th International Conference on Flow Processes in Composite Materials,* Ascona, Switzerland, July 2010.

LinkedIn Profile: www.linkedin.com/in/sg-evans

ANAND AGGARWAL

anand.aggarwal@mac.com | 555-789-6754 | linkedin.com/in/anand-agarwal

SENIOR EXECUTIVE: PAYMENTS—FINTECH—SOFTWARE
General Management | Business Development | Product Management | M&A

SIGNATURE STRENGTHS
- **Growth Driver:** Proven ability to grow revenue by launching new products and forming strategic partnerships.
- **Leader:** Strong general management capabilities and talent for building energized, high-performing teams.
- **FinTech Expert:** Deep domain expertise and a broad network of trusted relationships.

CAREER SNAPSHOT
- **PayWhiz:** Transformed the Payments line of business, driving 32% revenue growth in 1 year.
- **PayCard:** Launched the global platform powering mobile payment systems worldwide.
- **Big-Bell:** Negotiated HBO partnership that generated $100M+ annual revenue.
- **Cranford Partners:** Identified company that delivered 12X return on VC investment.

PROFESSIONAL EXPERIENCE

PAYWHIZ, INC., Boston, MA—*Leading provider of SaaS and integrated payments for the restaurant industry*

Vice President, Commerce and Payments   2020–2023

Steered growth of PayWhiz into a global commerce platform processing $6B annual payments volume across 18 countries. Recruited for strategic mindset, deep domain expertise, and ability to drive programs from vision to launch. Full P&L responsibility for $65M+ revenue; led 55-person team.

- **Delivered** 32% YoY revenue growth while keeping expenses flat.
- **Reimagined** the entire Payments line of business to drive growth and profitably scale the business.
  - Executed a global partnership with WePay, positioning PayWhiz to improve the customer experience, scale its B2C marketplace, and expand into new countries.
  - Renegotiated existing partnership deals to cut costs and terminated underperforming relationships.
  - Developed product vision for the next-generation payments platform. Engaged with key clients to gain insights and drive payments adoption.
- **Launched** new products (smart terminal, account updater) and new markets (Germany, Australia, Iceland).
- **Strengthened** the team through key outside hires, role reorganization, and development of existing talent.

PAYCARD, INC., New York, NY—*Leading global payments technology company*

Vice President, Digital and Mobile Payment Solutions   2016–2020

Hired to develop strategies, partnerships and products to establish Visa as a leader in the burgeoning mobile and digital payments arena. Built strategic partnerships with smartphone OEMs, mobile operators, banks, and processors. Managed 25-person team.

- **Envisioned** and developed a SaaS-based mobile payments platform adopted as a de facto industry standard. Mobilized resources across the company to pursue the opportunity and drive product development.
  - Engaged and negotiated deals with Apple, Google, Samsung, AT&T, Verizon, and T-Mobile.
  - Frequent speaker at industry conferences to publicize PayCard's leadership in mobile payments.
  - Achieved adoption by 800+ banks in 10 countries within 24 months of launch.
- **Defined** and executed strategy to bring mobile financial services to unbanked consumers in developing economies. Orchestrated $110M acquisition of PayNow, provider of mobile payment solutions for the unbanked.

Louise Kursmark, MRW, CPRW, JCTC, CEIP, CCM • Best Impression Career Services • louisekursmark.com

Note: Following a headline that immediately places Anand in the context of his target roles, the Summary contains 2 brief, easy-to-skim sections that clearly define what Anand does and how well he does it. Those claims are supported by measurable achievements in each Experience listing.

ANAND AGGARWAL   PAGE 2

BIG-BELL CORP., Wilmington, DE—*Fortune 100 voice/internet/video/wireless provider; acquired by AT&T in 2016*
Executive Director, Corporate Development   2006–2016

Promoted to leadership role identifying, negotiating, and closing M&A deals, alliances, joint ventures, and VC investments, both domestic and international. Managed junior professionals and led due diligence teams.

- **Created** Big-Bell's VC program, building a portfolio of 18 strategic investments that generated double-digit returns. Held board seats and observer roles.
- **Filled** coverage gap in Big-Bell's wireless footprint through 4 complex acquisitions totaling $210M.
- **Generated** $18M in proceeds (versus expected write-off) by selling Big-Bell's internet hosting business in a difficult market environment.
- **Executed** strategic alliance with HBO, adding video to the product portfolio and generating $100M+ revenue in year 2.

PRIOR

- **Senior Financial Analyst**—BIG-BELL: Built complex valuation models supporting domestic and international M&A transactions. Aided deal negotiations and participated in due diligence.
- **Associate**—CRANFORD PARTNERS: Joined top-tier VC/PE firm and identified promising investments by attending trade shows, reviewing industry publications, and making 2,500+ cold calls to target firm CEOs.
  - Initiated investment in Xtasy Software that delivered 12X return on Cranford's investment.

EDUCATION

MBA—University of Pennsylvania, Wharton School of Business
BS Management—Northwestern University

BOARD POSITIONS

Current   Advisory Board, CyberSets—Provider of security tools for software and IoT devices

Prior   Advisor to Board and CEO, SafeCo—Fast growing VC-backed SaaS provider to insurance carriers
          Board of Directors—Numerous joint ventures and VC investments during tenure at Big-Bell
          Board of Directors, Consolidated Products, Inc.—Venture investment of Cranford Partners

TIMOTHY WALDEN

New York, NY | (201) 887-4223 | timothy@timothywalden.com
www.linkedin.com/in/timothywalden.com

EXECUTIVE PROFILE

Performance-driven leader providing vision for profitable growth strategies, products, services, and new market entries. Delivered tens of millions of dollars in revenue at technology companies.

Experience... — P&L accountability for multimillion-dollar technology businesses
Startup and new venture leadership

Technology Expertise ... — Data Analytics | Cyber Security | Cloud Infrastructure | Unified Communications | Contact Center

Areas of Impact ... — Strategy. Business turnarounds. Spotting emerging opportunities. Product development and management. Complex mergers and acquisitions. Business development/partnering with startup technology companies. Securing funding for new ventures. Creating investor returns in early-stage and mature organizations. Exit planning. Hiring and leading top IT and business development talent.

Vast national and regional contacts: angel investors, VCs, and senior technology executives.

CAREER MILESTONES

Steered strategy, marketing, product, and technology initiatives in 6 companies that resulted in multimillion-dollar impact on revenues, cost reductions, or enterprise value. Examples:

- **Turned around, grew revenues, and boosted net income 20% at IT solutions business (Tech Institute).**
- **Secured $15M in venture funding from the board and $45M partnership agreement; landed anchor customer to launch business; set stage for company's successful IPO (Morrow, Inc.).**
- **Brought deal to SA Communications and developed business plan to enter contact center software market with potential to generate $35M in Q4 2023.**
- **Steered 100% cash exit for $19.7M, returning 4X to investors at ecommerce startup (CPT Advisory Group).**

PROFESSIONAL EXPERIENCE

SA COMMUNICATIONS, New York, NY • 2021 to Present

VICE PRESIDENT, CORPORATE DEVELOPMENT

Hired to create a new managed services business and lead corporate development at a provider of on-demand, cloud-based communications services for businesses and contact centers. Authored business plans; researched MS Lync-based contact center software companies and ecosystem. Modeled economics of perpetual licensing vs. subscription models.

- ➤ **Within 30 days, presented business plan** that identified key positioning opportunities and entry strategies.
- ➤ **Delivered 2 strategic business opportunities valued at $5.3M,** following preparation of customer pitch and product package for flagship offering.
- ➤ **Developed business plan for entering contact center software market**; qualified, negotiated, and presented an acquisition candidate that fit 100% of board's screening criteria.
- ➤ **Authored fundraising pitch and differentiation strategy**—based on strategic, technical, financial, and market conditions—to secure a new round of venture funding.
- ➤ **Closed a strategic partnership** and implemented solution to enter hosted unified communications and hosted contact center markets.

Louise Garver, CERM, CJSS, PRW, CCMC, IJCTC, CMP, MCDP • Career Directions Intl, LLC • careerdirections.com

Note: Timothy's resume conveys urgency and action through the use of strong verbs, bold type, and high-impact statements. All content is crisp and to the point.

TIMOTHY WALDEN – PAGE 2   (201) 887-4223 | timothy@timothywalden.com

CPT ADVISORY GROUP, New York, NY • 2014 to 2021

PRESIDENT

Built a business focused on strategy, commercialization, and operations consulting. Created company's operational infrastructure and grew business to $8.5M/annual. Selected engagement highlights:

➢ **As Interim CEO of Torrington, LLC (2019 to 2020),** took over a financially troubled data protection and backup business, lowered debt service 95%, and enabled company to begin reestablishing market position. Streamlined accounting and operational processes, resulting in 75% greater sales capacity and 50% faster sales-to-cash intervals.

➢ **Led development of a trademark clearinghouse critical to supporting launch of global top-level domains for next-generation technology initiative program ($150M+ revenue).** Worked with often competing stakeholders to gain consensus in a first-of-its-kind initiative.

➢ **Analyzed commercialization potential of a cyber security research portfolio for Tech Institute.** Mapped out supply chain, developed forecast model, and outlined pursuit plan for commercialization.

➢ **Conducted due diligence leading to successful funding ($24M) for a tech startup.**

TECH INSTITUTE, New York, NY • 2010 to 2014

VICE PRESIDENT, IT SOLUTIONS & KNOWLEDGE MANAGEMENT

Recruited to drive business development and reestablish growth trajectory for division of world's largest non-profit research and development organization. Within 60 days, selected to lead the $50M IT solutions business unit to energize and inspire 250 employees through 6 direct reports. Held full P&L and operations management accountability.

➢ **Revitalized IT solutions business; grew revenues and increased net income 20%** without increasing overhead.

➢ **Defined strategy, added 3 new practice areas** (knowledge management, information assurance/security, enterprise architecture), restarted IP development to create differentiation, and secured CMMI level-2 certification.

➢ **Created new strategy for effective enterprise-wide knowledge sharing** by leveraging influencing skills to garner support of major knowledge and information purveyors across company.

MORROW, INC., NEW YORK, NY • 2008 to 2010

VICE PRESIDENT, IP SERVICES

Brought on board to develop strategy and launch plan for a new convergence business unit. Established strategic direction, goals, and priorities for new entity. Staffed business unit and managed $10M budget. Led IP development project that introduced Morrow's SIP-based number translation service in the market.

➢ **Created a funded, sustainable new business by securing $15M in venture funding from the Morrow board.**

➢ **Helped legitimize company in a nascent market and generate $250K in revenue immediately** by securing level-3 rating as an anchor customer.

➢ **Negotiated $45M agreement** to partner on identity management product with an IT industry leader.

GLOBAL SYSTEMS, NEW YORK, NY • 2007 to 2008

PRESIDENT, GLOBAL ALLIANCES & PARTNERSHIPS

Served on senior management team that developed and presented strategic plan for the first pan-European broadband telecom company and one of the largest Tier-1 Internet service providers in Europe.

➢ **Built business plan for entering web hosting business.** Executed co-marketing deals with 2 technology companies.

EDUCATION

COLUMBIA UNIVERSITY, New York, NY
Master of Business Administration | Bachelor of Science, Computer Science

Part VIII:
Resources to Write, Format & Design Better & Faster

No resume book would be complete without practical resume and LinkedIn profile tools and resources.

On the following pages you will find:

- **Goal-Setting Worksheet**, a tool that will help you define your current career objective—the starting point for every successful resume.

- **Career Vault,** a structured guideline for gathering all of your resume and LinkedIn information in one place so it's easier and faster to work with.

- **Dig-Deep Questions** to guide you in uncovering, quantifying, and writing about your accomplishments.

- **Verbs With Verve,** our favorite list of **440 Resume Writing Verbs** to aid you in writing with power and distinction—while avoiding repetition.

Goal-Setting Worksheet

Define Your Objective Before Writing Your Resume

As you read in Chapter 3, most modern resumes do not start with a "Career Objective" as was standard in decades past. But that doesn't mean you don't have to think about your current career goals. In fact, the #1 step in resume and LinkedIn profile development is to know your objective, because it determines *what* you write, *how* you write it, *where* you position it, and *why*.

Give some thought to these questions:
- What new jobs combine your skills and your interests—what you do well and what you love to do?
- Look at job postings that interest you. Do you have the skills, experience, and qualifications the employer is looking for? Can you recall specific examples of when you've used those core skills?
- Do the salary range, benefits, working conditions, locations, and other details meet your needs? In other words, are your goals realistic?
- What industries are most intriguing to you? Do you have any experience in those industries? If not, how will you connect your background to a different industry?

Next, fill in the blanks below to create a clear objective statement and position yourself to appeal to your target audience.

Targeted Job Titles (Profession)

_____
_____
_____
_____

Targeted Industries

_____
_____
_____
_____

Top Skills & Attributes to Showcase

_____
_____
_____
_____
_____
_____

Geographic Preferences

_____
_____
_____

In-Person, Remote, or Hybrid Preferences

_____
_____
_____

Salary Requirements

_____
_____
_____

Additional Requirements & Specific Needs

_____
_____
_____
_____
_____

Career Vault

Capture Your Career Information Once—Use It Forever

To begin the resume and LinkedIn writing process you must collect all of the data you'll need—everything from the basics of job titles, company names, dates of employment, and college degrees to more detailed information about job responsibilities, career achievements, special training, and more.

Your "Career Vault" becomes the single document for all of your data. You'll use it when writing your resume, completing applications, or otherwise providing information to employers, and to recall specific facts for other career communications—letters, bios, career profiles, and more. Add to your Vault with every new position to maintain an easy-to-access record that you'll find valuable throughout your career.

> **PRO TIP: Answer all of the questions and record all of the data**—even if you don't think you're going to use all of the information you've assembled. You never know, until your resume and LI profile finished, what specifics you'll use and what you'll omit, so it's best to collect it all at the beginning.

Our recommendation is to create a Word file to capture all of this information and, when complete, make a backup copy. You'll never again have to go through the exercise of recreating all of the facts, figures, dates, and detailed data from your entire career. It's all safely stored in your Career Vault!

Job & Career Objective

You've read a lot about clarifying your objective in Chapter 3, and we hope you've taken the time to complete the Goal-Setting Worksheet on page 227.

You now know that even though you most likely won't include an objective statement on your resume, your objective is the driving force that guides everything about your resume and LI profile.

- Begin your Career Vault by writing down your current career objective, so that you're always focused on this all-important information that will guide everything that you write.

Education

Create a comprehensive list of your education. It might include multiple items from the list below:

- Degree • Major • College/University Name • Location • Honors and Awards • Graduation Date (year only unless you're a graduating student or very recent graduate, in which case you can add the month)

- College Leadership, Sports, and Activities (only if you are a graduating student or recent grad, or if you did something in college that is truly noteworthy even many years later)

- Certification and/or License • Organization/Agency/College/University • Date (year only)

- Professional Training and Development Program • College/University/Organization • Location (optional and if important) • Date (year only)

Experience

For each position you've held, document the following:

- Job Title • Company • Company Description • Location • Dates (include months in your Career Vault; you may need them for a job application, although we don't recommend adding them to your resume or LI profile unless you are a young professional or graduating student).

- Scope of Responsibility—Functions • Projects • Operations • Organizations • Budgets • Staff— everything that you are/were responsible for. Quantify as much information as you can—e.g., $2M project, operations in 14 states, $30M annual operating budget, staff of 47.

- Your Achievements and Success Stories. This is the material that will set you apart from the competition, so be comprehensive in documenting all that you've accomplished, contributed, improved, increased, reduced … all the ways that you've been valuable to your company, colleagues, customers, and other important stakeholders.

  As you are recording your success stories, at this point don't worry about writing tight, lean, and clean or otherwise writing with impact. You'll apply those lessons when you begin to work on your resume and LI profile. For your Career Vault, include details and tell the whole story. Details *now* will jog your memory *later*, so that these stories will remain rich and meaningful when you refer to them in the future.

> **PRO TIP: Use a professional resume writing technique: CAR Stories.** CAR is an acronym for Challenge–Action–Result. Follow the CAR structure to describe each particular challenge, obstacle, or opportunity in your career; what actions you took; and what happened as a result. The specifics that you uncover will be valuable additions to your resume, LinkedIn profile, and interview responses. Or you might prefer another acronym that is a slight variation on the CAR theme. Consider SAT: Situation—Action—Results; SPAR: Situation or Problem, Action, Results; STAR: Situation, Task, Action, Results; SOAR: Situation, Opportunity, Action, Results.

Refer to Dig-Deep Questions on pages 231–32 for more ideas to help you identify, describe, and quantify your unique and valuable achievements.

Technology / Technical Qualifications

Create a comprehensive list of your technical skills, knowledge, and expertise: hardware, software, systems, telecommunications, new media, tools, equipment … whatever is appropriate to you and your career:

- If technical expertise is a prime qualification for your job (e.g., programmers, designers, some engineers and skilled trades workers), Technology Qualifications, Technical Qualifications, or Equipment Skills are particularly important and should be listed in detail, often at or near the beginning of your resume.

- If you're an IT senior manager or executive, you may want to include a brief listing of relevant technologies (normally at the end of your resume), unless you have already interwoven them into your summary, job descriptions, and/or achievements.

- For every profession, if there is relevant technology (e.g., SAP in manufacturing; HRIS in human resources) and you're experienced with it, be certain to mention it in your summary or experience.

Honors & Awards

Document the recognition you've received throughout your career:

- Name of Honor/Award • Reason for Award • Bestowing Company/School/Organization • Date

Project Profile

If you work in a profession or industry where projects are the mainstay, or you work as a consultant, you will want to capture all of these details:

- Name of Project • Date • Scope of Work • Project Partners • Budget • Outcomes/Results/Problems Solved (quantified as best as possible)

Professional Affiliations / Community Memberships

For every professional association and every community, nonprofit, or volunteer organization to which you belong now or have belonged in the past, list:

- Name of Organization • Committee or Board Positions • Achievements • Projects • Location • Date (option to include in your resume, but helpful to have in your Career Vault)

Publications

Capture all of the data for each book, online or print article, white paper, or other publication you've written or where you've been featured:

- Title • Publisher/Magazine Name/Website Name • Co-Authors • Date of Publication • URL if published online. Be sure to also capture and save a hard copy.

Public Speaking

For each presentation, record:

- Title of Presentation • Audience • Sponsoring Company or Association • Location • Date (again, optional to list in your career documents but helpful to include here)

Languages

List all languages you speak, read, and/or write, and your level of fluency.

For most people reading this book, English will be your primary language and is not necessary to state unless it is a particularly rare job search situation.

Personal Profile

It is rare to include personal information on a resume in the US. However, as you are creating your Career Vault, make a note of personal items that you might briefly list at the end of your resume. If you live and/or work outside the US, list whatever personal information is customary in that country.

Dig-Deep Questions

Uncover and Quantify Your Career Successes

Having difficulty identifying your achievements? Don't worry; you're not the only one. Use this compilation of thought-provoking questions to pinpoint your career highlights and successes that ultimately become the foundation and showpieces of your resume and LinkedIn profile.

General Questions About the Company

- What is the company's primary line of business?
- What are its annual revenues and have those revenues increased during your employment?
- What markets or customers does the company service/supply/support?
- Is the company local, regional, national, or international?

General Questions About Your Position

- What is the scope of your responsibility; specifically, the daily business functions for which you are responsible?
- Do you have any management responsibilities for personnel, projects, functions, organizations, revenues, profits, or anything else?
- Have there been any particular challenges associated with your position?
- Have there been any specific opportunities associated with your position?
- Where you promoted from one position to another? How quickly? Based on anything in particular?
- Do you have budget or any other type of financial responsibility?
- What other departments or organizations do you "touch" as a routine part of your job?

Questions About Making Money

- Did the company's revenue increase during your tenure? If so, by what dollar amount or percentage?
- Would you say that the increase was average, above average, or phenomenal?
- Did you help impact (directly or indirectly) that increase? How?
- How did the company rank in comparison to other branches or to other competitors?
- Did market share increase? Were you directly or indirectly responsible or contribute in any way?

Questions About Saving Money

- Did you suggest any ways to cut costs in your team, department, unit, branch, or company?
- What were the before and after numbers or percentages of the savings?
- Were the savings significant in comparison to the total budget?
- Did the savings give you or the company a competitive advantage? If so, how, and what was the final result?

Questions About Saving Time & Improving Productivity

- Was there a reduction-in-force while you were there? Or, did you find yourself managing the work previously done by more than one person?
- Can you describe any tasks that used to take a lot longer to accomplish and what you did to streamline the process, function, or activity? Were the savings sustainable over time?
- What part did you have in reducing the time to complete these tasks?
- Did you regularly meet all your deadlines?

Comparisons With Your Performance

How did you do in comparison to your competitors?

- … to industry averages?
- … to company averages?
- … to your predecessor in the position?

Questions About Performance & Overall Qualifications

- What are you most proud of?
- What did supervisors compliment you for?
- What do your performance evaluations say?
- What were your performance goals? Did you meet them? Exceed them? How does that compare to … (see comparison questions above)?
- What are you best known for?
- What do you do that others can't or don't do?
- What would "fall apart" or "slide downhill" if you weren't at your job for a week?
- What did you do that saved the company money or time?
- How did you contribute to the bottom line?
- Were you the first, best, or most effective in any particular function or organization?

Good "Support" Phrasing for Accomplishments

(If you didn't take the lead or can't take full credit for an accomplishment—but want to feature it on your resume or in your LI profile)

- Contributed to …
- Partnered with …
- Co-managed with …
- Aided in …
- Helped to …
- Instrumental in …
- Member of 7-person task force that …
- Collaborated with department manager to …
- Participated on committee that …
- Supported a …
- Company-wide efforts led to …
- Departmental efforts led to …
- Selected for team that …

Verbs With Verve

Write with Power, Punch & Pizzazz!

Accelerate	Capitalize	Convey	Earn	Export
Accentuate	Captain	Coordinate	Edit	Extract
Accommodate	Capture	Correct	Educate	Extricate
Accomplish	Catalog	Corroborate	Effect	Facilitate
Achieve	Catalyze	Counsel	Effectuate	Finalize
Acquire	Catapult	Craft	Elect	Finance
Adapt	Centralize	Create	Elevate	Focus
Address	Champion	Critique	Eliminate	Follow up
Adjudicate	Change	Crystallize	Emphasize	Forecast
Administer	Chart	Curtail	Empower	Forge
Advance	Clarify	Cut	Enact	Form
Advise	Classify	Decipher	Encourage	Formalize
Advocate	Close	Decrease	Endeavor	Formulate
Align	Coach	Define	Endorse	Foster
Allocate	Cobble	Delegate	Endure	Found
Alter	Collaborate	Deliver	Energize	Freshen
Analyze	Collect	Demonstrate	Enforce	Fulfill
Anchor	Command	Deploy	Engineer	Gain
Apply	Commercialize	Derive	Enhance	Garner
Appoint	Commoditize	Design	Enjoy	Generate
Appreciate	Communicate	Detail	Enlist	Govern
Arbitrate	Compare	Detect	Enliven	Graduate
Architect	Compel	Determine	Ensure	Guide
Arrange	Compile	Develop	Entrench	Halt
Articulate	Complete	Devise	Equalize	Handle
Ascertain	Comply	Differentiate	Eradicate	Head
Assemble	Compute	Diminish	Espouse	Helmed
Assess	Conceive	Direct	Establish	Hire
Assist	Conceptualize	Discard	Estimate	Honor
Attain	Conclude	Discern	Evaluate	Hypothesize
Augment	Conduct	Discover	Examine	Identify
Authenticate	Configure	Dispense	Exceed	Illuminate
Author	Conserve	Display	Excel	Illustrate
Authorize	Consolidate	Distinguish	Execute	Imagine
Balance	Construct	Distribute	Exhibit	Implement
Believe	Consult	Diversify	Exhort	Import
Bestow	Contemporize	Divert	Expand	Improve
Brainstorm	Continue	Document	Expedite	Improvise
Brief	Contract	Dominate	Experiment	Increase
Budget	Control	Double	Explode	Influence
Build	Converse	Draft	Exploit	Inform
Calculate	Convert	Drive	Explore	Initiate

Innovate	Model	Prevent	Relate	Strategize
Inspect	Moderate	Process	Remedy	Streamline
Inspire	Modify	Procure	Render	Strengthen
Install	Monetize	Produce	Renegotiate	Structure
Institute	Monitor	Program	Renew	Study
Instruct	Motivate	Progress	Renovate	Substantiate
Integrate	Navigate	Project	Reorganize	Succeed
Intensify	Negotiate	Project manage	Report	Suggest
Interact	Network	Proliferate	Reposition	Summarize
Interpret	Nominate	Promote	Represent	Supervise
Interview	Normalize	Propel	Research	Supplement
Interweave	Obfuscate	Propose	Resolve	Supply
Introduce	Obliterate	Prospect	Respond	Support
Invent	Observe	Prove	Restore	Surpass
Inventory	Obtain	Provide	Restructure	Synergize
Investigate	Offer	Publicize	Retain	Synthesize
Judge	Officiate	Purchase	Retrieve	Systematize
Jump-start	Operate	Purify	Reuse	Tabulate
Justify	Optimize	Qualify	Review	Tailor
Knit	Orchestrate	Quantify	Revise	Target
Knot	Order	Query	Revitalize	Teach
Land	Organize	Question	Salvage	Terminate
Launch	Orient	Raise	Sanctify	Test
Lead	Originate	Rate	Satisfy	Thwart
Lecture	Outpace	Ratify	Save	Train
Leverage	Outperform	Realign	Schedule	Transcribe
Liaise	Outsource	Rebuild	Secure	Transfer
License	Overcome	Recapture	Select	Transform
Listen	Overhaul	Receive	Separate	Transition
Locate	Oversee	Recognize	Serve	Translate
Lower	Participate	Recommend	Service	Trim
Maintain	Partner	Reconcile	Set up	Troubleshoot
Manage	Perceive	Record	Shepherd	Uncover
Manipulate	Perfect	Recruit	Simplify	Unify
Manufacture	Perform	Rectify	Slash	Unite
Map	Persuade	Recycle	Sold	Update
Market	Pilot	Redefine	Solidify	Upgrade
Marshall	Pinpoint	Redesign	Solve	Use
Master	Pioneer	Reduce	Spark	Utilize
Mastermind	Plan	Reengineer	Speak	Validate
Maximize	Position	Regain	Spearhead	Verbalize
Measure	Predict	Regulate	Specialize	Verify
Mediate	Prepare	Rehabilitate	Specify	Win
Mentor	Prescribe	Reimagine	Standardize	Work
Merge	Present	Reinforce	Steer	Write
Minimize	Preside	Rejuvenate	Stimulate	Zero in

Part IX:
Resume & LinkedIn Profile Index

This is one of the most valuable resources in the book—an index of every resume and LinkedIn profile sample, sliced and diced in countless ways. You can search by:

- **Industry or Profession:** Samples for jobs you've held in the past or those you are now pursuing.
- **Circumstance:** Resumes that have worked for those dealing with issues that put a wrinkle in the job search and resume development process—career change, consulting and freelance, military transition, return-to-work.

In each category, you'll find the page numbers for relevant resumes.

Use the index wisely to find the right resume samples to guide you in writing, formatting, and designing a resume that works for you—that will help you *get noticed and get hired.*

Search by Industries and Professions

ACCOUNTING & FINANCE: Accounting • Auditing • Banking & Lending • Consulting • Corporate Finance • Economics • Financial Analysis & Reporting • Financial Services • Regulatory Affairs • Risk Management
Visit these pages for samples and ideas: 5, 142, 205, 206–207, 208–209, 230, 237–238

ADVERTISING, MEDIA & PUBLIC RELATIONS: Corporate Communications • Digital Media • Marketing Communications • Multimedia Advertising • Print Advertising • Outreach • Public Relations
Visit these pages for samples and ideas: 91–92, 98–99, 123–125, 193, 199

DIGITAL AND SOCIAL MEDIA: Customer Support • Product Design & Market Launch • Solutions Development • User Experience
Visit these pages for samples and ideas: 7–8, 75, 91–92, 192, 193, 226–227

EDUCATION & TRAINING: Coaching • Classroom & Virtual Teaching • Corporate Training • Curriculum Design & Development • Education Administration • Education Management • Organizational Development • Training & Development
Visit these pages for samples and ideas: 15, 179–180, 181–182

ENGINEERING & SCIENCE: Aerospace • Architecture • Biomedical Engineering • Construction • Defense • Electrical Engineering • Electronics • Environmental Sciences • Mechanical Engineering • Meteorology • Product Design & Engineering • Project Management • Skilled Trades
Visit these pages for samples and ideas: 68–69, 134–135, 212, 213, 214–215, 218, 219, 235–236

EXECUTIVE AND SENIOR MANAGEMENT: Board of Directors • Business Development • Change Management • Consulting • Executive Leadership • Executive Negotiations • Global Business Affairs • Operations Management • P&L Management • Strategic Planning & Leadership
Visit these pages for samples and ideas: 7–8, 10–11, 24–25, 37–38, 39–40, 51–52, 76–77, 100–101, 104, 107–108, 113–114, 115–116, 134–135, 163–166, 169–172, 185–186, 187–188, 189–190, 193, 195–196, 197–198, 203–204, 206–207, 208–209, 214–215, 216–217, 237–238, 239–240

Search by Career Circumstance